Maximization, Whatever the Cost

Maximization, Whatever the Cost

Race, Redistricting, and the Department of Justice

MAURICE T. CUNNINGHAM

PRAEGER

Westport, Connecticut
London

Library of Congress Cataloging-in-Publication Data

Cunningham, Maurice T.
Maximization, whatever the cost : race, redistricting, and the Department of Justice / Maurice T. Cunningham.
p. cm.
Includes bibliographical references and index.
ISBN 0–275–96649–6 (alk. paper)
1. United States. Congress. House—Election districts. 2. United States. Dept. of Justice. Civil Rights Division—Decision making. 3. Election districts—United States. 4. Apportionment (Election law)—United States. 5. Afro-Americans—Segregation. I. Title.
KF4905.C86 2001
328.73′07345—dc21 00–035969

British Library Cataloguing in Publication Data is available.

Library of Congress Catalog Card Number: 00–035969
ISBN: 0–275–96649–6

First published in 2001

Praeger Publishers, 88 Post Road West, Westport, CT 06881
An imprint of Greewood Publishing Group, Inc.
www.praeger.com

Printed in the United States of America

The paper used in this book complies with the Permanent Paper Standard issued by the National Information Standards Organization (Z39.48–1984).

10 9 8 7 6 5 4 3 2 1

Copyright Acknowledgments

The author and publisher gratefully acknowledge permission for use of the following material:

Excerpts from interviews conducted by the author with John R. Dunne, David Simon, Tiare B. Smiley, J. Gerald Hebert, and James P. Turner. Used by permission of interviewees.

FOR MARY

"(W)e have been placed in the unenviable position of depriving black citizens of a privilege the Justice Department never had the right to grant: maximization of the black vote, whatever the cost."

Johnson v Miller, 864 F. Supp. 1354, 1369 (S.D.Ga. 1994)

Contents

Preface

In the early nineties I was an assistant attorney general in Massachusetts. The commonwealth was sued under the Voting Rights Act (VRA) by an alliance of African-American, Latino, and Asian groups. The basis of the action was somewhat obscure, having to do with the commonwealth's practice of redistricting not after the federal decennial census, but after our own state census conducted mid-decade. The ultimate aim seemed to be that the state legislature should redistrict immediately and should provide proportional representation for groups that claimed to be underrepresented based on their percentage of the commonwealth's population. A federal district court disposed of the action. But I was left with a good deal of curiosity about the Act and the advocates' claim for proportional representation and even more curiosity about the co-plaintiff and apparent funding agent for the suit: the Republican Party. It struck me as unusual that the Republican Party would be advocating for proportional representation. I wondered about that, and it soon became apparent that the Republicans believed that if they could help maximize minority legislative districts, the surrounding districts would be more white, less liberal, less Democratic, and thus, more Republican.

A while after the case was placed on hold by the court, we received a communication from an assistant attorney general from the United States Department of Justice (DOJ). He stated that he had heard of the Voting Rights Act litigation and would like to discuss it with counsel for the commonwealth. We met with him in Boston and he raised concerns about the number of minority state legislative districts drawn by the Massachusetts house and senate. We discussed the legislature's rationale, he went back to Washington, we sent him some data, and we never heard from him again. I began to wonder about the suspicions that animated this assistant attorney general back in

Washington and his power to review and potentially challenge the judgment of the Massachusetts legislature. I understood that under Section Two of the Voting Rights Act, the DOJ or private plaintiffs might challenge practices of any state that result in less opportunity for minority citizens to participate in the electoral process and to elect candidates of their choice. It just didn't seem to me that the legislature was doing anything other than participating in the grand game of redistricting politics: accommodating the powers of a Republican governor and Democratic legislature, responding to interest groups, acknowledging concentrations of racial and ethnic groups, protecting incumbents, or making life difficult for disfavored officials. Perhaps proportional representation could trump those other concerns, but I did not read the Voting Rights Act to require it, though clearly many others did.

My very minor role in that obscure Voting Rights Act case yielded the salutary benefit of providing me with a constant topic of interest as I began work at Boston College. I came across a number of judicial decisions in which federal courts, including the Supreme Court, were critical of the DOJ for exercising its powers under Section Five of the VRA. The VRA recognizes the intransigence of some jurisdictions in devising methods to disenfranchise minority voters. Therefore a number of covered jurisdictions, mostly but not all in the South, must preclear their election-law changes with the DOJ or get a court order before the changes can go into effect. The Supreme Court found that the DOJ used its preclearance power to force covered jurisdictions to create the maximum number of minority congressional districts in North Carolina and Georgia. District courts recognized similar machinations in other states.

There has certainly been no shortage of commentary on the court decisions that reversed maximization, or concerning the possible effects on minority representation. But I did, and still do, believe that there has not been a systematic review of the Department's maximization of congressional districts in the nineties. Moreover, though several excellent scholars have examined different facets of DOJ enforcement, there has been no book-length examination of DOJ administration of Section Five since 1982.

I owe a great debt of gratitude to the community of scholars at Boston College for helping to nurture this project. Robert Scigliano, R. Shep Melnick, John Tierney, and Marc Landy were patient shepherds. Bob Scigliano and Shep Melnick both re-read the manuscript and provided critiques as I tore it apart and transformed it into a book manuscript; Shep was particularly detailed in identifying shortcomings and, even better, advising how to fix them. Keith Bybee of Harvard has made his own thoughtful contribution to VRA literature and was kind enough to critique my work as well. The University of Massachusetts and university President William M. Bulger have provided a fine environment for further work.

A number of participants in the nineties' redistricting were generous with their time and experience. I'd especially like to thank the chiefs of the Civil Rights Division under presidents Bush and Clinton, John R. Dunne and Deval L. Patrick, both honorable public servants. James P. Turner, deputy assistant attorney general for civil rights for many years, was thoughtful in answering questions and in deterring me from too many mistakes. David Simon, legal counsel to Mr. Dunne, and J. Gerald Hebert provided valuable perspectives. Lawyers from different sides of litigation provided a diversity of views, and I thank assistant attorneys general Tiare B. Smiley of North Carolina and Angie LaPlace of Louisiana. Brenda Wright was helpful in explaining the positions taken by voting rights advocate litigators and their wary relationship with their putative allies in the Republican Party. Attorneys Robinson O. Everett of Duke University Law School and Doug Markham of Texas offered a perspective from those who challenged the Department and the states' redistricting plans in the courts. Even magnanimous and patient assistance from so many able people cannot prevent all mistakes. Needless to say, any errors in this volume are my own, and all opinions are mine unless clearly expressed otherwise.

There are special people to thank closer to home. My parents Edward and Rita Cunningham are not alive to read this book, but they would have been proud to see it in print and amazed at how it could be produced by the indifferent student they spent years trying to encourage. Sisters Maureen Reid-Cunningham and Rita Robertson and their family members Jim, Allison, Edward, Paul and Catherine are a source of comfort. All the Devlins—Paul, Joan, Libby, Paul, Jr., Sarah, Peter, Chris, and Patrick—have provided support and much needed respite. No one ever had a grander friend than Patrick Halley; he's been with me every step of the way. My cousin Richard D. Joy, a hero to his country and to so many he touched, is also not alive to see this book. He taught me how to read, a pretty important predicate to writing a book. Thanks, Ricky.

Finally I thank my partner, Mary Devlin, whose patience, understanding, and love sustain me. Lucky guy, I am.

1

The Mystery of Racial Redistricting in the Nineties

As Congress gathered for its 103rd Session in 1993 its membership had undergone a notable change, wrought in great part from the perceived command of the Voting Rights Act (VRA). Sixteen African-American freshmen House members from newly drawn black districts stepped forward to take the oath of office. Many of the new congresspersons were elected from the old Confederacy. North Carolina, South Carolina, Florida, Virginia, and Alabama sent African-American representatives to Congress for the first time since the last black Reconstruction congressman retired in 1901. Congressional Black Caucus (CBC) membership increased from twenty-five members in the 102nd Congress to thirty-eight members in the 103rd Congress. CBC membership grew from four Southern members to seventeen Southern members from 1990 to 1994. Nine new Hispanic members swelled the ranks of that delegation to nineteen.[1] The catalyst for the increased minority membership was the Department of Justice's Civil Rights Division (CRD), which used its power to object to election-law changes in states covered by Section Five of the VRA to force those states to maximize the number of minority congressional districts. It was a triumphant time for the Division and its supporters in the civil rights community.

Only three years later the Department's maximization strategy lay in ruins, set aside by harshly critical federal district courts and ultimately by the Supreme Court, which found that the Department had a "policy of maximizing majority-black districts."[2] The courts ordered that many of the plans the Department had forced upon the states, including those in North Carolina, Georgia, Louisiana, Texas, and New York, be undone for having been conceived with an unconstitutional racial motivation. Several new minority seats were redrawn. Litigation in one state, North Carolina, was still ongoing to settle upon a congressional redistricting plan in 1999, as the new decennial census and redistricting loomed in 2000. The sea change and retrenchment was not inevitable. This book explains how and why choices were made in particular institutional, legal, technological, and political contexts and offers suggestions that might ameliorate damage incurred by the Division.

The Voting Rights Act of 1965 reflected a congressional judgment that drastic action was needed to secure the right to vote for African-American citizens. That right had been rendered nearly meaningless by Jim Crow laws and practices in Southern jurisdictions. Section Five of the VRA is the provision that imposes upon the Division or the federal district court in Washington, DC, the obligation to examine certain states' voting-law changes and either object to them or grant preclearance, allowing the laws to go into effect. The preclearance authority covers a limited number of jurisdictions, mostly in the South. The provision grew out of the congressional recognition in 1965 that unless a check was placed upon the covered states, some of them would devise new methods to disenfranchise African-American voters. The jurisdictions may choose to submit their proposal to either the district court or the CRD, but most choose to send them to the Division. Section Five requires the Department of Justice (DOJ) to determine that the change "does not have the purpose and will not have the effect of denying or abridging the right to vote on account of race or color," or certain language provisions.[3] If the Department objects to a plan, the state can choose to seek a declaratory judgment in the federal district court in Washington, DC, or can try to address the reasons for the objection and resubmit the plan.

Section Five exists for a good reason. As the Supreme Court explained in 1966 in *South Carolina v Katzenbach*, Congress designed Section Five pursuant to its Fifteenth Amendment power to assure black citizens the franchise. Federal approval of Southern voting law changes became necessary because of a century-long record of discrimination that mocked the Fifteenth Amendment's promise of the right to vote. Every incremental success in the courts by the federal government to improve black access to the ballot had been succeeded by a new Southern stratagem to defeat the right to vote. The Court therefore approved the creative measure, stating that "Congress might well decide to shift the advantage of time and inertia from the perpetrators of the evil to its victims."[4]

That the Department of Justice exceeded its role in legal policy making in the nineties has been established in numerous court decisions reaching all the way to the Supreme Court. The Department relied upon Section Five's prohibition against purposeful discrimination to force jurisdictions to maximize in case after case where no intentional discrimination existed. Part of the mystery of enforcement in the nineties lies in the fact that in over twenty-five years of administering the Act, the Department had established a record of moderate progressivism. Yet in the nineties the DOJ exercised poorly what it had exercised wisely for so long—it's power to protect minority political participation while maintaining respect for federalism. Its judgments had vast implications for racial representation, elected officials, and partisan control of the Congress. Perhaps no institution incurred more damage than the CRD itself. That damage must be undone if the Division is to be restored to its respected role in evaluating redistricting changes submitted by jurisdictions with a history of racial discrimination in electoral practices.

Though maximization appeared to be a logical step to many participants in the preclearance process, there were solid reasons why the Division might have continued to follow a restrained course. The Supreme Court seemed to increasingly question affirmative action claims that depended upon racial-disparity analysis and looked to proportional-result remedies. The Bush administration was opposed to affirmative action plans that relied upon quotas or preferences. The president vetoed legislation aimed at battling discriminatory practices and racial harassment in the workplace, labeling it a "quota" bill. As the civil rights establishment changed the terms of the voting debate from a focus on unfettered access to the ballot to proportional representation by race, its moral monopoly on voting issues dissipated. Yet the Division bought into and implemented a policy that forced states to create nearly every minority congressional district that imagination and technological advances would allow.

One cannot help but be impressed with the numerical increase in minority representation as an indicator of the force of the Division's approach in the nineties. There were no majority-black districts in the South in the seventies, though there were three African-American representatives from majority-white districts. In 1985 there were only two black congresspersons from the region, then four after the 1986 and 1988 elections. Three of those four representatives came from majority-black districts, and the fourth came from a district in which African Americans and Hispanics combined to form a majority. Three of the majority-black districts in the eighties came about through voting rights litigation. In 1994 voting rights scholars Bernard Grofman and Lisa Handley concluded that black-majority districts would continue to be needed to produce African-American officeholders in the South. They called for persistent DOJ diligence in requiring majority black districts where feasible. The scholars also suggested that part of the reason for the dearth of black-majority congressional districts in the seventies and eighties lay in the geographic reality that it is difficult to bond together sufficient numbers of African-American voters. That factor too would change in the nineties, due to computer technology.[5]

The evidence that a major change in the Division's approach to redistricting occurred is more extensive than a simple tally of the number of minority congresspersons. The Division had established a twenty-five-year example of vigilance for minority rights accompanied by respect for federalism. The prior full-scale redistricting cycles, in the seventies and eighties, had been occasions of moderate interventions into congressional plans by the Division. The objections taken were neither systematic nor intrusive into state decision making. The CRD made some use of disparate impact as a standard prior to the nineties, but not often in congressional cases. When disparate impact was considered, it was commonly used in conjunction with other circumstances pointing toward intentional discrimination. This is especially true in the congressional cases, where the CRD stepped in to remedy some ugly instances of intentional discrimination. The Division rejected entreaties from civil rights groups to use proportional representation as a talisman of fair districting.

There are a number of contributing factors to the shift in the Department's enforcement and the results it engendered. One consideration always present is the mystique of moral rightness that is invested in the civil rights claims of minority, especially African-American, citizens. The Voting Rights Act of 1965 was a product of that most fertile period of the civil rights movement. The Act is generally recognized as the most effective civil rights law in the nation's history. As legislation directed to redress disenfranchisement of minority citizens, the appeal of the Act is fundamental to American democracy.

The evolution of the concept of fair treatment is related to the mystique of moral rightness. When the movement was at its moral peak during the sixties, the general framework for fairness was the eradication of discrimination against African Americans in order to promote equality of opportunity for individuals. That understanding, however, was short-lived and was replaced by the idea that historical and institutional racism is so prevalent in American society that disparate-impact analysis is necessary to accurately measure discrimination and proportional representation is required to rectify shortcomings. This involves the familiar affirmative action debate concerning whether minority citizens are found in the workplace or in schools in ratio to their proportion of the population.[6] In nineties' redistricting, fair districting came to be equated with maximization, or proportional representation. The terms "proportional representation" and "maximization" are often used interchangeably with no great harm, but each can connote different outcomes. Proportional representation means representation in accord with a racial group's ratio in the overall population. Maximization can theoretically exceed that number, but more commonly it refers to maximization of the number of minority districts that can be drawn.

The CRD Voting Section's role in rights enforcement tracks the changing concepts of affirmative action and equal opportunity. The Division recognized in the early years of Voting Rights Act implementation that its role should be to remove barriers to black Americans' exercising the franchise. It tried to utilize the minimum amount of intrusion upon the states that would be effective and placed the lion's share of responsibility on African-American organizations to promote registration and voting, but as the dominant interpretation of equality by civil rights and public law activists changed to an exaltation of proportionate results, the Division's interpretation changed as well.

The evolving meaning of discrimination and fair treatment was crucial to the mission of increasing minority seats in Congress in the nineties. State legislatures must pass redistricting laws following each decennial census. Civil rights groups and the Republican Party were adept at placing maximization plans before the state legislatures. Proponents of maximization and Division attorneys came to focus upon Section Five's prohibition against purposeful discrimination. Though that term connotes some act taken with the intention to impair minority participation, the CRD came to accept another interpretation. The CRD accepted a reading whereby a failure to adopt a maximization plan if one had been presented to the state would raise a presumption of discriminatory purpose. This transformed the historical parameters by which the Division assessed purpose.

The Act itself underwent a significant modification in 1982. Section Two of the VRA, as amended, was designed to go further than Section Five's prohibitions against purposeful discrimination or a retreat from existing numbers of minority districts. Section Two prohibits any state from imposing or applying any voting law or practice that "results" in the denial or abridgement of the right to vote on account of race, color, or certain guarantees having to do with language. The results test is violated if it is shown, based on the "totality of the circumstances," that the political process is "not equally open to participation by members of a [protected] class of citizens . . . in that its members have less opportunity than other members of the electorate to participate in the political process and to elect representatives of their choice."[7] The passage of amended Section Two engendered debates in Congress, including accusations that the new language would lead courts to prescribe proportional representation by race. Civil rights advocates and their congressional allies dismissed such claims. A compromise was reached in which a proviso was included in Section Two indicating that proportional representation was not to be required.

Section Two is nationwide in scope but has no preclearance provision. Its results test, however, is vastly more far reaching than the purpose or effects tests under Section Five. Therefore, it became an appealing strategy to incorporate the results test into the Section Five preclearance process. By January 1987 proponents of fusing the results test into the preclearance process were able to overcome opposition from the Reagan administration and incorporate a clear violation of the results test into the regulations governing Section Five enforcement.

No less important than the amendment to Section Two was the Supreme Court's 1986 interpretation of it in *Thornburg v Gingles*. The decision of the Court, written by Justice Brennan, set forth three preconditions needed to establish a violation of Section Two. "First, the minority group must be able to demonstrate that it is sufficiently large and geographically compact to constitute a majority in a single-member district . . . Second, the minority group must be able to show that it is politically cohesive. . . . Third, the minority must be able to demonstrate that the white majority votes sufficiently as a bloc to enable it . . . usually to defeat the minority's preferred candidate."[8] In an opinion concurring in the judgment, Justice O'Connor warned that the majority's formulation would result in claims that only proportional representation would satisfy the Court's interpretation. Justice O'Connor's augury proved correct, a circumstance that made incorporation even more valuable to those within and outside the Department who advocated for maximization.

Maximization proponents outside of the CRD were concentrated in two groups, voting rights advocates who would naturally be expected to push for more minority seats—and a somewhat unusual and suspicious ally, the Republican Party. Drawing on the moral authority of the civil rights cause, public interest law firms such as the American Civil Liberties Union (ACLU) and organizations such as the National Association for the Advancement of Colored People (NAACP) fought for more minority seats. The nineties redistricting round was played out against the backdrop of civil rights advocates' muscular definition of racial fairness: that fair districting as contemplated by Section Two and *Gingles* means proportional representation. The advocates are repeat players at the Section Five preclearance process, aided not only by the public interest law firms but by a cadre of politically sophisticated and persuasive academics and social science experts. The advocates, including state elected officials aspiring to use the process to move up to a congressional seat, successfully melded the high cause of voting rights with their interest in the creation of more minority districts.

The Voting Section came to tilt toward the interpretation favored by the civil rights groups. In doing so the CRD affirmed its historical alliance with civil rights organizations, but in fostering the policy goals of the civil rights groups, the Division encountered the wrath of the courts. The Division was described by one federal district court as the captive of the American Civil Liberties Union.[9]

The other great promoter of maximization, the Republican Party (GOP), was less plausible in its claim for the mantle of moral rectitude. On principle, the GOP should have taken a contrary position: the party has long been recognized for opposition to affirmative action remedies that countenance quotas or proportional representation. Neither proportional representation by race nor alliances with civil rights groups are routine features of Republican Party ideology, but here self-interest intruded. Party strategists calculated that packing black and Hispanic voters into a certain number of districts so that they could elect minority representatives would leave surrounding districts whiter and more conservative—and produce a net gain for the Republicans. The Republican National Committee and state parties therefore embarked upon a campaign that rested explicitly on claims for proportional representation.

Nonetheless, the Republican administration of President George Bush had set itself against the notion of quotas or racial preferences. In most areas of civil rights, the administration frustrated and disappointed civil rights advocates. But in the review of Section Five submissions concerning congressional redistricting, the administration's Civil Rights Division could hardly have been more accommodating. The collision of aggressive enforcement and apparent treason to principle inspired some to conjecture that a "Republican Plot" was afoot—that the Republican administration was using the Division to obtain the partisan goal of increased numbers of Republican congresspersons.

The Republican Party plan seems to have worked. Political scientists differ on how many districts maximization may have cost the Democrats, but a moderate consensus is that seven to twelve seats were lost to the Democrats in 1992 and 1994 due to racial redistricting. Such a few seats can have a large impact. The Republican Party took control over the House of Representatives in 1994, and after losing seats in the 1996 election, it held a slim eleven-seat majority in the 105th Congress. The gains in the number of minority officeholders were real, but as the new congressmen found their way around the Capitol, senior members of the CBC lost three chairmanships and seventeen subcommittee chairmanships when the Republicans took over. Minority concerns got short shrift from the Republican House majority. Speaker Newt Gingrich even defunded the CBC. When the 1998 impeachment firestorm hit the House, President Clinton's most devoted allies were the members of the CBC, but their efforts to stave off impeachment failed on a partisan vote in the House. The House was composed of 228 Republicans, 206 Democrats, and 1 Independent who usually voted with the Democrats. Impeachment Article I passed the Judiciary Committee on a straight party vote, 21–16; it passed the full House by 228–205. Article III also passed the Committee by a party-line vote of 21–16, and it passed the entire House by a vote of

221–212. The difference between a Republican-led House and a Democratic-led House was a mere eleven seats, which quite likely would have meant a different impeachment dynamic and outcome.[10]

The actual account of administration involvement in the preclearance process is more complicated than the simple one-to-one relationship that Republican Plot theorists have advanced. A number of actors would have had to be involved in such a conspiracy—party operatives, high administration officials, the leadership of the CRD, and career staff of the Division. While all of these necessary groups came to desire maximization, not all needed to take action—the administration higher-ups only needed to look the other way, for instance; and while the Party was surely inspired by interest rather than principle, other actors came to favor maximization as a just and proper measure.

A good deal of the controversy swirled about the head of the man chosen by President Bush to head the Civil Rights Division. John R. Dunne arrived in the position with little direct experience in civil rights and voting rights. He understood affirmative action as contemplating the eradication of barriers to individual achievement—a formulation generally accepted when the Act was passed but not the position held in the nineties by advocates and many CRD careerists. Yet Dunne's tenure in the post brought him to believe that creating as many African-American and Hispanic seats as feasible constituted a proper advance for minority representation. He became determined to use the power of his office to increase minority representational opportunities. His efforts brought down upon him the accusation that he had manipulated the process for partisan advantage. While a neat hypothesis, the evidence lies in another direction.

Many career attorneys and support staff in the CRD almost naturally came to accept that pushing for maximization was a desirable civil rights standard. The careerists enter their profession with a desire to serve the important missions of destroying all vestiges of racial bias and promoting equality. They work in an agency steeped in a history of fighting against emerging and inventive techniques of discrimination. Activists who identify new contexts for claims of discrimination and push proportional representation importune them. Among those claims in the nineties was the argument that a failure to maximize indicated discriminatory purpose by state legislatures. The careerists enjoy a high reputation for professionalism. Nonetheless, it is only natural for them to be susceptible to arguments that seem to increase minority representational opportunities.

As with many other areas of life and politics, the explosion of technological capability transformed the practice of redistricting in the nineties. The mapmaking that brought constitutional challenges and the condemnation of the courts featured misshapened, bizarre-looking districts. The plans were drawn in such contorted fashion in order to link up far-flung populations of minority residents. Minority advocates and public interest group lawyers urged such plans upon state legislators, intimating that the activists had it on good authority that the CRD would require maximization. The linkages were dependent on the capacity of computers to sort out enclaves of residents by race and connect them together in ways unimaginable before the advent of sophisticated software. Computers were indispensable to all parties in constructing new districts and all had access to advanced hardware and software—states, advocates, and the CRD.

The successes shared among the Division, civil rights advocates, and the Republican Party came at a cost to the states. State redistricting leaders came to believe that nothing short of maximization of minority congressional seats would satisfy the Division. The application of pressure differed among the states, but the result was acquiescence in the maximization plans. State political leaders bristled at the Division's interference. One argued in an editorial released to his state's newspapers that the Division's interference to force an additional black congressional district was born of partisan politics. He contended that the arguments against the state's preferred plan were evidence of the need to either amend the Voting Rights Act or to elect a president who would appoint a less partisan chief of the Civil Rights Division. That editorial, entitled "Justice Department Has the Last Word," was authored by Daniel T. Blue, the first African-American Speaker of the House in North Carolina since Reconstruction.[11]

The eighties brought important developments in the voting rights environment. Amended Section 2, *Gingles*, the push to incorporate the results test into the preclearance process, advanced technology—all promoted the logic of proportional representation. Those factors had time to develop with some public attention but nowhere near the thorough scrutiny attendant to the redistricting that follows each federal census. These accretions became much more visible in the crucible of biennial submission of redistricting plans for the Department's preclearance determination. The every-ten-years element tends to make preclearance policy nonincremental, an unusual aspect of this policy arena. Piece by piece, changes can combine and explode on the political landscape.

The Division is the tribune through which minority voting rights have been assured by the federal government. But a shifting Supreme Court majority, challenges from academia, the willingness of voters in covered states to challenge the Voting Rights Act on constitutional grounds, and the linguistic and interpretative battleground over such terms as discriminatory purpose and racial fairness have cast the Division into turbulence. As the controversies of the nineties' redistricting cycle recede and we prepare for the first redistricting round of the new millennium, significant questions remain to vex us.

How much can we trust the states not to discriminate against minority voting aspirations?

Should the CRD judge fair districting by a standard of means or of ends?

Does the opportunity to elect a candidate of choice require a guarantee that the candidate will share race or ethnicity with a majority of the districts' voters?

Can white officeholders represent minority interests as well as minority officials?

Since favoring substantive representation could aid the Democratic Party, while advancing maximum descriptive representation redounds to the Republicans' benefit, can the Division escape the "political thicket?"

The station of the Division has been unique in voting rights enforcement—indeed, in all of federalism. By virtue of its Section Five power to approve or object to election-law changes, it is a decider of whether election-law changes are just. In no other area of federal-state relations must a state seek the approval of a federal agency before its legislation may go into effect.

This book examines a critical civil rights enforcement agency at the center of a matrix of historical antecedents, interests, meanings, and values. How does an agency function when its closest allies and political nurturers push it to be an unabashed champion of minority interests while its statutory design and own regulations command it to act with the objectivity and detachment of a court of law? What effect does it have when the prevailing liberal ethos of professional staffers interacts with the policy commands of a more conservative administration? As technology changes the world around us, can it also affect how we give legal definition to terms such as equality and fairness? This book examines factors that help explain the Department of Justice's central role in achieving—at least for a time—the maximization of minority congressional districts in Southern states.

This study shows that despite fears in the sixties that the Department would treat the states as conquered provinces, such concerns were not borne out—until the Department overreached in the nineties' round of redistricting. Chapter 2 looks at the history of Department enforcement and reveals the constant interpretative tension between those who believe that the Department has done too little and those who believe the Department has done too much.

The bureaucratic history and culture of the Civil Rights Division play an explanatory role. The Division attracts professional staffers who are interested in the Division's mission and in progressive notions of civil rights law. As recent years have proven, the nomination to serve as Division chief is one of the most hotly contested domestic policy appointments, rife with interest group politics and ideological disputes. Chapter 3 examines how the Voting Section professionals and their politically appointed superiors go about their task.

Chapter 4 analyzes the methods by which the Department interprets the Voting Rights Act and important judicial precedent. Narrow Supreme Court majorities, and especially Justices Scalia and Thomas, have encouraged a text-based approach to legal interpretation in the past decade. The CRD's efforts to increase minority representation in the nineties required a more expansive mode. The Division offered a new definition for Section Five's purpose element, then attempted to stretch *Gingles* in order to defend bizarre looking districts. The Department, advocates, and the states were not able to persuade the courts that the districts were inspired by anything but racial motivation. Courts repeatedly rejected their rationales for the districts as pretextual.

Contending interests buffet the Department. Most states submit their plans for departmental review, rather than opt for a full judicial proceeding before the district court in Washington, DC. This decision has consequences, because although the Department is to make the same substantive decision as would the court, the process is more permeable. Interests from the states to public interest litigators to the political parties are free to file comments with the Department and to lobby for their positions. This process creates odd alliances and political arrangements that produce different kinds of interest group configurations around the Department's decision making. In

Chapter 5, I discuss how organized interests have formed around the Voting Section and their influence on legal policy making.

Chapter 6 focuses in greater detail on how the stage was set for enforcement in the nineties and provides a detailed consideration of the process in several critical states including North Carolina, Georgia, and Louisiana, where judicial proceedings have rendered fully developed records.

Finally, Chapter 7 discusses processes that brought the Division to its present critical juncture and the products of the Division's policy-making choices. The Division cannot continue to hunker down in defense of the old ways but must alter its approach in order to avoid a repeat of the disaster of the nineties and restore its necessary leadership position in voting rights enforcement.

The Division has enforced the Voting Rights Act for nearly thirty-five years and has met with substantial controversy at times. It would necessarily be so, since the agency stands at the center of the storm, buffeted by officials attempting to perpetuate racial dominance and aggressive advocates pushing a definition of proportional representation as fairness and equality; but in all the years and across all the battles, the Division never before engendered the criticism from the courts, and even attacks on its integrity, that it drew in the nineties. The credibility of the Division and its capacity to act has been damaged. How deep those wounds are and what measures the Division might utilize to repair the damage and retrieve its leadership role in voting rights enforcement are also considered here. Because of its unique role in enforcement, and because civil rights organizations have not been regarded by the courts with the same credibility as the Division, it is important that the CRD restore its reputation. But to do so it cannot return to the advocacy posture of the last redistricting round, as its supporters in the civil rights community might wish. Rather, it must recapture the balance missing from its efforts in the nineties.

NOTES

1. "Black Caucus Grows, Moves Toward Center," *1992 Congressional Quarterly Almanac*, 18–19. "103rd's Hispanic Contingent Largest Ever," *1992 Congressional Quarterly Almanac*, 21. The Hispanic delegation includes delegates with limited voting privileges from the U.S. Virgin Islands and Puerto Rico.
2. *Miller v Johnson*, 515 U.S. 900 (1995).
3. *Voting Rights Act, Section Five*, U.S. Code, vol. 42, sec. 1973b (1994).
4. *South Carolina v Katzenbach*, 383 U.S. 301, 328 (1966).
5. Lisa Handley and Bernard Grofman, "The Impact of the Voting Rights Act on Minority Representation: Black Officeholding in Southern State Legislatures and Congressional Delegations," in Chandler Davidson and Bernard Grofman, *Quiet Revolution in the South: The Impact of the Voting Rights Act, 1965–1990* (Princeton, N.J.: Princeton University Press, 1994), 343–350.
6. Hugh Davis Graham, *The Civil Rights Era: Origins and Development of National Policy, 1960–1972* (New York: Oxford University Press, 1990).
7. *Voting Rights Act, Section Two*, U.S. Code, vol. 42, sec. 1973 (1994).
8. *Thornburg v Gingles*, 478 U.S. 30, 50 (1986).
9. *Johnson v Miller*, 864 F. Supp. 1354 (S.D. Ga. 1994).

10. David Lublin, *The Paradox of Representation: Racial Gerrymandering and Minority Rights in Congress* (Princeton, NJ: Princeton University Press, 1997), 109–114; Steven A. Holmes, "Did Racial Redistricting Undermine Democrats?" *New York Times*, 13 November 1998; Alison Mitchell and Lizette Alvarez, "President Urges 'Conscience' Vote on House Inquiry," *New York Times*, 8 October 1998; CNN, "House Impeaches Clinton," http://cnn.com./ALLPOLITICS/stories/1998/12/19/impeachment.01/.

11. Daniel T. Blue, "Justice Department Has the Last Word," submitted to the Supreme Court in "Appendix," *Shaw v Hunt*, Nos. 94-923, 94-924, 163.

2

Transformation

> What happened in Selma is part of a far larger movement which reaches into every section and State of America. It is the effort of American Negroes to secure for themselves the full blessings of American life.
> Their cause must be our cause too. Because it is not just Negroes, but really it is all of us, who must overcome the crippling legacy of bigotry and injustice.
> And we shall overcome.
>
> President Lyndon Baines Johnson.
> Special Message to the Congress: The American Promise
> 15 March 1965

In order to make the case that the Civil Rights Division engaged in a novel approach to 1990s enforcement, it is necessary to review how it implemented the Voting Rights Act in the twenty-five plus years it had already been responsible for carrying out the Act's requirements. The sensitive nature of civil rights enforcement guaranteed that the Division would become enmeshed in conflict. Controversies came, though none were as transformative as the strife of the nineties. From 1965 through 1990 the CRD staff pursued a progressive but measured approach, but during the eighties, elements developed that were to transform the nineties preclearance process.

The controversial character of Department of Justice enforcement grows out of three omnipresent subtextual elements to voting rights disputes. These are accusations of politicized enforcement, claims of moral right, and the question of how to define equality. Each of these factors has been present from the passage of the VRA under the Johnson administration through the maximization of majority-minority districts by the Bush DOJ and the defense of those districts by the Clinton administration.

It is in the nature of policy advocates never to be either satisfied or quiescent, and voting rights proponents do not disappoint. Nonetheless, there has been a fair degree of comfort in the civil rights community with the performance of the Voting Section over the years, with two lengthy exceptions: the administrations of Richard M. Nixon and Ronald Reagan. The pragmatism and persistence of legal professionals within the Voting Section cushioned the political and ideological squalls of those administrations. The moderate progressivism of the professionals also helped prevent the CRD from overstepping the boundaries set by the VRA. The Act establishes federal action to guarantee a right to electoral participation, and interests that have grown up around the Act have always beseeched the CRD for greater activism. For twenty-five years under several administrations, the CRD careerists maintained an even keel between civil rights demands and state interests.

This is not to say that there have not been sharply divergent viewpoints expressed about implementation. There have been. Activists have let their discontents be known over the years, and the Division has sometimes been put on the defensive. Efforts have been made to push the Division toward more proactive positions. Divergent views grow out of polarized expectations concerning the VRA. Observers such as Steven Lawson, Bernard Grofman, and Lisa Handley assert that Nixon's Southern Strategy and Reagan's ideological blinders led them to only grudging enforcement. Yet critics such as Abigail Thernstrom argue that the DOJ has behaved overzealously almost without reserve.[1]

Although charges of "politicization" are often made concerning the Department's conduct of civil rights enforcement, the term is not used precisely. Politicization can have two meanings. First, it may be taken to be an ideological or philosophical approach to government. One example might be that of contrasting the approaches of the Reagan and Clinton Civil Rights Divisions. Reagan's Division advocated that antidiscrimination laws focus upon individual rather than group rights, and in voting rights matters such as the Supreme Court case of *Thornburg v Gingles,* it granted deference to the states. The Clinton Division favors group rights and has acted aggressively on behalf of the preferences of civil rights organizations.

A second definition of politicization would be "a corruption or abuse of power." Examples would be that of the Nixon administration opposing key provisions of the Act as part of its Southern Strategy to appeal to white voters, or accusations that the Bush administration used its preclearance powers to assist Republican chances in legislative redistricting efforts. The second usage denotes something improper, but the first meaning opens a debate concerning the extent to which the governing philosophy of an administration should and does affect its approach to law and public policy.[2]

Some contend that the attorney general and his political appointees should approach the enforcement of law in a neutral fashion, regardless of the political philosophy of the sitting administration. A neutral appointee would be more concerned with implementing existing precedent than the policy goals of the administration. Another kind of appointee, the advocate, would consider the job to entail the promotion of administration policies within the law, including challenging existing interpretations the administration opposes. The attorney general is usually expected to be a part of the president's team, to form and not just to implement policy, and to share the president's governing philosophy. Burke Marshall, a former assistant attorney general for civil rights during John F. Kennedy's term, has stated that an administration should give policy direction in the area of civil rights. Drew S. Days III, the assistant attorney general for civil rights during the Carter administration and solicitor general in the Clinton administration, has acknowledged that CRD attorneys are policy makers through their management of the Division's litigation strategies and resources.[3]

That the attorney general and the assistant attorney general for civil rights are expected to be team players is significant because the 1964 Civil Rights Act and the 1965 VRA recognized that the attorney general and the courts would be critical national policy makers in civil rights. Moreover, the DOJ and the civil rights movement associated closely through the administrations of Truman, Eisenhower, Kennedy, Johnson, and Carter. The relationship was less comfortable during the Nixon and Reagan administrations. We should not be surprised to find that political appointees bring their administration's ideological predilections to the CRD. Disputes can occur within the Division as administration appointees clash with career staff whose mission is informed by the moral imperatives of the civil rights movement.

There is a unique character to civil rights statutes. They are imbued with a mystique of moral rightness. This is particularly true of the VRA, because it is intended to safeguard the most fundamental and precious right of citizenship—the right to participate in a government that acts by the consent of the people. Those called upon to guarantee the right to vote for their fellow citizens should recognize a high moral calling in their mission.

The formative years of an agency can establish its direction.[4] By the time the 1965 VRA had passed, Department attorneys had been engaged for years in case-by-case voting litigation in Southern states. The CRD itself was created by the 1957 Civil Rights Act, and Division lawyers set to work litigating cases where Southern officials were impeding blacks from exercising their right to vote. Southern jurisdictions, and often Southern judges, delayed and battled the CRD in almost every case. Progress was slow and frustrating, remedies limited. Incremental success achieved in one case was met by new Southern stratagems to disenfranchise black voters in others. Thus, Section Five of the VRA was intended to obviate the need for case-by-case litigation by subjecting voting-law changes to preclearance.[5]

Nonetheless, the Division's intensive Section Five interventions in Southern electoral decision making did not immediately follow the 1965 enactment. It was dependent on later developments in the courts, especially the Supreme Court's rulings in the 1969 cases of *Allen v State Board of Elections* and *Gaston County, North Carolina v United States*. The developing tasks were subject to expansive definition by Division lawyers. Their political parents, civil rights advocates and key legislators, surrounded the voting lawyers. Over the years, those allies adopted a normative vision of group rights. Moreover, opposition voices were tainted by the horrific discrimination that made passage of a federal voting statute a necessity. CRD attorneys have an abiding sense of the historical mission of their Division and their unique place in righting the wrongs of racism.

The same forces that changed the conception of equality that informs affirmative action policy have transformed voting rights. Hugh Davis Graham has categorized two phases of affirmative action. In Phase One, which culminated in the Civil Rights Act of 1964 and the Voting Rights Act of 1965, the goal was to incorporate African Americans into the general competition for success. The theory was grounded in the tenets of classical liberalism: society should eradicate discrimination so that the individual would have the opportunity to succeed based on merit. The nation was to provide assistance to help African Americans achieve equal opportunity.

Phase Two, which informs the position of many civil rights advocates today, transformed the meaning of equality and affirmative action. By the late 1960s some civil rights leaders had come to argue that racism so suffused American society that simply providing compensatory programs with the aim to help blacks compete was insufficient. They argued from the premise of historical racism, a form of the disease perhaps more tenacious than open, intentional discrimination. The theory is that if not for the presence of racism built into the political (or educational, or employment) structure, racial groups would be found in the environment in proportion to their ratio in the general population. Discrimination is detected by statistical disparity analysis and redressed by proportional representation. The remedies of classical liberalism aimed at individual instances of discrimination would not suffice. Thus, the theorists of Phase Two's definition of affirmative action devised group solutions, dependent not upon equal opportunity but upon equal results for each group. It is the Phase Two definition that now dominates the claims of civil rights activists. Daniel Bell observed in 1973 that the change had occurred virtually without debate. "[T]he principle has changed from discrimination to representation."[6]

Graham argues that the VRA of 1965 was designed on the New Deal model of administrative economic regulation, a tort model that enumerates harmful acts and orders the transgressor to halt; but as Phase Two developed, the emphasis shifted from a model of intentional torts and equal treatment to a model of no-fault and equal results.[7] The Phase Two definition adds the concepts of negligent discrimination or strict liability for discriminatory effects. Phase Two argues that but for historical discrimination, minorities would have a place in the political structure in ratio to their presence in the population. Therefore, the remedy is proportional representation.

ENFORCEMENT OF THE VOTING RIGHTS ACT OF 1965

The Johnson Administration and the Early Years

With the nation focused upon the crisis of black voting rights by violent white reaction to a 1965 protest march in Selma, Alabama, President Lyndon B. Johnson asked his attorney general for the "goddamnedest, toughest voting rights bill" that his staff could produce. Attorney General Nicholas deB. Katzenbach, whose staff had been preparing drafts of such a bill as early as two days after the 1964 election and throughout the crisis in Selma, obliged. Katzenbach and CRD chief Burke Marshall fought for the bill before Congress.[8]

From their experiences in the South, Division lawyers knew that the most widely used and effective tool of voter disenfranchisement was the literacy test. They determined that by using a formula that focused on literacy-test jurisdictions in which either vote registration or voter turnout fell below 50 percent in the 1964 presidential election, the drafters would identify those states and counties that had employed the literacy test to discriminate against blacks. In those areas, Section Four of the Act banned the use of the literacy test for five years. It was feared that a permanent ban might be found unconstitutional; Congress extended the ban nationwide in 1970 and made it permanent in 1975. The covered states were Alabama, Georgia, Louisiana, Mississippi, South Carolina, Virginia, forty counties in North Carolina, and scattered counties elsewhere. The attorneys also knew that Southern judges could not be trusted on racial issues, and that provision must be made to counteract Southern habits of devising new roadblocks to black enfranchisement. Section Five of the Act was therefore designed to protect against new schemes by requiring that voting-law changes in covered states be approved first by the federal government before they could go into effect. Moreover, approval could not be obtained from friendly local jurists; covered states would be required to present their new laws to the United States District Court for the District of Columbia or the CRD.[9]

The attorney general's key role in passage of the VRA confirmed the pre-eminent function of the Department in civil rights and voting rights policy. The Department had played a crucial role in the one-person one-vote case of *Baker v Carr* and the reapportionment case *Reynolds v Sims*. Solicitor General Archibald Cox wrote Attorney General Robert Kennedy that "it is no exaggeration to recognize among ourselves that we played the most important role in *Baker v Carr*, and our brief and argument may even have determined the result."[10]

President Johnson signed the VRA on 6 August 1965. By 9 August the attorney general had designated nine Southern counties for federal registration examiners. By September of 1965, leaders of the NAACP, Congress of Racial Equality (CORE), National Urban League, and Southern Christian Leadership Conference (SCLC) had already complained to Vice President Hubert Humphrey of an inadequate federal presence in the South. On the one-year anniversary of the Act, 46 percent of African Americans in the Deep South were registered, doubling the number of registered black citizens. From 1965 through 1969, black registration in five Deep South states increased from just over 24 percent to slightly less than 61 percent, an improvement attributed to the Act's limit upon literacy tests and the presence of federal registrars. A great preponderance of the registration was accomplished by local, not federal, officials, although the local registrars were acting with the knowledge and fear that federal workers would do the job if they did not. As former Division attorney Brian K. Landsberg points out, a policy premised on mistrust of Southern officials was carried out successfully by local institutions.[11]

In 1966, the Supreme Court decided the first challenge brought against the constitutionality of the VRA in *South Carolina v Katzenbach*. South Carolina, assisted by several other Southern states, attacked the entire remedial structure of the VRA. The Department offered a robust defense of the Act's constitutionality. Its brief explained that Section Five was necessary because of the frequency with which covered jurisdictions had resorted to new inventions to frustrate black voting rights. The Department cited the "long history of changing qualifications designed to defeat negro suffrage" and the "remarkably persistent record of varied schemes devised for that purpose—from the crudest to the most ingenious." Therefore, the Department argued, the Congress was fully justified in legislating a prophylactic against such future schemes.[12] In an eight-to-one decision over a strong dissent from Justice Hugo Black, the Court held that the preclearance provision of Section Five is an appropriate use of Congress's power to effectuate the Fifteenth Amendment's prohibition against racial discrimination in voting. The Court found that when Congress required selected states to submit their election-law changes to the federal district court in Washington or to the DOJ, it had acted in an "inventive manner." But the Court recognized that Congress's hearings on voting rights had revealed a system in which case-by-case litigation by the DOJ and private parties was inadequate to defeat Southern intransigence. The Court therefore upheld Section Five's requirement that the covered states seek approval of voting-law changes before they could go into effect.[13]

The Department's approach in the early years was to go slowly and respect federalism. Some in the civil rights community were dissatisfied with the Department's deference to local voluntary compliance. In 1966, the United States Commission on Civil Rights issued a report criticizing the Department's restraint and urged the government to begin an aggressive program of voter education and registration. The Voter Education Project, a program of the Southern Regional Council, argued that federal presence was the most important variable in increasing black registration. The president, the attorney general, and the chief of the CRD responded that black leaders, not the federal government, should spur registration and voting efforts. Federal presence was to be a last resort. Katzenbach wished to assure the ability of black Southerners to register and vote, and he believed that success in that endeavor would naturally induce Southern politicians to respond to their newly enfranchised constituents, out of self-interest at least. The attorney general also desired to keep confrontation with Southern political leaders to a minimum in order to facilitate a return to normal federal-state relations as soon as possible. That policy of effective restraint set the CRD's approach for the next twenty-five years.[14]

In addition to advocates' requests for more federal activity in registering voters, the Johnson administration was also criticized for bowing to political considerations. Steven Lawson maintains that the Department delayed in sending examiners to the home counties of Senators Eastland of Mississippi and Russell of Georgia, since both legislators were important to President Johnson's legislative program (Russell was also a close friend and early mentor of the president). Eastland even bragged that the Department would warn him of designs to send examiners to Mississippi and that he was able to block some plans (though it was a routine courtesy of the CRD to notify members of Congress of pending action). The Department was thus in crossfire between Southern congressmen and civil rights advocates.[15]

The Nixon Administration and the Seventies

Such political controversies were only to grow as President Richard M. Nixon came to power. As a 1968 Republican presidential candidate, Nixon made the performance of the DOJ and federal courts a powerful issue. He followed through on his criticism of departmental activism by appointing as attorney general his former law partner and campaign manager, John Mitchell. The new attorney general viewed the office as an instrument of advocacy for conservative public policy. Nixon came to office wishing to pursue a "Southern Strategy" in order to appeal to Southern whites on issues of racial and social conservatism. One scholar of the Nixon presidency argues that the attempt to limit implementation of the VRA was the most evident manifestation of the Southern Strategy. Nixon and Mitchell set out to do the minimum required by law on civil rights in the South and to underenforce the VRA where possible.[16]

One far-reaching decision came in September of 1969, when Mitchell reorganized the CRD. The restructuring did away with the geographic organization of the Division and rearranged it based upon function, including the creation of a new Voting Section. Many Division staffers were dismayed at what they regarded as Nixon administration partisan political interference in school desegregation policy. The birth of the Voting Section "furnished an unforeseen opportunity for disgruntled attorneys to move into it." Nixon's Southern Strategy demanded that the Justice Department slow down zealous civil rights advocates, but the Voting Section attorneys successfully resisted.[17]

The Johnson administration had taken the narrow view that open access to registration and assurance that a cast ballot would be fairly counted set the boundaries of the VRA, but the ingenuity of some Southern jurisdictions in attempting to limit black voting power soon brought the Department to argue for an expanded interpretation of Section Five. The Department joined plaintiffs before the Supreme Court in *Allen v State Board of Elections*, a 1969 decision that was to transform and extend Section Five jurisprudence beyond mere access to registration and ballot-counting issues. *Allen* was a consolidation of four cases, three from Mississippi and one from Virginia. The Mississippi cases represented bald efforts to minimize the power of newly enfranchised black voters. The most important matter focused upon whether Mississippi could change district elections in some counties to at-large voting without obtaining preclearance. The state's new system would dilute the voting power of newly enfranchised blacks. Dilutive schemes are those that minimize or cancel minority voting strength by techniques such as fragmenting or unnecessarily concentrating a group's voting strength.[18] Mississippi's changes were not barriers to registration or a fair count, but were they a "standard, practice, or procedure with respect to voting" and thus subject to Section Five?

The Department sided with the parties that were challenging Mississippi's obviously discriminatory election-law ploy. The solicitor general's brief asserted that Section Five was meant to reach not only changes that directly affect registration and casting a ballot, but also those that could dilute or impair the effectiveness of black votes. Section Five, in the Department's view, was meant to free the right to vote from impairments of any character, and however devised.[19]

The DOJ's interpretation carried the day. In an opinion expressing the views of seven members of the Court, Chief Justice Warren wrote "the right to vote can be affected by a dilution of voting power as well as by an absolute prohibition on casting a ballot." A ploy such as that exercised by Mississippi could be as effective in denying black voters the ability to elect a candidate of their choice as could an outright prohibition on voting. The Court therefore found that Section Five could be employed to invalidate any state enactment that might dilute or harm minority voting rights in even a minor way.[20] By centering on dilution *Allen* promoted a focus on group rights.

Allen provided a clear signal that some covered jurisdictions intended to implement a range of discriminatory practices to impede black political power. Division staff advised new Assistant Attorney General for Civil Rights Jerris Leonard that *Allen* required the Department to seek an injunction against any election going forward in which a covered jurisdiction had failed to preclear any change to its electoral procedures. The effect of *Allen* on Section Five administration was immediate. From 1965 through 1968, the Division handled 189 Section Five submissions. In 1970, the year following *Allen*, the Division handled 255 submissions and in 1971 it reviewed 1,118 submissions. Redistricting submissions in the early years were a trickle: 201 in 1971 and 97 in 1972, following the decennial census. Between 1991 and mid-1995, almost 3,000 redistricting plans were submitted to the CRD.[21]

The Court also expanded the reach of the VRA and thus the Department in 1969 in *Gaston County, North Carolina v United States*.[22] Section Four of the Act included a provision allowing a jurisdiction that had not conducted a racially discriminatory literacy test for five years to petition to "bail out" of Section Five coverage. Gaston County contended it could meet this standard and brought a bail-out suit in order to reinstate a literacy test. The United States opposed the county's effort, arguing that historical educational discrimination had rendered black voters less able to pass a literacy test than white citizens.[23] The Court upheld a lower court's ruling that Gaston County had historically denied black citizens equal educational opportunity, which therefore deprived them of an equal opportunity to pass a literacy test. Therefore, Gaston County could not bail out. As Graham points out, *Gaston County* relied upon the notion of compensatory protection for historical discrimination.[24]

This account reinforces what Graham argues was the transformation of meanings within the civil rights movement itself. After 1969, voting rights activists shifted from a concern with registration and voting to claims focusing upon historical discrimination. *Allen* recognized not just a right to register and vote, but a group's right to an undiluted vote. In *Gaston County* the Court accepted the notion that states should be held accountable for past injustice.

Following *Allen,* civil rights groups pushed the Voting Section to fully utilize the Section Five preclearance provision to intervene in Southern election-law changes. As the Act came up for renewal in 1970, the Nixon administration devised a legislative strategy designed to placate white Southerners. The administration proposed that the literacy-test ban should be extended nationwide and preclearance eliminated. It would thus fall to the DOJ to seek out discriminatory voting changes wherever they might exist and seek to enjoin them. The administration also sought to extend Section Five jurisdiction to all federal district courts and to place the burden of proof upon the party asserting a discriminatory purpose or effect. John Mitchell contended that the proposal would fight discrimination wherever it existed and would reduce the stigma on one part of the country.[25]

Civil rights advocates shot back. They asserted that the administration's posture was a smoke screen, designed to weaken Section Five by extending it beyond the Department's enforcement capabilities. Clarence Mitchell Jr., director of the Washington, DC, bureau of the NAACP, contended that 2 million Southern blacks remained unregistered and that the attorney general's proposal "would throw every single one of those persons to the wolves." Clarence Mitchell connected the administration proposal to the Republican Party platform's promise to end "regional legislation." The president's version passed in the House, and Clarence Mitchell proclaimed that the administration had "sold us out in order to get the segregation vote in the South."[26]

The Senate passed a compromise bill offered by moderate Republican Senator Hugh Scott of Pennsylvania. The Scott compromise extended the temporary provisions, including preclearance, for another five years. It banned literacy tests nationwide and expanded Section Five coverage to a number of counties outside the South that used literacy tests and had a voter turnout of less than 50 percent in 1968. Scott's bill was acceptable to, if not enthusiastically greeted by, civil rights leaders. The Senate version prevailed in conference committee and was signed into law. Nonetheless, the advocates could not have been encouraged after the renewal when the attorney general was quoted as saying that he could not fulfill the preclearance requirements properly.[27]

Southern efforts to limit black voting power continued. In 1970 the Mississippi legislature passed an open-primary law designed to limit the opportunities for third-party candidates. The law would have harmed the prospects for an African American to run and win outside the confines of the racially biased major parties. Under prior law an independent African-American candidate might win in a three-way general election if two white major-party candidates split the white vote. The open-primary law abolished party primaries and required all candidates to run in an open primary, with the top two finishers to face off in a general election requiring a majority vote. Although the intent of the law seemed clear, the attorney general declined to file an objection, demurring that he lacked sufficient time to sort out the competing claims. In essence the Department was placing the burden to show discriminatory purpose on those challenging the plan, not on the state. Controversy erupted, as civil rights activists and members of Congress pressed upon the administration the need to place the burden on the submitting states. In a privately initiated suit, a district court in Mississippi harshly criticized the attorney general's failure to decide and suspended the open-primary law. (The Supreme Court later ruled in another case that if no objection was rendered within the statutory sixty-day period established for the Department to decide whether or not to object, then the changes should go into effect.) The district court, no friend of the VRA, criticized the attorney general's failure to act as "an obtuse, patronizing failure by the federal government official to discharge the duties Congress placed upon him."[28]

The influx of submissions in the wake of *Allen* and confusion over decisional rules in the Mississippi open-primary case made it apparent that a regulatory structure for handling submissions was necessary. Discontent continued in 1971 as the Department prepared to propose regulations. Assistant Attorney General for Civil Rights David Norman asserted that the burden to prove discriminatory purpose or effect should be placed upon complainants. Civil rights advocates contended that the burden should be carried by the states—that the attorney general should not preclear a change unless the state could prove the absence of discriminatory purpose or effect. There would therefore be a presumption against the validity of state action.

The advocates met the threat from the Department with a bipartisan strategy. This included lobbying by the civil rights establishment and its allies as well as the active engagement of senators such as Democrat Philip Hart and moderate Republicans Hugh Scott and Jacob Javits. Northern moderate Republicans were concerned about how a perceived administration assault on civil rights would play in the 1972 election. They threatened to turn the proposed regulations into a replay of the vitriolic nomination battle of G. Harrold Carswell to the Supreme Court, which Nixon had lost. As the pressure increased and House hearings devoted to examining VRA enforcement loomed, Norman continued to negotiate the regulatory language with the concerned senators and finally acquiesced. The regulations would place the burden on the states to prove nondiscrimination.[29]

The proposed regulations were issued on 25 May 1971 and House hearings on VRA enforcement, led by Democratic Congressman Don Edwards, commenced the next day. Edwards opened the hearings with the observation that "Some have suggested that the Attorney General is attempting to accomplish by administrative action in 1971 what he failed to accomplish in 1970 by legislative action." Nevertheless, voting rights litigator Armand Derfner praised the career attorneys in the Voting Section. Assistant Attorney General Norman testified that the Division's first priority was voluntary compliance, the model established by the Johnson administration.[30]

The Act needed renewal yet again, in 1975, but with Gerald Ford having replaced Richard Nixon as president and John Mitchell having been forced from office in disgrace, the political atmosphere was far more conciliatory. Even after the controversies of the Nixon administration, the committed careerists of the CRD maintained a continuum of policy across administrations. J. Stanley Pottinger, assistant attorney general for civil rights, told Representative Edwards's Subcommittee in 1975 that "enforcement of Section Five is the highest priority of the Voting Section." The United States Commission on Civil Rights noted approvingly that the Department was going beyond a consideration of the purpose of proposed changes to examine results.[31]

In the 1976 Supreme Court case of *Beer v United States* the Court issued another major VRA decision. New Orleans had a city council composed of five councilmanic districts and two seats elected at large. The city population was 55 percent white and 45 percent African American. Following the 1970 census, the city reapportioned its districts. The DOJ denied preclearance to a plan that created two districts with African-American population majorities, but neither with a majority of voting-age population. A second submission included majority populations in two districts with a majority of black registered voters in one. The Department found that the second plan had a discriminatory effect in that it diluted potential black voting strength and again refused preclearance. The city brought a declaratory judgment action in the district court, seeking approval of the second plan. The district court upheld the Department's position and the case was appealed to the Supreme Court. There, the Department argued that limiting Section Five's effects test to a mere determination that the change would be no worse than the pre-existing procedure would defeat congressional intent. The Court decided in favor of the city, ruling that electoral changes have a discriminatory effect under Section Five only when retrogression in minority voting strength occurs. The Court's ruling greatly restricted the utility of an objection for discriminatory effect.[32]

The Department objected to only one congressional redistricting plan in the seventies redistricting cycle, in Georgia. This was not because the Department failed to recognize dilutive schemes. Indeed, the Department objected to dilutive state legislature redistricting plans in Louisiana, South Carolina, and Georgia. The original Georgia congressional plan, which included a 38 percent black Fifth Congressional District, discriminated in three ways. It divided black populations, snaked its way through Atlanta so as to exclude the homes of strong African-American potential candidates Andrew Young and Maynard Jackson, and awkwardly jutted so as to pick up the home of a favored white candidate. The Department objected for purposive discrimination and the Georgia legislature produced a plan with a 44 percent black Fifth District, including the homes of Young and Jackson. The Department precleared this plan, and Young ran and won the seat.[33]

Even as the administration of President Jimmy Carter managed the Department with a friendlier posture toward civil rights, advocates for aggressive intervention found fault with restrained enforcement. Howard Ball, Dale Krane, and Thomas P. Lauth argued in 1982 in *Compromised Compliance: Implementation of the 1965 Voting Rights Act* that Department intervention in the South from 1965 to 1981 had been disappointing. A 1978 Government Accounting Office report criticized the Division for administrative inefficiencies. Assistant Attorney General for Civil Rights Drew S. Days III responded that although the Department was given a large measure of responsibility for enforcement of the Act, it was to share responsibility with private entities—an interpretation that was consistent with that of attorneys general since the Act's passage. Despite the arguments of academics and the policy preferences of some attorneys within the Voting Section, Days's testimony represented the prevailing dimension of voting rights enforcement through the years. CRD political appointees and the dominant proportion of professional staff agreed that the VRA empowered them to eradicate barriers to political participation, but not to intercede in favor of specific outcomes.[34]

The Division followed a temperately progressive enforcement strategy in the administrations from Johnson through Carter. The emphasis upon voluntary compliance and negotiation mollified Southern intransigence; but the same strategy led one critic to argue that the Department's position left minority voters without an advocate against covered jurisdictions.[35] With the coming of the Reagan administration, the philosophical battles over the meaning of nondiscrimination were about to be joined.

The Reagan Administration—Conflict Masks a Transformation

Ronald Reagan came to office offering a conservative direction to civil rights policy. The president and Assistant Attorney General for Civil Rights William Bradford Reynolds argued for a color-blind vision of nondiscrimination based upon individual rights. Reynolds asserted that federal antidiscrimination laws are not the province of any discrete group but should be applied to all Americans.[36] Civil rights activists however, considered Reynolds's concern with reverse discrimination as antithetical to the movement and their model of historical discrimination, institutional racism, and racial compensation. Moreover, they regarded the CRD as their special ally within the government. The relationship between Reynolds and the advocates was poisoned significantly by his decision to reverse the Division's position in the pending case of *Bob Jones University v United States*, in which the Reagan administration supported a tax exemption for religious institutions that discriminate on the basis of race. Following that dispute, critics often imputed political interference in the work of the Division.[37]

Voting rights law in the eighties and nineties was to be greatly influenced by a 1980 Supreme Court decision and the statutory change it spawned. In *City of Mobile v Bolden*, the Supreme Court decided that intent to discriminate must be shown in a suit brought to enforce the promise of the Fifteenth Amendment, and consequently its cognate statutory provision, Section Two of the VRA. Mobile, Alabama, had an at-large system for electing city commissioners. The at-large method often dilutes minority votes, because where voting is racially polarized and whites are in the majority, they will outvote blacks. No African American had ever been elected to the city council in Mobile, though blacks comprised a third of the population of the city. The Department (still under the Carter administration) supported the voting rights advocates and argued that the at-large system amounted to official action that enhanced the effects of racially polarized voting and thus constituted a purposive effort to cancel out black voting strength. The Department concentrated its arguments on what it described as a violation of the Fourteenth Amendment's Equal Protection Clause and extended that argument to the Fifteenth Amendment and Section Two of the VRA, but the Supreme Court held that a showing based upon disparate impact could not support a finding of unconstitutional vote dilution—invidious intent to discriminate must be shown. "A plaintiff must prove that the disputed plan was 'conceived or operated as [a] purposeful devic[e] to further racial . . . discrimination.'"[38]

The civil rights community declaimed that *Bolden* was a misinterpretation and a break with the Supreme Court's ruling in *White v Regester*, in which the Court had set a "totality of the circumstances" test for determining dilution. The temporary provisions of the Act came up for renewal in 1982. A coalition of advocacy groups working under the umbrella of the Leadership Conference on Civil Rights was ready with proposals to repair the *Bolden* damage. Working with an obliging Democratic majority in the House, advocates altered Section Two of the Act to get at dilutive impact by amending the section to reach electoral "standards, practices and procedures" that "result" in the denial or abridgement of the right to vote. Amended Section Two would now be nationwide in scope and applicable to any electoral system, so long as the arrangement could be said to have some discriminatory result.[39]

Reagan administration officials and other critics argued that the courts would reach for some measure to determine discriminatory results and settle on the mathematical standard of proportional representation according to race. President Reagan made this argument in a press conference in December of 1981: "[T]he effect rule could lead to the type of thing in which effect could be judged if there was some disproportion in the number of elected officials who were elected at any governmental level." (The president's use of the word "effect" reflects that the word is commonly used interchangeably with "result"; the statutory meanings are quite different.) Both Attorney General William French Smith and Reynolds argued in the Senate hearings that the proposed amendment would lead to proportional representation. Professor Walter Berns agreed and recounted that the Founders had sought to diminish the importance of faction by creating large congressional districts so that a representative would not be beholden to particularized interests.[40]

The civil rights lobbyists disputed the administration's arguments. The Lawyers' Committee for Civil Rights Under Law said Reynolds's concerns about proportional representation were made from whole cloth; there was no interest in proportional representation. The House Report indicated that "The proposed amendment does not create a right to proportional representation."[41] Revised Section Two was passed into law after the concerns of Senator Orrin Hatch and others were partially assuaged by a compromise offered by Senator Robert Dole. The Dole language indicated that the results test of new Section Two would be violated if members of a racial minority have less opportunity to participate in electoral processes and less opportunity to elect candidates of their choice than do white citizens. While the proportion of minority members elected in a jurisdiction could be "one circumstance" taken into account in determining whether a violation existed, a proviso was added "That nothing in this section establishes a right to have members of a protected class elected in numbers equal to their proportion in the population."[42] Yet it was still open to plaintiffs to argue that a lack of proportional representation is evidence of discrimination and to seek proportional representation as a remedy.

By 1982, the model of the civil rights community was not discrimination against the individual, but equivalence of results—proportional representation. The advocates sought to achieve this goal by the 1982 amendment. The Department's use of its preclearance powers in 1992 to force Southern states to draw the maximum possible number of minority districts indicates that the concerns of Reynolds, Smith, and Hatch were borne out. In congressional cases during the 1990s the Department objected under Section Five's purpose prong. Yet opposing litigants and reviewing courts recognized the objections as having a Section Two results basis.

Given the maximization agenda that obtained in the next redistricting cycle following the Section Two amendment, it is interesting to give further attention to the remarks in 1982 of key players concerning disparate impact and proportional representation. Reynolds denied that the Department was then imposing mathematical standards upon its objection determinations. Nevertheless, Senator Hatch's Subcommittee on the Constitution found that the Department had required maximization in some cases. Even before the 1982 amendment, Reynolds had signed Section Five objection letters based upon a jurisdiction's failure to show a result that fairly reflected minority voting strength. Thernstrom argued in 1987 that the Division under Reynolds continued to ignore the *Beer* retrogression test in favor of a "fairly drawn" test. She wrote: "'Fairly drawn' plans are those that give blacks 'safe' seats in proportion to the black population—to the degree possible." Following the 1982 amendment, the Department adopted incorporation of Section Two into Section Five in at least two district court cases. In its post-trial brief in *Sumter County v United States* in 1984, the Department asserted that "each time the issue is addressed the conclusion is that Section Two is to be applied in Section Five proceedings."[43]

The approach outlined here is incompatible with the policy positions advocated by Reynolds. Such inconsistencies were probably attributable to the tug-of-war between Reynolds and career staff. The professionals would bang away at Reynolds, whose predisposition was not to object to submissions. The careerists sometimes succeeded, but frequently Reynolds stubbornly refused to accede to their arguments.[44]

Former Assistant Attorney General Days, a strong advocate for the Act, also testified at the House and Senate hearings. Days testified that during his tenure, the CRD evaluated Section Five submissions to see if minority voting strength was augmented, decreased, or not affected at all. He continued that where no change in voting strength or retrogression occurred, the Division would inquire whether an acceptable alternative could have been devised "that would have given minorities a fairer opportunity to elect candidates of their choice." Nonetheless, Days asserted, the Department would not "demand that the jurisdiction adopt a crazy-quilt, gerrymandered districting plan to ensure . . . proportional minority representation." Days further testified that during his tenure he was under constant pressure from voting advocates to dictate gerrymandered proportional representation, but he refused to do so.[45] This testimony is telling because "crazy-quilt, gerrymandered" districts were exactly the results engendered by the Department's maximization agenda under the Bush administration—and later defended before the Supreme Court by Days, as solicitor general in the Clinton administration.

Reynolds sparked criticism in May of 1985 when the Department issued proposed revisions to its regulations governing Section Five enforcement. The revisions included a tepid incorporation of the Section Two results test into the preclearance process; Reynolds indicated little commitment to even a modest form of incorporation. The proposed incorporation provision stated that a Section Five objection would be lodged upon a "clear and convincing" violation of Section Two, and it placed the burden of proof upon the party alleging the violation rather than the submitting authority.[46] Congressman Edwards's Subcommittee held hearings on the proposed regulations in November. Reynolds termed the decision whether to incorporate as being very difficult, because the Section Five process is brief in nature and a Section Two inquiry calls for a full evidentiary process. Therefore, he asserted that incorporation might be used only in those rare circumstances where it was quite clear that a Section Two violation existed.

The Edwards Subcommittee received evidence that went even further than Reynolds's doubts about the scope of incorporation. A written analysis by political scientist Timothy G. O'Rourke was admitted, in which he argued:

> [I]ncorporation at least would open the door for the inclusion of a straight-forward requirement of proportional representation on covered jurisdictions.
>
> Under a results-oriented standard, Section Five could easily evolve into a mandate for maximizing the number of safe minority districts. . . . In this event, even the pretext of federalism would be lost and, more important, the goal of equal access would be sacrificed in favor of a quota-based politics that amounts to a "resegregation" of the electoral system.[47]

These doubts were expressed in the face of a well-organized campaign by proponents of incorporation. The activists generated an overwhelming number of comments to the Department in favor of incorporation and placing the burden of proof on the states. The Subcommittee Report came out in favor of incorporation. Edwards later termed Reynolds's approach "an outrageous retreat on the Voting Rights Act by the Justice Department." [48]

When the final regulations were promulgated, the Department relented. The new regulation stated that where DOJ could find no discriminatory purpose or effect but could find evidence of a "clear violation of amended section 2," it would withhold Section Five preclearance.[49] Civil rights groups praised the decision, though complaining of continued ambiguity on the burden question. In a front-page article in the *Washington Post* of 7 January 1987, Mary Thornton reported in an article entitled "New Rules Strengthen VRA" that voting rights litigator Frank Parker proclaimed a "great victory. Reynolds has flip-flopped."

The key Supreme Court pronouncement on the amended Section Two occurred in the 1986 case of *Thornburg v Gingles*. Black citizens of North Carolina challenged the state's 1982 redistricting plan for state legislative seats, which relied upon multimember districts. They alleged that the multimember districts interacted with white bloc voting to dilute African-American voting power. The Department, nearly always a strong supporter of minority voting aspirations before the Court, instead aided North Carolina's position. The DOJ's brief was a product of the solicitor general and the conservative political appointees in the Division; CRD professionals were literally out of the loop. A linchpin of the solicitor general's argument was that recent African-American electoral successes in the challenged locales indicated that black North Carolinians enjoyed an equal opportunity to participate in political affairs. In a sharp rebuke to the administration several congressmen, including Senator Dole, filed their own *amicus* brief arguing that the solicitor general had misread the amended Section Two and misrepresented congressional intent. The congressmen asserted that under the totality-of-the-circumstances test, recent or sporadic black electoral success is not enough to preclude a Section Two violation.[50]

The Court narrowly ruled in favor of the challenge from the African-American citizens in a decision authored by Justice Brennan. The Court rejected the Department's position and found that proof of some recent minority electoral success does not foreclose a Section Two claim. The significance was great, for the decision was widely interpreted as virtually requiring proportional representation. Supporters of that remedy were able to argue quite convincingly that only proportional representation would satisfy *Gingles*. The DOJ and even some covered jurisdictions came to accede to that interpretation.

In 1992 Days argued the Department's position that Congress had mandated incorporation in 1982, and that the limitation of *Beer's* nonretrogression test therefore no longer presented an obstacle to objections to plans that failed to maximize. Thus the question for the Voting Section (which Days acknowledged would require resolution by the Supreme Court) became "whether the changes provide minority voters with the greatest feasible access to the political process in light of the 'totality of the circumstances.'"[51]

There appeared to be good authority that the Department could require states to draw districts on a racial basis under the Voting Rights Act in the Supreme Court's 1977 decision in *United Jewish Organizations (UJO) v Carey. UJO* was a case in which members of a New York City Hasidic neighborhood alleged that the state legislative redistricting plan unconstitutionally diluted the votes of community members. The legislature had originally submitted a plan to the Department for certain counties covered by Section Five, and the Department objected because it appeared that minority voters had unnecessarily been packed into a single senate district when their votes might have been more effectively dispersed into surrounding districts. Similarly, African-American and Hispanic voters appeared to have been concentrated into three assembly districts, leaving adjoining districts with few minority voters. The CRD objected to the submission. The state then went back to work and submitted a revised plan that did not change the number of minority state house and senate seats in Kings County, but did change the size of the nonwhite majorities in those districts. The alteration made certain of the districts safer for minority candidates by assuring a 65 percent minority population, but the plan split apart a Hasidic neighborhood. A New York legislative staffer testified that from meetings and conversations he had held with Department officials he had drawn the conclusion that districts with 65 percent minority populations would be precleared. The Court agreed that in the circumstances 65 percent would grant the minority population a reasonable chance to elect a candidate, and it stated that the petitioners "have not shown that New York did more than accede to a position taken by the Attorney General that was authorized by our constitutionally permissible construction of Section 5."[52] The 65 percent figure became a kind of informal standard thereafter, with courts requiring a 65 percent minority population to correct for assumed lower minority voting-age population, registration, and voter turnout.

Reynolds's color-blind approach to enforcement and preoccupation with reverse discrimination disturbed the civil rights activists. They helped to defeat his nomination to become associate attorney general in 1985. The moral fervor and political rhetoric concerning Reynolds is captured in Parker's statement that Reynolds's Division acted as "the friend and advocate for the white perpetrators and beneficiaries of racial discrimination." Reynolds was attacked not only for politicizing the office in the ideological sense, but also for responding to the political concerns of Southern politicians.

In 1982 the Lawyers' Committee for Civil Rights Under Law produced a report entitled "Justice Department Voting Rights Enforcement: Political Interference and Retreats." The report accused the Division of backing off vigorous enforcement after inquiries from Southern politicians such as Senator Strom Thurmond and Representative Trent Lott. To be sure, an official who can respond to the importuning of congressional allies in a manner consistent with administration policy finds himself in a precious state indeed. That such a criticism came from advocates who themselves enjoyed a synergistic relationship with congressional staff and Voting Section careerists shows the sense of illegitimacy attached to opposing views by the advocates.[53]

The conflict over the Reagan administration's approach to voting rights enforcement is a good illustration of the two aspects of "politicized" enforcement. The administration's strategy reflected a genuine ideological predisposition to interpret the VRA narrowly more than a partisan corruption. This was what Reagan had promised in his campaign for the presidency in 1980, and the policy appealed to his political base. The Lawyers' Committee complained in 1982 that the political appeals made to the Department were all to the effect that the Department should reflect the wishes of Reagan's electorate.[54] Aside from the overstatement (it is hard to believe that civil rights advocates were not petitioning the professional staff of the Voting Section in this period), the argument ignores the tension in agency policy making when political appointees of a democratically elected official clash with professional holdovers of different ideological predisposition. The contention that political appointees are somehow sullied by responding to the constituents of a democratically elected president is dubious.

Raymond Wolters adds a nice distinction to the argument over narrow enforcement. Reynolds's critics asserted that if the administration disputed prevailing interpretations of civil rights laws, it could go to Congress with amendments or outright repeal of offensive provisions. Wolters replies:

> Under the U.S. system of government, a bill can become law only if it surmounts a host of obstacles that have been deliberately embedded in the structure of the Constitution. But the racial preferences of the 1970s, unlike the nondiscrimination of the civil rights laws of the 1960s, had become a social policy without ever having been subjected to the conventional legislative process.
>
> The critics were demanding that Reynolds do more to repeal racial preferences and forced busing than the initiators of the policies had done in the 1970s. The policies had been created administratively and judicially, but the critics were saying that to change things the Reagan administration should surmount the checks and balances associated with the usual legislative process. This tilted the playing field for, as Richard E. Morgan has noted, the same set of interest groups that are "insufficient to persuade Congress to adopt a policy in the first place, may be quite sufficient, if the policy can be put in place judicially or bureaucratically, to keep the legislature from disestablishing it."[55]

Paradoxically, Reynolds's performance also attracted criticisms that he overzealously enforced voting rights. Charles Bullock and Katharine Butler show that in areas such as numbers of submissions handled, objections filed and percentage of objections and new cases, the Reynolds Division performed much as had the Division under Days in the Carter administration. Thernstrom argues that the Division consistently exceeded the boundaries set by *Beer* in pursuit of "fairly drawn" plans. Rather than backing off, these commentators argue that the Reynolds Division had gotten tougher.[56]

How can these assessments be reconciled? By distinguishing the political appointees from the career staff. Chandler Davidson and Bernard Grofman argue that the Voting Section careerists have historically been able to resist political appointees who favor restrained enforcement.[57] I believe that on large policy matters Reynolds was able to impose the administration's ideology. Yet in many less visible ways the careerists pushed for an expansive vision of the Act. One example of this is the Division's 1982 objection to Texas's first congressional plan for its discriminatory purpose; the objection relied on a results theory of vote dilution. The brief in *Sumter County* that argues for incorporation of the Section Two results test into Section Five is another example. Those positions are policy making by enforcement.

Grofman and Davidson have assessed why the careerists have prevailed so frequently. First, there have been only a handful of controversial Section Five cases where political pressure was brought to bear, and thus staff could usually proceed without interference. Second, only during the tenure of Reynolds was political interference especially troublesome. Grofman and Davidson seem to define political interference as an abusive response to political figures. I believe that this sort of politicized conduct was more manifest in the Nixon-Mitchell Southern Strategy. In the case of the Reagan-Reynolds Division, I would characterize the political concerns as ideological, though there is evidence of partisan consideration, as in Reynolds's treatment of Louisiana's Governor Treen in a redistricting case in which the governor sought to protect a favored congressman (none other than 1998's failed Speaker-elect, Robert Livingston); but even where a political appointee might wish to take partisan action, the official is often constrained by the professional staff.[58]

Third, Grofman and Davidson assert that conflict was generally over high-level issues and conclude: "[D]uring the Reagan administration, the resolution of those high level conflicts was in ways generally in far closer accord with the views of line staff than with the views of their political bosses. Voting rights attorneys could simply lie low and wait until their views were vindicated." The Department's decisions on large policy matters such as the 1982 renewal or the Department's brief in *Gingles* reflected the administration's preferences. In fact, on the 1982 renewal, the careerists had little or no influence upon Reynolds and his inner circle. The policy victories of the careerists were in the day-to-day enforcement decisions.[59]

Grofman and Davidson's fourth reason for the general prevalence of the careerists is the seniority, bureaucratic expertise, and strong personal commitment of the Voting Section professional staff. Indeed, Bullock and Butler argue that the Voting Section was largely unaffected by Reynolds's designs and conclude that after 1982 the political appointees had simply lost the fight to careerists and forfeited control of voting rights policy.[60]

Notwithstanding the staff's ability to overcome Reynolds's qualms over objections in certain enforcement cases, the Division was not ready in 1982 to force maximization in congressional districts, but it did object to several plans on purpose or effect grounds. Georgia again earned an objection when the Department refused preclearance to a plan that created a Fifth Congressional District with a black population in excess of 57 percent, but a 54 percent white voting-age population. Georgia took the matter, *Busbee v Smith*, to the District Court for the District of Columbia. In 1982 the court found the plan not technically retrogressive but the product of a discriminatory purpose—a finding buttressed by evidence of ugly racist statements by the chair of the house redistricting committee, deliberate fragmentation of geographically compact black voting populations, historical discrimination, and the want of any legitimate non-racial reason for splitting black voters.[61]

The DOJ also objected to Mississippi and Texas's congressional redistricting plans. As recounted in the 1982 Mississippi case *Jordan v Winter*, the state's submission tracked the existing 1972 plan that had been precleared by the Department and made some one-person one-vote adjustments. The Department formally claimed retrogression, a seemingly pretextual claim for a plan that did not backslide; but the objection letter revealed the true basis, the accusation that Mississippi's new plan had been drawn "to dismember the black population concentration and effectively dilute its voting strength." The Department noted that alternative plans had been submitted that would have created a black-majority seat, but they had been rejected without satisfactory reasons.[62]

The objection to Texas's first congressional redistricting plan was made on 29 January 1982. It noted that in an area of South Texas, one congressional district had been drawn with a population just over 80 percent Mexican-American; an adjoining district was just shy of 53 percent Mexican-American, sustaining allegations that minority voting strength had been diluted. The objection letter also pointed out that the Division was aware that alternative plans that would have ameliorated this outcome were rejected. The dilution grounds in the Texas and Mississippi cases are substantially the same as those claimed to show purposeful discrimination in the 1990s redistricting.

The congressional redistricting matter that caused Reynolds the most grief was that of Louisiana. The Democratic legislature had approved a plan with a new 54 percent black congressional district. This legislation was adopted not out of solicitude for African-American constituents but because of other political considerations. Republican Governor David C. Treen threatened a veto, claiming he wished to protect Republican Congressman Robert Livingston. The legislature bowed to the governor's threat and passed a new plan without the black district. Treen signed the bill.

Voting Section staff attorney Victor Kwan examined the submission. Kwan reviewed Treen's past participation in the states' rights movement, the governor's proffered justification, and indications that he disfavored a black district. The attorney also obtained a confidential report that one key legislator had stated that "we already have a nigger mayor, and we don't need another nigger bigshot." Kwan concluded that Louisiana had not met its Section Five burden to prove lack of discriminatory purpose. Reynolds, after meeting with Governor Treen but not with Louisiana voting rights advocates, declined to object. The matter was litigated, and the court found for plaintiffs on the basis of amended Section Two, which was not available to Reynolds at the time he reviewed the submission. Nonetheless, given the state's burden under Section Five, Reynolds might well have lodged an objection. Some Voting Section staff suspected that Reynolds had succumbed to political pressure from the governor.[63] None of this endeared Reynolds to voting rights advocates, who continued to battle him and receive succor from Voting Section careerists throughout the remainder of the Reagan administration.

Despite the lengthy battles with Reynolds, the advocates were winning many of the enforcement battles (with the aid of Voting Section staff). They were also making substantial progress toward their goal of proportional representation. The Section Two amendment, *Gingles*, and incorporation all advanced the agenda, even against Reagan administration opposition.

THE TECHNOLOGICAL REVOLUTION

The revolution in computer capacity that began to pervade society in the late eighties and early nineties was to have a profound effect on redistricting. One explanation for the limited number of challenges to redistricting plans for failure to maximize before the nineties round is that there were few opportunities for map drawers to link together significant concentrations of minority residents. That changed. Software engineers had developed programs capable of searching out and grouping residents of similar demographic characteristics. The programs and the hardware necessary to run them were widely accessible by the time the 1990 census tapes became available.

The increased sophistication of technology was to play a revolutionary role in the nineties round of redistricting. A process recently reliant on legislators' experiential knowledge of the demographic and electoral characteristics of their states, plus calculators and colored pencils for filling in maps, was now transformed by the ability to manipulate racial data at the census-block level, the smallest unit measured by the Census Bureau. This newfound computer power was matched with increased availability so that interested parties outside of the legislature could readily create their own plans, sometimes with the legislature's own hardware and software.

In a June 1990 speech to the National Conference of State Legislators, Bush administration CRD chief John R. Dunne explained that the Division possessed the latest state-of-the art hardware and software with which to review the jurisdictions' handiwork. He added that those who wished to participate in the redistricting process would have similar capabilities, giving each interest the ability to draw lines in whatever configuration might be most favorable, whether it be partisan, racial, or otherwise. Dunne warned the legislators that a state must be able to justify its racial line drawing in light of competing plans that were proposed but not adopted. He cautioned that interest groups could almost instantly analyze each adjustment to district lines for racial and electoral impact, and could readily produce maps to illustrate state-plan shortcomings and the purported superiority of alternative plans. These participants, Dunne stated, would be able to analyze every plan drawn by the state and lodge protests to the Department over perceived deficiencies. The states had thus better be ready not only to defend their own plans, but also to make a rational argument for the rejection of each alternative plan. "Move a district line one block north or one block south and I assure you that someone will have a color chart and tables of statistics to show the impact. And you'll see similar presentations analyzing the failure to move that same district line one block north or south." Dunne told *Congressional Quarterly* that the technological capabilities could spawn literally thousands of people who could bring a credible case to court.[64]

The system used by the CRD in the nineties was called the Geographic Information System (GIS). The GIS uses census data and can incorporate other data sources. The potential and power of the system was described in the Spring 1995 edition of the CRD's quarterly publication the *Civil Rights Forum*:

> The Division's GIS can analyze and map data at the census block level, the smallest aggregate level provided by the Census Bureau. . . . In many urban areas, a census block is literally a city block. The Division's GIS uses two types of census data: TIGER Lines that provide the geographic references for creating maps, and Public Law 94–171 data that provide various aggregations of demographic data collected by the Census Bureau. Using this data, GIS can produce extremely detailed maps. For example, if one wanted a series of maps for a geographic area showing households without indoor plumbing broken out by race, income, education, and age of the head of the household, GIS could produce it down to the city block level.
>
> [The] primary user application, the Justice Application, was designed so that end users with approximately two hours of training can do any number of analytical tasks and generate presentation quality color maps. The Justice application is described as so user friendly that even a lawyer can use it.[65]

Notwithstanding the availability of the Census Bureau's TIGER files and the computer technology to tailor a district to meet particular demographic or political profiles, the era of desktop redistricting was not quite upon the nation in the early nineties. The amount of data needed to draw a map of an entire state could not be handled by an ordinary personal computer, but one of the most damaging complaints against the states in the eighties had been that they ran their redistricting processes as closed shops. To avoid such complaints in the nineties, many states offered public terminals and even advisory staff to assist citizens who wanted to draw or analyze maps. North Carolina's chief technician reported that among those who took advantage of that state's public terminals were political consultants, journalists, the Republican National Committee, the NAACP, the ACLU, and the Southern Regional Council. The most frequent users in North Carolina were the legislators themselves. Interested parties produced over 800 plans.[66]

North Carolina Assistant Attorney General Tiare B. Smiley, who has represented the state in several redistricting cases, describes the capacity of the technology available in the nineties:

> You put up a map of an area, and hit a button, and you can look at every precinct and it will show you . . . racial data and would also show election results. . . . And you could see the percentages there on the screen, and the machine allows you [to click the mouse] and the precinct would go into the district. Or the other thing you could do was called a lasso, and you kind of drew on the screen, so what you could do [was] lasso the precincts with the highest percentages of whatever you were looking for, and click it and the computer would stick that in the district.[67]

A typical example of the new technological capacity occurred in Texas, where the state's plan was challenged. The Texas computer program was known as "REDAPPL." The system allowed redistricters to manipulate lines on maps, to which racial and socioeconomic data were imposed. As lines were moved, the racial implications were simultaneously tracked. The fact that racial statistics were available on REDAPPL down to the census-block level permitted a nearly perfect fit between race and district boundaries. Recognizing the racial component of the gerrymander, the district court found that "the borders of Districts 18, 29, and 30 change from block to block, from one side of the street to the other, and traverse streets, bodies of water, and commercially developed areas in seemingly arbitrary fashion until one realizes that those corridors connect minority populations." The Supreme Court noted that REDAPPL's capabilities were vastly more sophisticated for manipulating racial statistics than other data, providing evidence of the legislature's racial motivations. This factor also played a role in a Virginia district court's reversal of that state's congressional plan.[68]

The vastly improved computer technology available in the early nineties must be recognized as a significant factor in developing oddly shaped racial gerrymanders. The most sophisticated data available was racial, and the intentions that drove the process were racial. The technology allowed those intentions to be accomplished in ways unimaginable even ten years earlier. As promised by Dunne, the Department used the plans developed by the Republican Party, the ACLU, and other advocates as alternatives to measure the racial potential of state submissions. When those plans were found not to maximize, the Department objected in many cases.

CONCLUSION

Battles over voting rights almost always reveal something about the subtextual elements of politicized enforcement, moral claims, and how we define equality. Claims of politicized enforcement have sometimes encompassed accusations of partisan advantage, and at other times, accusations of an ideological hijacking of the VRA. Moral claims are not as powerful for proportional representation based upon race as they were for ensuring that the racist discrimination that denied black citizens the right to vote should be destroyed forever. Nonetheless, they are made sincerely and with sufficiently compelling appeal that courts and advocates nearly always regard racial representational disparity as a rationale for close scrutiny of redistricting plans. In conducting that examination, reviewers are faced with the question of whether to define equality as the elimination of obstacles to political opportunity or as a guarantee of proportional results. Each of these subtextual elements was present in the historical view of voting rights enforcement, and as we shall see, each was present in the controversies of the nineties that encompassed Bush administration objections to nonmaximization plans and Clinton administration defenses of the resulting state legislative enactments.

The historical review also shows that from the advent of the VRA the DOJ placed great stress on community involvement to register and mobilize black citizens. The early norm was one of restrained enforcement, reliance on state compliance unless faced with deep intractability, and dependence on the minority community to promote registration and voting. In this respect, an expectation that the early years of agency implementation establishes the standard for enforcement began to break down as theories of discrimination and equal opportunity changed. The norm of federal intervention to remove obstacles to the individual right to vote began to give way to what would become the logic of proportional representation and finally to the maximization agenda of the nineties. As the theory of equal opportunity changed, so too did emphasis begin to shift from the democratic efforts to increase registration and voting toward theories of proportional representation and maximization propounded by social scientists and lawyers. Elite control of the parameters of voting rights debate continued into the controversial redistricting round of the nineties.

Notwithstanding the emotional battles over Reynolds and his ideological or political postures, the Reagan administration was unable to significantly slow the career attorneys in the Voting Section. The Bush administration came to office promising a less conflictual administration. One early assessment concluded that by taking liberal positions in attacking electoral mechanisms in Texas, Georgia, and Louisiana, and siding with minorities in the 1991 Supreme Court case *Chisom v Roemer*, the Bush administration indeed appeared to be "kinder and gentler" than the Reagan administration.[69] The administration was to exceed kind and gentle in its handling of the 1990s congressional redistricting.

NOTES

1. Steven F. Lawson, *In Pursuit of Power: Southern Blacks and Electoral Politics, 1965–1982* (New York: Columbia University Press, 1985); Bernard Grofman and Lisa Handley, "1990s Issues in Voting Rights," *Mississippi Law Journal* 65, (winter 1995), 205, 207, note 7; Abigail M. Thernstrom, *Whose Votes Count? Affirmative Action and Minority Voting Rights* (Cambridge, Mass.: Harvard University Press, 1987), 166–168.

2. Cornell Clayton, "Introduction: Politics and the Legal Bureaucracy," in Cornell Clayton, ed., *Government Lawyers: The Federal Legal Bureaucracy and Presidential Politics* (Lawrence, Kans.: University Press of Kansas, 1995), 16.

3. Nancy V. Baker, *Conflicting Loyalties: Law and Politics in the Attorney General's Office, 1789–1990* (Lawrence, Kans.: University Press of Kansas, 1992); Cornell Clayton, *The Politics of Justice: The Attorney General and the Making of Legal Policy* (Armonk, N.Y.: M.E. Sharpe, Inc., 1992), 57; Brian K. Landsberg, "The Role of Civil Service Attorneys and Political Appointees in Making Policy in the Civil Rights Division of the United States Department of Justice," *Journal of Law and Politics* 9 (1993), 275, 281, note 26; U.S. Senate Committee on the Judiciary, *Confirmation of William C. Lucas, to be Assistant Attorney General for Civil Rights, Department of Justice.*, 101st Cong., 1st sess., 1989, 262.

4. James Q. Wilson, *Bureaucracy: What Government Agencies Do and Why They Do It*, (New York: Basic Books, 1989), 67.

5. Thernstrom, *Whose Votes Count?*, 12.

6. Hugh Davis Graham, *The Civil Rights Era: Origins and Development of National Policy, 1960–1972* (New York: Oxford University Press, 1990); Daniel Bell, *The Coming of Post-Industrial Society* (New York: Basic Books, 1973), 417.

7. Hugh Davis Graham, "Voting Rights and the American Regulatory State," in Bernard Grofman and Chandler Davidson, eds., *Controversies in Minority Voting: The Voting Rights Act in Perspective* (Washington, DC: Brookings Institution, 1992).

8. Chandler Davidson, "The Voting Rights Act: A Brief History," in Grofman and Davidson, *Controversies in Minority Voting*, 17–21. Davidson in turn cites Howell Raines, *My Soul Is Rested: Movement Days in the Deep South Remembered* (New York: Putnam, 1977). A fine detailed account of the effort that went into drafting the bill and preparing it for passage can be found in David Garrow, *Protest at Selma: Martin Luther King, Jr. and the Voting Rights Act of 1965* (New Haven, Conn.: Yale University Press, 1978).

9. Thernstrom, *Whose Votes Count?*, 15–17, 34, 52.

10. Clayton, *Politics of Justice*, 134–135.

11. Lawson, *Pursuit of Power*, 25, 29; Steven F. Lawson, *Black Ballots: Voting Rights in the South, 1944–1969* (New York: Columbia University Press, 1976), 329–334; Brian K. Landsberg, *Enforcing Civil Rights: Race Discrimination and the Department of Justice* (Lawrence, Kans.: University Press of Kansas, 1997), 31–32.

12. U.S. Department of Justice, *Brief for the Defendants*, submitted in *South Carolina v Katzenbach*, No. 22.

13. *South Carolina v Katzenbach*, 383 U.S. 301 (1966).

14. Lawson, *Pursuit of Power*, 16–42; Lawson, *Black Ballots*, 330–337.

15. Lawson, *Black Ballots*, 334–35; Lawson, *Pursuit of Power*, 21.

16. Clayton, *Politics of Justice*, 138–139; Michael A. Genovese, *The Nixon Presidency: Power and Politics in Turbulent Times* (New York: Greenwood Press, 1990), 84–85.

17. Graham, *Civil Rights Era*, 362; Lawson, *Pursuit of Power*, 162–163; Landsberg, *Enforcing Civil Rights*, 112–113.

18. Bernard Grofman, "An Expert Witness Perspective on Continuing and Emerging Voting Rights Controversies: From One Person, One Vote to Partisan Gerrymandering," *Stetson Law Review* 21 (1992), 783.

19. U.S. Department of Justice, *Memorandum for the United States as Amicus Curiae*, submitted to Supreme Court in *Allen v State Board of Elections*, Nos. 3, 25, 26, 36 (1969), 12–15.

20. *Allen v State Board of Elections*, 393 U.S. 544 (1969).

21. Lawson, *Pursuit of Power*, 162; Howard Ball, Dale Krane, and Thomas P. Lauth, *Compromised Compliance: Implementation of the 1965 Voting Rights Act* (Westport, Conn.: Greenwood Press, 1982), Appendix C, Appendix D; Mark A. Posner, "Post-1990 Redistrictings and the Preclearance Requirement of Section 5 of the Voting Rights Act," in Bernard Grofman, ed., *Race and Redistricting in the 1990s* (New York: Agathon Press, 1998).

22. *Gaston County, North Carolina v United States*, 395 U.S. 285 (1969).

23. U.S. Department of Justice, *Motion to Affirm*, submitted to the Supreme Court in *Gaston County, North Carolina v United States*, No. 701 (Washington, DC: 1968), 29.

24. Graham, *Civil Rights Era*, 377.

25. United States Commission on Civil Rights, "Political Participation: A Study of Participation by Negroes in the Electoral and Political Processes in 10 Southern States Since the Passage of the Voting Rights Act of 1965" (Washington, DC: 1968), 197; Ball, Krane, and Lauth, *Compromised Compliance*, 71; Lawson, *Pursuit of Power*, 133, 138.

26. Lawson, *Pursuit of Power*, 136–137; House Subcommittee No. 5 of the Committee on the Judiciary, *Hearings on Voting Rights Act Extension*, 91st Cong., 1st sess., 1969, 248–253.

27. Lawson, *Pursuit of Power*, 146–157; Paul N. McCloskey Jr., *Truth and Untruth: Political Deceit in America* (New York: Simon and Schuster, 1972), 169.

28. Lawson, *Pursuit of Power*, 163–173; *Evers v State Board of Election Commissioners*, 327 F. Supp. 640, 641–42 (S.D. Miss. 1971).

29. Lawson, *Pursuit of Power*, 172.

30. House Civil Rights Oversight Subcommittee (No. 4) of the Committee on the Judiciary, *Hearings on the Enforcement of the Voting Rights Act,* 92nd Cong., 1st sess., 1971, 2–3, 52–69, 268.

31. Lawson, *Pursuit of Power*, 225–227; Thernstrom, *Whose Votes Count?*, 44; United States Commission on Civil Rights, "The Voting Rights Act: Ten Years After" (Washington, DC: 1975).

32. *Beer v United States*, 425 U.S. 130 (1976).

33. Chandler Davidson and Bernard Grofman, *Quiet Revolution in the South: The Impact of the Voting Rights Act, 1965–1990* (Princeton, N.J.: Princeton University Press, 1994), 88.

34. Ball, Krane, and Lauth, *Compromised Compliance*; General Accounting Office, "Voting Rights Act Needs Strengthening" (Washington, DC: 1978); House Subcommittee on Civil and Constitutional Rights of the Committee on the Judiciary, *Hearings on General Accounting Office Report on the Voting Rights Act*, 95th Cong., 2d sess., 1978.

35. Lorn Foster, "Section 5 of the Voting Rights Act: Implementation of an Administrative Remedy," *Publius* 16, No. 4 (fall 1986), 37.

36. William Bradford Reynolds, "The Reagan Administration and Civil Rights: Winning the War Against Discrimination," *University of Illinois Law Review* 4 (1986), 1001, 1023.

37. James P. Turner, interview by author, tape recording, Accokeek, Md., 27 August 1997.

38. *City of Mobile v Bolden*, 446 U.S. 55, 66 (1980).

39. Davidson, "Voting Rights Act: A Brief History," in Grofman and Davidson, *Controversies in Minority Voting*, 37–41.

40. *Congressional Quarterly Weekly Report* (Washington, DC: Congressional Quarterly, 26 December 1981), 2605 (quoting presidential press conference); Senate Subcommittee on the Constitution of the Committee on the Judiciary, *Hearings on Sen. 53, Sen. 1761, Sen. 1975, Sen. 1992, and H.R. 3112*, 97th Cong., 2d sess., 1983, 233–236, 1660.

41. Senate Subcommittee on the Constitution, *Hearings on Sen. 53, Sen. 1761, Sen. 1975, Sen. 1992, and H.R. 3112*, 82, 744; House Committee on the Judiciary, *Voting Rights Act Extension*, Report 97-227, 97th Cong., 1st sess., 1981, 2.

42. *Voting Rights Act, Section Two*, U.S. Code, vol. 42, sec. 1973 (1994); Thernstrom, *Whose Votes Count?*, 135–136.

43. Senate Subcommittee on the Constitution, *Hearings on Sen. 53, Sen. 1761, Sen. 1975, Sen. 1992, and H.R. 3112*, 52–53; Charles S. Bullock III and Katharine Inglis Butler, "Voting Rights," in Tinsley E. Yarbrough, ed., *The Reagan Administration and Human Rights* (New York: Praeger, 1985), 39–44; Thernstrom, *Whose Votes Count?*, 171; U.S. Department of Justice, *Post-Trial Brief*, submitted to the district court in *County Council of Sumter County, South Carolina v United States*, No. 82-912 (D. D.C.), 15–18.

44. Turner interview.

45. House Subcommittee on Civil and Constitutional Rights of the Committee on the Judiciary, *Extension of the Voting Rights Act*, 97th Cong., 1st sess., 2119; Senate Subcommittee on the Constitution of the Committee on the Judiciary, *Hearings on Sen 53, Sen. 1761, Sen. 1975, Sen. 1992, and H.R. 3112*, 97th Cong., 2d sess., 1375–77.

46. U.S. Department of Justice, "Procedures for the Administration of Section 5 of the Voting Rights Act of 1965: Proposed Rules," *Federal Register 50*, No. 87 (6 May 1985).

47. In House Subcommittee on Civil and Constitutional Rights of the Committee on the Judiciary, *Proposed Changes to Regulations Governing Section 5 of the Voting Rights Act*, 99th Cong., 1st sess., 1986, 38–41.

48. Report of the House Subcommittee on Civil and Constitutional Rights of the Committee on the Judiciary, *Voting Rights Act: Proposed Section 5 Regulations* 1986, 99th Cong., 2d sess., 1986; Howard Kurtz, "Justice Dept. Won't Assess Possible Bias in Election Plans," *Washington Post*, 30 August 1986.

49. Department of Justice, "Revision of Procedures for the Administration of Section 5 of the Voting Rights Act of 1965, Final Rule," *Federal Register* 42, No. 3 (6 January 1987), 28 CFR sec. 51(b)(2).

50. U.S. Department of Justice, *Brief for the United States as Amicus Curiae* and *Brief for the United States as Amicus Curiae Supporting Appellants* and *Brief of Senator Dennis DeConcini, et al., and Representative Don Edwards, et al., as Amici Curiae in Support of Appellees*, submitted to the Supreme Court in *Thornburg v Gingles*, No. 83-1968 (1985).

51. Drews S. Days III, "Section 5 Enforcement and the Role of the Justice Department," in Grofman and Davidson, *Controversies in Minority Voting*, 57.

52. *United Jewish Organizations v Carey*, 430 U.S. 144, 164 (1977).

53. Frank R. Parker, "Voting Rights Enforcement in the Reagan Administration," in Reginald C. Govan and William L. Taylor, eds., *One Nation Indivisible: The Civil Rights Challenge for the 1990s* (Washington, DC: Citizen's Commission on Civil Rights, 1989), 362, 369–370; Lawyers' Committee for Civil Rights Under Law, "Justice Department Voting Rights Enforcement: Political Interference and Retreats" (Washington, DC: Lawyers' Committee for Civil Rights Under Law, 20 January 1982).

54. Clayton, *Politics of Justice*, 146–148, 204; Lawyers' Committee for Civil Rights Under Law, "Without Justice: A Report on the Conduct of the Justice Department in Civil Rights in 1981–82" (Washington, DC: Lawyers' Committee for Civil Rights Under Law, February 1982), 204.

55. Raymond Wolters, *Right Turn: William Bradford Reynolds, the Reagan Administration, and Black Civil Rights* (New Brunswick, N.J.: Transaction, 1996), 10.

56. Thernstrom, *Whose Votes Count?*, 171; Bullock and Butler, "Voting Rights," 33–34, 43.

57. Bernard Grofman and Chandler Davidson, "The Enforcement of the Voting Rights Act by the U.S. Department of Justice: Compromised Compliance? Republican Plot? Or Great American Success Story?" note 17 (paper presented at the annual meeting of the American Political Science Association, 1992).

58. Grofman and Davidson, "The Enforcement of the Voting Rights Act by the U.S. Department of Justice," note 17; Turner interview.

59. Grofman and Davidson, "The Enforcement of the Voting Rights Act by the U.S. Department of Justice," note 17; Turner interview.

60. Grofman and Davidson, "The Enforcement of the Voting Rights Act by the U.S. Department of Justice," note 17; Turner interview; Bullock and Butler, "Voting Rights," 46.

61. *Busbee v Smith*, 549 F. Supp. 494 (D. D.C. 1982).

62. *Jordan v Winter*, 541 F. Supp. 1135 (N.D. Miss. 1982).

63. Joel Selig, "The Reagan Justice Department and Civil Rights: What Went Wrong," *University of Illinois Law Reviev* 4 (1985), 785, 834.

64. John R. Dunne, "Remarks to National Conference of State Legislators," Orlando, Fla., 13 August 1991; Peter Bragdon, "Eyes on Dunne at Justice," *Congressional Quarterly*, Vol. 48, no. 22, 2 June 1990.

65. U.S. Department of Justice, Civil Rights Division, "The Computer, Data, and Discrimination," *Civil Rights Forum* 9, No. 1 (Washington, DC: Civil Rights Division, spring 1995). The term "TIGER" refers to the Topologically Integrated Geographic Encoding and Referencing system and database developed by the Census Bureau.

66. Rob Gurwitt, "The Messiest Job in Politics," *Governing*, November 1993.

67. Tiare B. Smiley, telephone conversation with author, 31 December 1997.

68. *Vera v Richards*, 861 F. Supp. 1309, 1318–19, 1336; *Bush v Vera*, 517 U.S. 952, 961–63 (1996); *Moon v Meadows*, 952 F. Supp. 1141, 1147, and note 6 (E.D. Va. 1997).

69. Augustus J. Jones Jr., "Kinder, Gentler? George Bush and Civil Rights," in Ryan J. Barilleaux and Mary E. Stuckey, eds., *Leadership and the Bush Presidency* (Westport, Conn.: Praeger, 1992), 182.

3

Bureaucratic Culture of the Voting Section

> Certainly a lot of the rank and file clerks in the Voting Section would look for ways to increase minority representation. That's the nature of this game. To increase it, but increase it in ways that were not reverse discrimination or were not fixing elections by deciding convoluted districts or other devices. So there is that tendency.
>
> James P. Turner

The Civil Rights Division makes voting rights policy through its preclearance functions. CRD leaders have denied that a maximization policy existed. James P. Turner, for twenty-five years a high-ranking careerist in the Division, argued in 1992 that the approach of the CRD has always been "case-specific"—that a practice that is objectionable in one jurisdiction may be proper in another, depending upon local circumstances.[1] That method served the CRD well until the nineties.

One element that complicates the Voting Section's existence is the fact that the Section has dual and conflicting roles. As an advocate and protector of minority voting rights, it aggressively seeks out and attempts to eradicate racially discriminatory practices. In fulfilling this role, the Division encounters new designs employed to limit minority voting power and creates strategies devised to block those schemes. The advocacy function can conflict with the Division's responsibilities under Section Five, which places it in a quasi-judicial role—the Voting Section attorneys are to act as would a court in considering submissions. There should be less room in the preclearance process for cutting-edge legal theories, but the Division adopted some while resisting the direction of the increasingly conservative courts. During the nineties CRD political appointees and Voting Section careerists agreed upon a mission of increasing electoral opportunities that encompassed maximization. The Division staff is naturally predisposed to advancing the civil rights mission. They are receptive to evolving definitions of discrimination backed by social science and legal theories. In contrast with the political leadership under the Reagan administration, CRD professionals found Bush Division chief John R. Dunne and Clinton administration chief Deval L. Patrick willing to aggressively promote increased minority representation.

FORGING A PATH

In the early 1990s, the Civil Rights Division determined that the critical task of the Voting Rights Act was to increase descriptive minority representation in legislative councils.[2] During the Reagan administration, advocates inside and outside of the Voting Section who wished to push for more minority representation were in conflict with Division Chief William Bradford Reynolds, who favored a limited application of the Act. When administrations changed, so did the view of the man at the top of the Civil Rights Division. Bush administration Assistant Attorney General for Civil Rights John R. Dunne originally seemed skeptical of proportional representation remedies but he came to regard an effective vote as nearly synonymous with the right to elect a candidate of choice. Many state legislators pondering Dunne's objection letters understood this to mean the creation of districts in which a minority candidate would be all but assured of victory. This is not to say that Dunne, or his Clinton administration successor Deval L. Patrick, held the position that only an African-American official could represent black interests. They did not. But the logic of voting rights enforcement often brought the result that creation of a district in which minorities could elect a candidate of their choice translated into districts calculated to afford victory by a minority candidate.

So the problem for the Department became how to increase the number of racial minority representatives in Congress. The method for solving this critical task was to use the preclearance power to require covered jurisdictions to create as many minority districts as possible. In order to effectuate the task, the Department began to regard a state's failure to maximize as evidence of a discriminatory purpose. Typically the Department would muster as evidence the state's rejection of an alternative plan, offered by an advocacy group or the Republican Party, that might create an additional minority district. Many of the proposed alternatives included grossly noncompact districts that split counties, municipalities, precincts, and communities of interest, but the Department would regard the states' rejection of such plans as "pretextual." The states, recognizing that the Department would only preclear plans that maximized minority districts, succumbed. Thus was the critical task advanced.

Another organizational imperative for the Department was to achieve agreement that the mission of the Division should be to increase the number of minority representatives in Congress.[3] In *Compromised Compliance* Howard Ball, Dale Krane, and Thomas P. Lauth found the Voting Section staff divided between a strong majority of pragmatists who favored a restrained approach mindful of federalism concerns and a smaller group of normativists who argued that the office should intervene whenever a state had declined to take all possible measures to increase minority representation. To the authors' dismay, the pragmatists held sway prior to 1982.[4] During the nineties' preclearance round there was widespread acceptance of the idea that increasing minority voting power would presumptively entail proportional representation.

One might have expected some form of internal contention over the expanded definition of the critical task. Little occurred. In contrast to the Reynolds days just past, Dunne favored the creation of as many minority districts as possible as a benign civil rights measure. In meetings at which the change was discussed, little protest from the Department's professionals was heard.[5] There was a gradual evolution at work. The concept of group remedy for historical discrimination had become the standard progressive curative. Voting rights litigators and attorneys for the states alike read *Thornburg v Gingles* and the Department's incorporation of Section Two's results test into Section Five as an evolution toward proportional representation. What eventuated in a political explosion appeared at the time to be a merely incremental step.

The third problem for the Department was to assure that it had the autonomy to follow its preferred direction, to adopt a sense of mission for increasing minority representation.[6] This was no small task. The Voting Section was under exacting scrutiny from interested advocates, submitting jurisdictions, political parties, congressional committees, and executive superiors. The position of assistant attorney general for civil rights was and continues to be an intense hot seat.

Yet the Department was able to gain sufficient autonomy to permit it to pursue its critical task. The advocacy groups most interested in its work, the civil rights organizations, had long-standing relationships with Division professionals and an ardent desire for maximization. Key congressional committees and subcommittees were in the hands of liberal Democrats, such as Representative Don Edwards and Senator Joseph Biden. The local jurisdictions had little ability to resist: the Department has a strong bargaining stick, the threat of objection, with which to encourage the states' compliance. The political parties differed in the strength of their support for maximization of minority districts. The Democrats acquiesced, because they could ill afford to alienate their most loyal constituency, African-American voters. The Republicans approved and often cooperated, contemplating the delicious irony of doing well while seeming to do good.

This left the executive as the remaining potential source of opposition. President Bush attempted to convey opposition to preferences without engendering the passionate bitterness that civil rights advocates directed at the Reagan administration. Early in his tenure, Dunne tried to distinguish the concept of affirmative action based on preferences from the notion of affirmative action based on opposition to discrimination against the individual. Yet Dunne came to believe that creating as many minority districts as possible was good civil rights policy. Many officials in the White House cared little for civil rights, and a preponderance of civil rights issues were managed from within the White House or by Attorney General Richard Thornburgh, but voting rights enforcement was left to Dunne's discretion.[7]

PERSONNEL IN THE CIVIL RIGHTS DIVISION

The legal staff of the Civil Rights Division is composed of political appointees who serve at the pleasure of the administration in power and professional (or career) attorneys and support staff. The Division is unique in its mission and in the people who are attracted to it, what they hope to accomplish, and their tenure.

The CRD pursues its mission within the moral and ideological milieu of the civil rights movement. The movement generated great moral force during the 1960s, culminating in passage of the 1964 Civil Rights Act and the 1965 Voting Rights Act. These historic civil rights measures were not enacted with ease, but were passed with a Democratic and Republican bipartisan agreement on the moral need for action. The movement of the sixties was directed at removing barriers of discrimination that stood in the way of equal opportunity. By the early seventies, much of the movement's energy had been redirected to affirmative action policies focusing upon institutional racism, disparate impact, and proportionate results. Advocacy under the Voting Rights Act followed this trajectory, leading toward proportional representation. As the movement became enmeshed in claims for proportionate results, some of its moral force dissipated. Bipartisan agreement on the moral appeal of affirmative action programs never has enjoyed the broad support achieved by the sixties drive to eradicate discrimination. Public opinion has divided, with white Americans favoring support when couched in terms of assistance to the disadvantaged, but opposing programs cast as racial preferences. Some surveys indicate that the races see the issue differently, with African Americans generally supporting affirmative action programs and whites more willing to see them phased out.[8] Conflicts about the meaning of discrimination, equality, fair treatment, affirmative action, and the VRA have played out in confirmation battles and court battles. When a conservative political appointee as chief has taken a different view than the predominantly progressive staff, these disputes have played out in the CRD itself.

Former CRD attorney Brian Landsberg recognizes that both civil service attorneys and political appointees influence legal policy making, and he therefore calls for a norm of mutual assistance between them. Landsberg raises the issue of who is the Division's client, a question with an answer not altogether clear. Some argue that the government lawyer is responsible to the public interest, others say to the government as a whole. Landsberg favors the idea that the employing agency should normally be considered the client. In such a case, the staff attorney would learn the client's preferences from the political appointee. Participation by career staff helps insulate the decision-making process from the appearance of partisanship, but problems posed by the issue of the indeterminate client persist. Civil service employees and political appointees each bring their own disadvantages to such an ambiguous legal practice. "The civil servant has no claim to represent the wishes of 'We the People'; the political appointee may take a narrow, partisan view of those wishes. The former may be tied to the positions of the past; the latter may not be aware of the lessons of the past." Landsberg suggests the value of close cooperation that builds on the strengths of careerists and political appointees.[9] One disadvantage of too harmonious a whole is that significant policy issues may not receive the full exploration they deserve.

Political Appointees

The official most responsible for setting policy is the chief of the Civil Rights Division, appointed by the president with the advice and consent of the Senate. Careerists and subordinate political appointees may make their case, but the chief has ultimate responsibility for a decision. Senate approval is hardly *pro forma*. Contending organized interests compete to elevate or shoot down a president's choice. The nomination process frequently serves as a battleground over not only presidential prerogative and interest group influence, but over the meaning of equality. The debate over whether equality means equal opportunity or proportionate results, discrimination against the individual or disparate impact, is fought out. These elements are evident in the processes concerning President Bush's two nominees for the post: William C. Lucas, opposed by the civil rights establishment and defeated by a Democratic Senate; and John R. Dunne, who became the architect of the Division's voting rights policy.

Since the stormy tenure of Reynolds as chief, organized interests on the right and the left have targeted the president's nominees. The sniping begins as soon as a potential candidate's name is made public, even before formal nomination. President Bush's first choice, William Lucas, attracted such attention. Lucas was the elected sheriff of Wayne County, Michigan, and, with his conversion from the Democratic Party in 1985, the highest ranking black Republican elected official in the nation. He was in private law practice at the time of his nomination. When his name became public, the Leadership Conference on Civil Rights (LCCR) expressed its concern over his lack of civil rights experience. LCCR executive director Ralph G. Neas stressed that it had not yet taken a position on the nominee, but the LCCR was simultaneously distributing news stories and editorials critical of Lucas to senators and reporters. Patrick McGuigan, a conservative scholar at the Free Congress Foundation, complained that Lucas "is being opposed because he will not recognize the infallibility of the reigning civil rights establishment in the nation's capital."[10]

The Bush administration made appeals for Lucas based upon his background as a successful African American who had overcome discrimination. Unfortunately for Lucas, he turned out to understand little about civil rights law, a flaw exposed in Senate confirmation hearings. He had few prominent African-American leaders among his supporters, but two were the Reverend Jesse Jackson and Congressman John Conyers. Lucas's fumbling testimony cost him the support of both. The LCCR, NAACP, NAACP Legal Defense and Educational Fund (LDF), Mexican American Legal Defense and Educational Fund (MALDEF), and People for the American Way, among the leaders in scuttling President Reagan's nomination of conservative jurist Robert Bork for the Supreme Court, coalesced against Lucas. Attorney General Thornburgh complained that the Democrats and civil rights advocates were seeking something they were not going to get—a nominee who would quarrel with the president on civil rights.[11] The Senate Judiciary Committee, split largely along partisan lines, eventually killed the nomination.

President Bush's second nominee, former New York state Senator John R. Dunne, faced similar doubts but less opposition from the civil rights advocates. When his nomination was announced, the director of the New York Civil Liberties Union expressed concerns about Dunne's understanding of civil rights issues. Neas of LCCR again expressed disappointment. Like Lucas, Dunne had little civil rights background, and thus almost no record to attack. Unlike Lucas, he was able to draw upon backing from New York's congressional delegation including its two senators, Democrat Daniel Patrick Moynihan and Republican Alfonse D'Amato. Governor Mario M. Cuomo and Congressman Charles B. Rangel also endorsed him. The initial reservations expressed by the groups that had routed the Lucas nomination were swamped by such influential support. The NAACP announced that it had investigated Dunne and found a lack of civil rights experience, but sensitivity toward important issues. It neither endorsed nor opposed Dunne. In contrast to Lucas's dismal performance at his confirmation hearing, Dunne was able to carefully skirt troublesome questions and persuade the senators of his good intentions. Congressman Rangel expressed the dilemma: if President Bush had to pick a Republican, he "couldn't pick a more decent person than John Dunne." Senate Democrats came to believe that they were not about to get a more agreeable nominee out of the Bush administration. Dunne's nomination easily gained the approval of the committee and full Senate.[12]

The nominations of Lucas and Dunne indicate the fervor with which organized interests approach the nomination process. The Republican administration of President Bush, trying to appear less confrontational on civil rights than the Reagan administration but observant of its conservative base, attempted twice to advance a nominee with little civil rights track record. On the Lucas nomination, organized interests were able to raise enough questions about his experience and character to kill the nomination, but on the Dunne nomination, the Bush strategy, as modified, worked. The civil rights groups that had been so formidable in the Bork and Lucas fights briefly huffed and puffed but quickly grew quiescent. A former state senator with almost no civil rights record but with respectful support from home state Democrats easily passed through the nomination process.

Dunne established the policies that eventuated in maximization of congressional seats in several Southern states, but it was the Clinton administration's first chief of the Civil Rights Division, Deval L. Patrick, who defended the districts when they came under attack. The background to his nomination shows the way in which the debate over equality and voting rights can roil the nomination of a Democratic nominee.

Patrick was not the initial selection of President Clinton. The president first nominated law professor and former LDF litigator Lani Guinier. Her nomination became extremely controversial because of views she had expressed in law-review articles that proposed pushing the VRA to new progressive frontiers. Conservative activists and Republicans on the Judiciary Committee derided Guinier as a "quota queen." As the controversy heated up, Guinier began to lose support among centrist Democrats. A senior Democratic senator revealed that up to two dozen Democratic senators had informed the White House that Guinier's nomination should be withdrawn. The president eventually withdrew her name from nomination. A new search was undertaken, and one potential nominee went far enough to be introduced to various civil rights groups, but he was found to have only recently registered to vote and the Congressional Black

Caucus felt that he would be too timid on voting rights enforcement, so he was never nominated.[13]

Finally, over a year into his first term on 2 February 1994, President Clinton nominated former LDF attorney Deval L. Patrick. Patrick was a polished practitioner, not a cutting-edge legal theorist like Guinier. He already knew many civil rights leaders (including Guinier) through his work with the LDF and was introduced by the Leadership Conference to union leaders and advocates for the disabled and women. He reports that there was not much discussion of voting rights during this process, but the Congressional Black Caucus did express concerns because *Shaw v Reno* had been decided recently. The only real opposition came from conservative activist Clint Bolick. Republicans who expressed a wait-and-see attitude came to support Patrick. Mainstream civil rights groups such as the Leadership Conference and Congressional Black Caucus endorsed his nomination, as did the *New York Times*, and he sailed through the Democratic Senate.[14]

Patrick could put his understanding of racial discrimination and poverty in personal terms. In many of his speeches as chief, he recounted in moving words his boyhood in an inner-city neighborhood of Chicago and America's troubled legacy of racial injustice. He saw his role as providing the opportunity to preserve and protect advances made by racial and language minorities. Patrick describes one of his greatest frustrations in the job as discerning exactly what the president wanted done in civil rights, where he wanted the emphasis to be placed. In the battle over the future of affirmative action fought in 1995, though, Patrick was one of the critical players. Following the Republican sweep of both houses of Congress in 1994, GOP leaders commenced an attack on affirmative action programs as racial preferences. The Supreme Court was in the process of issuing decisions contrary to the preferred policies of the civil rights establishment. At a time when President Clinton's "triangulation" re-election strategy pushed him toward Republican positions, Patrick was one of the advisers who helped persuade President Clinton that "mend it, don't end it" is the best approach to affirmative action. In voting rights, Patrick gave not an inch to challengers of maximization plans. In Louisiana, he fought on even after defeat was assured in the courts.[15]

Patrick fought fiercely for the newly created minority districts, but the critical decisions on which redistricting plans to preclear and which to object to were made under Dunne's watch. As a Bush administration political appointee, Dunne did not come to his post as a civil rights firebrand, but he did take the job with a willingness to learn and a reputation for independence.

In May of 1990 Dunne addressed a Law Day gathering at Fordham Law School. He promised vigorous enforcement of the VRA in general terms, but his remarks regarding affirmative action were of greater interest. Maximization policy, after all, is a form of results-oriented preference, and many civil rights leaders regard such preferences as the *sine qua non* of affirmative action. Dunne had a different view:

> We must invigorate affirmative action. Although it is often confused with racial preferences, affirmative action originally was intended to open up opportunities, secured by the civil right laws, for those individuals who previously had been excluded by racial, ethnic or gender discrimina-

tion—to provide those outside the economic mainstream with the tools necessary to take advantage of these opportunities.

It is now time to restore affirmative action to its original purpose.[16]

Dunne therefore expressed an idea of affirmative action consonant with the Phase One understanding, not the Phase Two interpretation preferred by the civil rights establishment.

On 2 June 1990 *Congressional Quarterly* reported upon the looming redistricting battles and their implications for minority representation. In an article entitled "Eyes on Dunne at Justice," Peter Bragdon described the eagerness of those involved in the process to know how the Department would approach submissions. Dunne was oblique in discussing the Division's criteria. He suggested that attention be paid to the Act, legal precedent, compactness, and contiguity and that states have a rational basis for line placement. He declined to be specific or even to define a majority or minority district, but he did declare that the Division would be vigilant in scrutinizing submissions for evidence of dilution of minority voting power. He indicated that the Department had been communicating with those interested in redistricting and would continue to do so. This seemed to bring hope to voting rights leaders, who expressed optimism that Dunne would vigorously enforce the Act.

Despite his friendship with Attorney General Thornburgh, Dunne found frustration in many aspects of his new role. On 10 January 1991 the *New York Times* assessed the first eight months of his tenure in an article entitled "Justice Department's Civil Rights Chief Is Sitting on Sidelines of Main Battle." The paper adjudged the Division as an outpost that had been demoralized under the Reagan administration and remained marginal under President Bush. The article stated that Thornburgh played the key role in civil rights policy, including the president's decision to veto a civil rights bill, with the Division left out of the loop. Neas of the LCCR assessed Dunne's overall performance as "a tremendous disappointment." One of the few areas in which the *Times* recognized Dunne had been active was in voting rights. It described his role in deciding whether to preclear plans due to be submitted in the wake of the 1990 census and noted that Dunne was already fending off accusations of partisan favoritism.[17]

His remarks at Fordham Law School in May of 1990 reflect his conception of affirmative action at the time. And the *New York Times* assessment was accurate: Dunne concedes that much of the administration's civil rights policy was handled by Attorney General Thornburgh or the White House. Thornburgh, however, left Dunne entirely on his own in setting voting rights enforcement policy, and Dunne was becoming educated in the ways that jurisdictions devise to diminish minority voting power. He was certainly aware of the political ramifications of his actions, and one could hardly expect him to be disappointed by Republican gains, but he was animated by what he saw as Southern intransigence against increased minority representation.

By May of 1991, civil rights leaders were well on their way to developing a bifurcated view of Dunne's tenure. They were particularly disappointed by his support for the president's veto of the 1990 Civil Rights Act. However, the Citizens' Commission on Civil Rights declared that Dunne "has repeatedly stated his goal of vigorously enforcing the Voting Rights Act, and the department appears to be making good on its promise." Some observers speculated that with many areas of civil rights enforcement being hamstrung by the White House, Dunne might regard vigorous voting rights enforcement as a legacy for the end of his public career. Reflecting on his tenure, Dunne recalled the criticism from advocates, whom he felt used the opportunity to attack a Republican appointee, perceiving this as more valuable than a sincere effort to work with him. To Dunne, much of the approval on voting policy was merely damning him by faint praise.[18]

The Division's approach appeared in clear outline by July of 1991. In its first decisions concerning plans drawn with 1990 census data, the CRD objected to Mississippi's submission of state house and senate plans and Louisiana's state senate plan. Analysts interpreted the objections to indicate that the Division under Dunne would aggressively interpret and enforce the Act. Shortly thereafter, the Division lodged an objection to the plan submitted for the Virginia House of Delegates. Near the end of July, Dunne revealed that his approach would not be confined to the South. The Division blocked a plan to redistrict the New York City Council, stating that it had diluted Hispanic votes. The *New York Times* considered the objection "further evidence of the new vigor with which the Justice Department is enforcing the Voting Rights Act."[19]

State legislative leaders throughout the country took note of the objections. An August 1991 article described the machinations in Texas and the observations of several Justice Department watchers who concluded that the Department's prior objections meant that Texas must create every minority district possible. Texas Democratic legislative leaders, who believed there was Republican partisan motivation afoot, contemplated bypassing the Department and seeking a declaratory judgment from the district court for the District of Columbia. In a measure of how positively activists had come to view Dunne's administration, voting rights litigators erupted in fury. Frank R. Parker, director of the Voting Rights Project of the Lawyers' Committee for Civil Rights Under Law, complained "It sounds like they are trying to pull something over on the court." Pamela Karlan, a law professor and prominent voting rights advocate, stated that "If they obeyed the law, it would be easier to go to the Justice Department."[20] Submission to the Department under Section Five is an option to a declaratory judgment action in the District of Columbia district court, not the other way around, but the activists had so come to esteem the Department's efforts that any state move to pursue its statutory right to go to court was viewed as a nefarious scheme. The legislators relented and submitted to the Department.

The Division's voting enforcement drew approval within the voting rights community. In 1992 a briefing paper published by the Southern Regional Council remarked that "increased standards, community vigilance and, in most cases, vigorous enforcement have led to substantial gains, making the Justice Department the preferred route for winning fair representation. Without resort to the courts, black legislators and leaders have won gains with aid from Justice Department objections."[21]

Both Republican Dunne, who had little civil rights experience prior to accepting the post, and Democrat Patrick, who had personal knowledge of discrimination and had litigated for the LDF, remark upon the educative nature of being confronted with voting rights cases. Dunne held a conventional Republican approach to affirmative action matters, believing that it applies to opportunity and not to preferences. Yet his views changed as he learned more about stratagems used to diminish minority voting strength, and this education made him more determined to enforce minority voting rights—so much so that he now concedes that the Division pushed toward maximization. Patrick recounts the alarm expressed by the Congressional Black Caucus in the wake of the Supreme Court's decision in *Shaw v Reno*. Yet he had to be convinced by them that a threat existed that was not abstract, but concerned "real problems in real people's lives. And the question of whether we were going to remain in these cases at this level was very much on the table. I needed to be persuaded that this was in that group of cases and eventually, I was."[22]

The Professionals

The political appointees at the head of the Division are important, but they come and go with some regularity. Career staffers tend to stay from administration to administration. The Civil Rights Division undertakes a historical mission with strong moral overtones. As an attractive place to work with an important mission, the CRD draws elite legal applicants. The typical Division lawyer was a high achiever in law school. Attorneys are hired laterally from law firms, from judicial clerkships, or from the Attorney General's Honors Program. The Honors Program comprises a pool of the top 10 percent of law school classes, from which the Division selects the most promising students. The Division looks for maturity, good judgment, analytical ability, interest in civil rights, and the ability to get along within the institution.[23]

There are any number of legal positions in the federal government that are regarded by bright and ambitious young attorneys as stepping-stones to experience and contacts for future lucrative private-sector employment. For example, DOJ antitrust division attorneys typically stay for a few years, gaining experience to be used upon their departure for well-compensated private practice.[24]

CRD attorneys are not in the business to burnish resumes for future opportunities. To many careerists, the nonmaterial satisfactions they garner from public service outweigh the monetary rewards available elsewhere. A number of CRD attorneys responsible for voting rights have enjoyed a long tenure and have only recently departed for retirement or private practice. James P. Turner entered the Division's employ in 1965. (He had earlier participated in the first Honors Program.) He served with the Division until his retirement in 1994, having acted since 1969 as the senior deputy for voting rights matters, as well as having other responsibilities. Gerald Jones, who served a lengthy period as head of the Voting Section's Section Five Unit, also recently retired.[25]

Most Division attorneys are attracted to the office because of their commitment to civil rights laws and the Division's reputation for granting experience in complex litigation. While some leave after a few years for law firms or posts with the U.S. Attorneys, others make the Division their career. Their chief motivation "is the feeling that their work promotes justice. In short, the Division has attracted employees looking for more than just another job, people committed to equality under the law and to litigation as the engine of securing that right."[26] Dunne confirms this motivation: "Unlike most of the other divisions, the folks in the Civil Rights Division stay much longer. They don't go in for two to three years to get their experience such as in environment or antitrust. They are there because they believe in the work."[27]

Prior organizational experience and its effect on the people involved molds them and the organization. The expectations of peers can affect how hard an employee works, as well as what the employee understands is important to accomplish. Landsberg writes: "The Civil Rights Division's type of work—litigation in federal court—tends to mold those who do it." He argues that Southern intransigence and biased courts in the South in the Division's early years engendered an ethic of careful, scrupulous lawyering. Joel Selig, another former Division attorney, asserts that the Division has traditionally followed a moderately progressive legal course and imbues its attorneys with that ethic. Career attorneys demand balance, moderation, and self-restraint of themselves and new hires.[28] Even so, the history of legal battles against racial intractability must lead to at least some natural (and often justifiable) predisposition against Southern sincerity.

In addition to distinguished academic and service records, the Division looks for lawyers who are analytical and good investigators. A sense of balance is a welcome quality, especially in those who must decide on Section Five submissions. Since the Section Five process places the examiner in a quasi-judicial role, the attorney must approach the job with the detachment of a judge.

In its FY 1991 budget request to Congress, the Division detailed the Voting Section's responsibilities, personnel distribution, and needs. The request described two components within the Section: a Section Five unit staffed by equal opportunity specialists under the supervision of attorneys; and a litigation group, which brings suits to enforce multiple provisions of the VRA, including Section Two. The Section counted sixty-eight full-time employees in FY 1990, including twenty-seven attorneys, twenty equal opportunity specialists, (paralegals who do the threshold examination of Section Five submissions), three paralegal specialists, and eighteen other support staff. Dunne requested sixteen additional positions specifically to handle the anticipated increase in redistricting submissions following the 1990 census. Three new attorneys would bolster the Section Five component and two would primarily assist with litigation. The proposal suggested that the new Section Five attorneys would help reduce the pressure to use litigators to decide preclearance cases. But the recommendation acknowledged that due to the heavy workload caused by the submissions, no clear division of labor could be maintained.[29]

Those familiar with the workings of the Division, including former chiefs Dunne and Patrick, emphasize the professionalism of the career attorneys. Nonetheless, some ideological preference is inevitable. Turner remarks: "I would have to agree there would be some tilt towards the left, toward the liberal positions, . . . it's perfectly natural, because you wouldn't be attracted to civil rights unless you believed in it . . . I'm thinking of things like busing or quotas . . . sure, there was a tilt in that direction, but any time the Court would say no, that was it for the Department."[30]

The equal opportunity specialists (as distinguished from the paralegal specialists, who primarily assist with Section Two cases) process and analyze Section Five submissions. The use of the equal opportunity specialists to handle initial processing is essential, because the volume of submissions is so high. The equal opportunity specialists receive instruction on procedures from their supervisor and training in legal definitions of discrimination by Division lawyers. The equal opportunity specialists are college graduates, supplemented with three-month student volunteers and full-time temporary personnel. They are always under legal supervision. Their recommendations receive multiple reviews, from their director, to the Section Five chief, to the deputy assistant, who forwards the recommendations to the assistant attorney general for civil rights. In its FY 1991 budget request, the Division sought four additional equal opportunity specialists. Even with the additional help, Dunne acknowledged that the Voting Section would have to continue to supplement their functions with less well-trained student volunteers and temporary employees.[31]

The relationship of professional career staff and political appointees involves inherent problems. Landsberg notes:

> First, the job of the law enforcer is to find violations of the law and correct them. Zeal to uncover wrongdoing may lead to a lack of rigor in critically evaluating cases and positions. Second, the civil service staff is hired by and serves under political appointees, each of whom may seek to mold that staff into the image most compatible with the policy views of the President. This may lead to a real or perceived lack of responsiveness to new leadership when administrations change. Third, some civil service staff may develop a degree of expertise and a commitment to particular law enforcement policies that can overwhelm a new leader. Fourth, civil service staff may form alliances with outside groups concerned with the laws that the staff enforces. Fifth, "there are significant pressures to place decisions beyond the control—even beyond the consideration—of policy making officials by identifying policy questions as questions of law and therefore as peculiarly within the province of the courts." Finally, we know that, over time, bureaucracies tend to ossify, lose their sense of purpose, look more to the past than to the future, and reject new ideas because they differ from what they have always done.[32]

The leadership of the Civil Rights Division is reliant upon the Voting Section professional staff. The staff had an uncomfortable relationship with Reagan administration chief Reynolds, and Dunne wished to improve that dynamic. There was a greater tendency to accept the recommendations of career staff under Dunne; in the judgment of voting rights advocate Brenda Wright, the staff had not changed its approach so much as had the leadership. The political appointees relied upon the staff's judgment both because decisions came to the leadership under time pressure and because they felt the staff were usually correct in their recommendations.[33] It is also true that the careerists had years of civil rights experience, while the political leadership was relatively unschooled.

Dunne indicates that relationships between his more conservative politically appointed deputies and the liberal Voting Section staff were not always harmonious. Dunne endorses the talent and professionalism of Voting Section staff. Deval Patrick expresses his respect for the Voting Section professionals in carrying out their jobs facing the "difficulty of doing it with a boss who for many of them is equated with the Christmas help . . . people who are just in seasonally and move on." He enjoyed a close working relationship with the Voting Section attorneys.[34]

REGULATORY FRAMEWORK

The Division's regulatory framework for exercising its authority under Section Five is found in *Procedures for the Administration of Section Five of the Voting Rights Act of 1965, as Amended*, 28 CFR sec. 51, et seq. The basic standard of decision making is set forth in 28 CFR sec. 51.52(a): "the Attorney General shall make the same determination that would be made by the court in an action for a declaratory judgment under Section Five: Whether the submitted change has the purpose or will have the effect of denying or abridging the right to vote on account of race, color, or membership in a language group."

No election-law change may go into effect in a covered jurisdiction unless either the federal district court for the District of Columbia grants a declaratory judgment or the Department determines that the change has neither a discriminatory effect nor purpose. Most jurisdictions that must preclear go to the Department rather than the district court because that avenue is quicker and less expensive. Seeking preclearance from the Department is thought to be "more subject to political pressures" and more desirable "than a full blown lawsuit in Washington, which didn't sit very well with the Southerners, anyway."[35]

In 28 CFR sec. 51.27, the Department sets forth the materials that a jurisdiction is required to submit. This regulation covers subjects such as the language of the proposed change, identification of the law being repealed or amended, a statement of the reasons for the change, and more mundane particulars. The next section, 28 CFR sec. 51.28, sets forth supplemental factors that may be required in certain circumstances, including two that are required for each redistricting change. These include both demographic information, stating total- and voting-age population of the affected area before and after the change by race and language group, and maps of the prior and new boundaries of the voting unit or units.

Jurisdictions are also encouraged to provide additional information. Maps may be required to show before- and after-views of precinct lines, location of racial or language groups, natural boundaries or geographical features that influenced line drawing, polling places, and registration sites. The Department may seek election data, including name and race or language group of each candidate, and election returns. The jurisdiction might be requested to explain how the change could affect minorities, the extent of notice given of the change, and opportunity for minority comment and participation in it. It could also be required to show the availability of materials to the minority community and to provide a list of minority contacts within the community who are familiar with the changes or have been active in the process.

Under 28 CFR sec. 51.58 a number of background factors relating to representation are considered. Among these are the extent to which minorities have been denied a meaningful opportunity to participate in the community's political life and the extent of denial of the opportunity to influence elections and official decision making. The jurisdiction may also be expected to provide evidence of the extent of racially polarized voting and racially segregated political activities, as well as the extent to which minority voter registration and participation has been hindered by present or past discrimination.

Section 51.59 deals specifically with redistricting. The Voting Section considers whether districts have been malapportioned to affect minority voting strength. It also inquires whether minority voting strength has been diminished, and whether minority voters have been "packed" into a small number of districts to limit their effectiveness, or "cracked" into a greater number of districts where they would be unable to elect candidates. The Voting Section is curious as to the availability of alternative plans. It also wants to know whether the submitted plan deviates from established or traditional redistricting criteria such as compactness or contiguity, and whether the plan is inconsistent with state redistricting standards. Any of these factors might indicate an effort to impair minority voting strength.

Among the most critical provisions in the regulations are those calling for public comment upon submissions. The Voting Section accepts input from groups or individuals wishing to comment on proposals. Requests for anonymity are honored to the extent that the Freedom of Information Act permits. The Section maintains a Registry of Interested Individuals and Groups and notifies those registered of submissions. Submissions are monitored by many local activists and outside interest groups, including the political parties and advocacy organizations such as the Southern Regional Council, LDF, ACLU, MALDEF, Lawyers' Committee for Civil Rights Under Law, and others. The Division now periodically posts notices of Section Five submissions and an invitation to submit comments on the CRD Web site.[36]

The Department has sixty days from the date of submission to object to a plan, though the time may toll for another sixty days if the attorney general requests additional information. The Department may not reset the clock again. A failure to object within the period constitutes preclearance, but preclearance does not certify that the change complies with any legal requirements beyond those of Section Five. Indeed, the process may expose problems that would render the jurisdiction vulnerable to a Section Two lawsuit from the Department or private parties. The decision to preclear is not reviewable by the courts, although a state that suffers an objection may still bring its submission to the United States District Court for the District of Columbia for declaratory judgment.

The attorney general must notify the jurisdiction of a decision to object and state the reasons for the objection. The jurisdiction may request that the Department's decision be reconsidered and that a conference be granted. Other interested commenters will be notified and offered an opportunity to confer, which may be in a separate meeting. In practice, conferences and communications in person, telephonically, and otherwise are part of the process from its earliest stage. Historically, overburdened Voting Section attorneys have been willing to help local officials get over the hurdles set by preclearance. Court decisions in the nineties recognized, sometimes in critical terms, Voting Section consultation with voting advocates.[37]

CRD attorneys are acculturated to adhere to procedural regularity. The Division operates under a structured review process, in which important decisions such as whether to object or litigate are overseen by experienced professional staff and political appointees. Operational integrity, "internal and external," is a valued component of CRD legal practice. It is important within the Division that proper procedures are followed and that careerists and political appointees are involved. External regularity concerns the notion that the Department should be perceived as proceeding in accord with fair and established practices. Selig wrote in 1985 that the Division follows an "incrementally progressive, middle of the road approach to legal interpretation." He argues that since the Division has resisted both maximalist approaches favored by civil rights advocates and the narrower approaches urged by the states, the Department is well positioned to criticize either extreme.[38] The Division's abandonment of the "incrementally progressive" approach in favor of maximization cost the Division in the nineties in terms of diminished respect from the courts.

The burden of proof is on the submitting jurisdiction to show the absence of discriminatory purpose or effect. If the evidence is conflicting, the burden means that the submitter loses and the plan will draw an objection. The regulations in the early nineties also permitted an objection to be lodged when the submission portrayed a clear violation of Section Two, but the 1990s objections were offered under the theory that absence of discriminatory purpose was not shown. When the Department determined that failure to maximize would constitute evidence of discriminatory purpose, it swallowed Section Two whole.

In *Compromised Compliance*, Ball, Krane, and Lauth break the Voting Section's review process down into four phases. In Phase One, the submission is received and logged in, noting such information as jurisdiction and type of change. The director of the Section Five Unit's paraprofessional staff reads the submission letter and assigns the case to a subordinate, giving consideration to the locale of the jurisdiction, complexity of the submission, and experience of the staffer. Phase Two is analysis by the equal opportunity specialist. That individual inspects the previous record for information on the jurisdiction and examines demographic and legal information provided. The staffer also will contact minority citizens and local officials in the affected area. On the basis of this information, the specialist will recommend that the submission cannot be reviewed, that additional information should be sought, that an objection should be interposed, or that preclearance should be granted.

In Phase Three, the specialist's superiors review the recommendation. The paraprofessional director reviews the analysis, then turns the file over to the senior attorney in the Section Five Unit. If the attorney decides not to object or that the matter cannot be reviewed at this time, a letter is sent to the jurisdiction to that effect. The process is ended. But if the recommendation is to object and the attorney agrees, then the Section Five attorney prepares an objection letter. The chief of the Voting Section and the deputy assistant attorney general for civil rights review that draft. The letter is finally reviewed and signed by the president's appointee as assistant attorney general, Civil Rights Division. As this process is ongoing, the staff meets to discuss issues of concern. Phase Four occurs as the follow-up process on requests for additional information.

The equal opportunity specialists are thus entrusted with the initial discretion to determine whether a change has a discriminatory purpose or effect. This has proven to be an elusive task. The very notion of discrimination has evolved over the years to focus less upon discrimination against individuals than upon institutional racism directed against groups. In the voting rights area the focus has metamorphosed from efforts to ensure registration and the right to cast a ballot, to detecting dilutive schemes, to advancing toward proportional representation. By the 1990s, voting rights advocates viewed the Act as a tool to increase minority descriptive representation to its limits.

While the regulations are extensive, they leave many definitions in an ambiguous state. What, for instance, constitutes a showing of discriminatory purpose? In 1992, a failure to maximize when alternative plans established that possibility constituted evidence of discriminatory purpose; in previous years, it did not. The equal opportunity specialists have had to keep abreast of changes affected by emerging paradigms of discrimination. There has been no official training memo for paralegal staff since the 1979 version, which is no longer used.[39] The Department requires flexibility in order to address the creativity of jurisdictions that continue to resist minority electoral power. The lack of a confining parameter may have contributed to the ease with which the Division stretched the Act's boundaries in the nineties, but the greater influence was an expanded definition of purpose, and that came from legal staff and political appointees.

Sophisticated computer programming supports the efforts of the equal opportunity specialists and the attorneys. Dunne requested $1.85 million in his FY 1992 budget for the implementation of a Geographic Information System to assist in handling the submissions. The GIS system enabled the Voting Section to analyze demographic characteristics of submissions down to the census-block level. Implementation of the GIS was essential to the Division's ability to process submissions.[40]

Dunne also explains that he spent a substantial amount of his time on voting rights matters, more so than his predecessors. Previous chiefs had awaited recommendations to reach them from the chain of command. Dunne got involved earlier in the controversial cases, sometimes attending two or three sit-down meetings to go over submissions. It was at these early meetings, Dunne recalls, that he would ask what percentage of the voting population in a given area was minority and whether some reasonable amount of representation might not approach that percentage. Proportional representation was not his goal, he states. "What we were trying to do was to see if within reasonable standards there could be an opportunity . . . for minority voters to have a more effective voice, but our goal was never [proportional representation]." Nonetheless, "these concepts kind of lap over into each other."[41]

The Appellees in *Miller v Johnson* argued that the Division's Section Five practice "has no established fact-finding procedures, no administrative hearing and no discernible standards for evaluating information."[42] While this statement reflects hyperbolic advocacy, it also contains some truth. Informal conferences substitute for an administrative hearing, which would be difficult to hold within sixty days. Standards can be malleable, as the ambiguity in statutory terms such as "discrimination" or "equal opportunity to participate and to elect" demonstrates.

Dunne concedes that his concern with the racial percentages in a given locale could have been taken as an interest in proportionality. The problems in the approach are evident in the objection letters. In the first Georgia objection letter on 21 January 1992, Dunne wrote "a concern was raised" that the leadership wished to limit the plan to two black districts. He also contended that alternative plans were suggested but the legislature did not make "a good faith effort to recognize the concentrations of black voters in the southwest" and ignored the "community of interest" that black voters in Baldwin County shared with African Americans in nearby counties. It was clear that much of the opposition was coming from the ACLU, though some commenters, including a front organization for Republican interests, sought to conceal their roles. Georgia did not have the chance in a hearing to confront those who raised concerns. The state tried to justify its rationale, but the CRD routinely dismissed such explanations as pretextual. Chief Dunne met with state officials, and Department officials also convened separately with representatives of interest groups and the Republican Party who opposed the submission. Following the rejection of Georgia's first plan, a second state plan was submitted with two majority-black districts and a 45 percent influence district, but the second plan was rejected because the senate had passed a plan, not acceptable to the house, which included a third majority-minority district. The objection came, as the district court in *Johnson v Miller* found, "despite the fact that the second submission addressed the criticisms leveled at the first."[43] It seemed that every time the state broke from the huddle, it found that the goal line had been moved ten yards farther downfield.

The Division sets itself the task of making an "intensely local appraisal" of redistricting submissions. The fact-finding process under Section Two may be too burdensome to be accomplished within the sixty-day deadline. Whereas the traditional Section Five review focuses upon retrogressive effect and discriminatory purpose, Section Two requires a more searching inquiry into whether an electoral plan results in dilution. Turner nonetheless argues that the intensely local appraisal can be done; if it cannot be accomplished the Division is to object, since the burden lies with the submitting jurisdiction.

It might be easy in the abstract to agree on how the Section's attorneys should approach a redistricting submission: the classic attorney's formulation, apply the law to the facts. Such abstract ideals fall, however, to the reality of applying an ambiguous statute imbued with interpretations subject to shifting ideological approaches. Turner describes the difficulty in determining objection decisions:

> Career staff ought to make the judgment calls . . . in a straightforward, non-political, no tilts, no moral judgments swaying it, just a strict legal application of the law to facts, get all the facts and apply the law to it and make a recommendation. That is easier to talk about than it is actually to do, because there is frequently more than one answer to these things. . . . You have to come down and make the recommendation based on what you think the proper spirit and reality of the statute is. [It is a] civil rights law intended to expand the right to vote, so that's one consideration. But you're not supposed to intrude and tell the states how to run their business, and that's another thing. Those things have to be balanced all the time. So you make a good faith balancing effort and make the recommendation. . . . [The political appointee] makes the final call. . . . Eighty to ninety percent of the cases are clear, nobody would argue that. . . . A few cases that are out on the fringes, either on the left or right, those are the ones that get all the ink.[44]

Turner here is describing, in a sense, a clash between the critical task (a civil rights law intended to increase the right to vote) and competing values (federalism, or not telling the states how to run their business). Dunne concedes, "I pushed the envelope about as far as it could go with regard to trying to maximize minority voting rights—not just opportunities but rights—and the courts struck it down." He acknowledges that there may have been an underemphasis on traditional redistricting criteria and possibly a lack of deference to federalism by the staff. Deval Patrick, however, argues that Congress settled the federalism question in passing a statute that requires federal preclearance of state election laws. He does not believe that the Division's approach in the nineties incorrectly balanced the federalism concerns expressed in the Act.[45]

In the nineties round, civil rights groups approached the careerists they knew from prior contact. Some participants believed that the Republicans approached the higher-ups in the Division, who were political appointees. The Republican Party operatives did lobby both careerists and political appointees, and they met with Dunne and his lieutenants, but the process was open, as Dunne met with Democratic Party representatives, state officials, and activist groups. Lawyers' Committee attorney Brenda Wright reported comfort in seeking and obtaining meetings with Dunne when the advocates believed they were warranted.[46]

Compromised Compliance found a norm of assistance by Voting Section attorneys to submitting jurisdictions. Helping the jurisdictions, negotiating and bargaining with them to get past the preclearance hurdles, was seen as a valuable tool to lessen a crushing workload, but former CRD legal counsel David Simon, who came from New York with Dunne, debunks the idea that the Voting Section's policy under Dunne was to negotiate and bargain. Simon states they were there to enforce the Act:

> The Voting Section felt strongly about enforcing the law. If a compromise could be worked out, great, but if it could not be worked out, we weren't supposed to compromise on the law. . . . You act like a judge, and judges don't compromise. . . . We didn't believe . . . that our lawyers should sit there negotiating with the jurisdiction and tell them how to draw their lines. . . . If you look at the objection letters, I don't think [Dunne] ever told them how to draw the lines, he simply told them what they did was not consistent with the Voting Rights Act.[47]

Simon acknowledges that courts in Georgia and elsewhere have found intervention by career staff in line drawing, but he asserts that this was contrary to Dunne's policy. Some line attorneys did rely upon voting rights advocacy groups. In Georgia, the district court found that Voting Section attorneys Keith Borders and Thomas Armstrong related to ACLU counsel Kathleen Wilde as peers in a common endeavor. "[T]he close working relationship between Ms. Wilde and the Voting Section, the repetition of Ms. Wilde's ideas in Mr. Dunne's objection letters, and the slow convergence of size and shape between the max-black plan and the plan DOJ finally precleared, bespeak a direct link between the max-black plan formulated by the ACLU and the preclearance requirements imposed by DOJ." The Voting Section attorneys were also unable to resist the temptation to mold state legislative redistricting in South Carolina. There a district court found that the CRD's close cooperation with the South Carolina Black Legislative Caucus, NAACP, and ACLU rendered the government attorneys as "advocates for the coalition that was seeking to maximize the number of majority BVAP [black voting-age population] districts in an effort to achieve proportionality."[48]

In Louisiana, as the legislature sought to draw a new congressional plan after a district court had found its first minority two-seat plan to be unconstitutional, Deval Patrick wrote Louisiana Legislative Black Caucus counsel Brenda Wright and Robert McDuff, reinforcing the Department's commitment to force two seats. In that letter of 20 April 1994, Patrick stressed the strong working relationship between the Department and the Louisiana Legislative Black Caucus in pursuing the case. Angie LaPlace, an asistant attorney general who represented the state, believes that Caucus members used the Patrick letter to push the legislature toward another two-seat plan.[49] While local activists were involved in each state, they played a secondary role to the lobbying of the Department by national advocacy organizations such as the ACLU and the Lawyers' Committee for Civil Rights Under Law.

As a continuous player in a repeat game, the Voting Section has a substantial advantage over the submitting jurisdictions, which are only sporadically involved in the preclearance process. It can balance litigation resources and risks against the specifics of a given case. A disappointed jurisdiction must sue in the United States District Court for the District of Columbia to overturn an objection. The DC court has historically been seen as hostile to Southern racial appeals, which is precisely the reason the Congress assigned Section Five cases to it in the first place. Thus, the preclearance process is a mighty hammer. Many of the most egregious plans never are passed by legislative bodies and forwarded to Washington because of the threat of objection.[50]

The Voting Section must review those submissions that do arrive in Washington, and here is a place where the administrative burdens placed upon the Section present a damaging problem. The two components of quasi-judicial objective decision making and aggressive litigation are too much in conflict. For example, in *Garza v County of Los Angeles*, the Division litigators won recognition of an expansive theory of discriminatory intent from the Ninth Circuit Court of Appeals.[51] The Division relied upon *Garza* as authority for the nineties' objection letters, but a more judicious approach might not have depended upon the furthest-reaching decision in the nation, from the most liberal court, in a time of general judicial retrenchment. There is a costly inelegance within the statute. The Voting Section must both advocate (sometimes pushing the Act toward the cutting edge) and stand as a surrogate for an objective judiciary. Even where efforts are made to separate the litigation and quasi-judicial functions, the sheer crush of submissions that follows the decennial census requires litigation attorneys to pitch in and help review submissions. The Division's FY 1991 budget request makes clear that when submissions flood the Section Five Unit, litigation attorneys must be pressed into service to decide submissions.

Separation of the advocacy and quasi-judicial functions is a sensible step. Turner has remarked upon the relationship within the Voting Section of litigators and preclearance personnel:

> It is something that needs to be separated. . . . In a perfect world, with unlimited lawyers . . . we would have a situation where the Section Five deciders wouldn't talk to the Section Two litigators, because frequently they would come to the table with a point of view or trying to litigate something instead of trying to decide something. But we didn't have that perfect world, so you do the best you can. . . . There might be instances where we would have problems that would not

amount to a conflict of interest, a formal one, but in that same neck of the woods we might be able to find a problem.[52]

HUNKERING DOWN IN THE CIVIL RIGHTS DIVISION

As the Department issued its objection letters in 1991 and 1992, it was faced with the criticism that it was following an agenda of maximization. State Democratic leaders in covered jurisdictions were suspicious of the Division's enforcement. When Democratic state legislators accommodated Division concerns while preserving incumbent protection, frustrated Republican partisans and local citizens brought the lawsuits that became *Shaw v Reno* and its progeny. These suits illuminated the Division's implementation of Section Five and brought more controversy and conflict. It is appropriate to review the Department's reaction to these accusations when considering its organizational culture. "When criticized, some organizations hunker down and others conduct a searching self-examination."[53]

In 1992 in remarks at Cardozo Law School, Dunne responded to criticisms that the Department required maximization of minority districts: "There is one thing the Civil Rights Division does not do: It does not require, because the law does not require, the maximization of minority representation. Jurisdictions are not required in all cases to create as many minority districts as possible. Nor are jurisdictions required to guarantee or to attempt to guarantee racial or ethnic proportional results." Dunne now concedes that his policies did drift into maximization.[54]

As Dunne handed over responsibility for the Division to the Clinton administration, however, the CRD still maintained that it had no policy of maximization. By 1993 and the *Shaw v Reno* decision, the voting rights legal environment began to change. Deval Patrick was convinced that *Shaw v Reno* was wrongly decided. In a speech before the NAACP National Convention in July 1994, Patrick assessed *Shaw v Reno* as "an alternately naive and venal decision." He criticized the Court for abandoning its sense of history and perspective on "how meaningful it is to have the largest Congressional Black Caucus in history and the largest Congressional Hispanic Caucus in history." The Court was accused of starting down the path of "an exclusion of Black and other minority representatives from positions of power." In October, Patrick argued that *Shaw v Reno* was an "abstraction" that turned "away from real problems and real people." In November he suggested that challenges to the Department's redistricting policies in *Shaw* and other cases "sounds a lot like 1901 all over again." (In 1901 George White of North Carolina, the last black Reconstruction congressman, departed Washington. It was twenty-eight years until another African American served in Congress. North Carolina did not send a black to Congress again until 1992.) Patrick repeated many of these remarks to the National Conference of State Legislators in July of 1996 and stated "that the department did not have then, and does not have now, a 'maximization' policy." Yet, even some of the Department's allies agree that the Department had used its preclearance powers to compel new majority-minority districts.[55]

In 1993 and 1994, as *Shaw* and *Miller* were working their way through the courts, the CRD disregarded cautions arising in those cases as they pursued maximization plans in other states. One such case was the redistricting of the South Carolina legislature. In *Smith v Beasley*, the court found that the Department was in close contact throughout the process with Dr. John Ruoff, a demographer working on behalf of the Statewide Reapportionment Adviory Committee, a group advocating for black interests. Dr. Ruoff had developed a "dream plan" for maximizing African-American districts, and he communicated with Voting Section line staff to report his progress and receive recommendations. During its consideration of the South Carolina submission, the Department stayed in contact with strategists for the dream plan, including Dr. Ruoff, representatives of the NAACP, and ACLU attorney Laughlin McDonald. The only issue involved in these conversations was the creation of race-based districts. The South Carolina Black Legislative Caucus and the Republican Party sought proportional representation. The court found that: "It is obvious from the notes of telephone conversations, memoranda, correspondence, and testimony presented that the Black Caucus, the South Carolina Republican Party, and the Department of Justice were seeking to maximize black representation in the South Carolina House of Representatives with little concern for compactness of districts, contiguity, or communities of interest." These same factors were cataloged in the Georgia congressional redistricting case, *Miller v Johnson*.

Deval Patrick testified in a deposition in *Smith v Beasley* that "I don't think there is any such thing as a bizarre or irregular shape"—a statement made after the decisions in *Shaw v Reno* and *Hays I* (and to which Patrick still adheres, arguing the impossibility of defining a "regular shape").[56] But the Division's Section Five enforcement regulations call for it to consider the regularity of shape in potential discriminatory gerrymanders. Under 28 CFR sec. 51.59(f) the Voting Section must review the "extent to which the plan departs from objective redistricting criteria set by the submitting jurisdiction, ignores other relevant factors such as compactness and contiguity, or displays a configuration that inexplicably disregards available natural or artificial boundaries." While this provision is aimed at the kinds of irregular districts historically drawn to dilute black voting power, the principle is applicable to any districting plan.

Smith is also similar to *Hays* in the extent of CRD intervention into legislative decision making. In Louisiana, Patrick sent a 20 April 1994 letter to counsel for the Louisiana Legislative Black Caucus that is believed to have been timed to influence legislative deliberations on a new congressional redistricting plan. In South Carolina, the court found that Patrick's objection letter of 2 May 1994 was used "as a directive for creating additional districts and the location of such districts." When *Shaw v Reno* might have portended caution, the Division plowed right ahead. Patrick objected in 1996 to Louisiana's legislative adoption of a plan already imposed on it by a federal court. Despite the battering from the courts, in 1996 a district court in Florida observed that the Department still seemed to be pursuing maximization.[57]

While Supreme Court arguments were pending in *Shaw v Hunt*, the recently retired James P. Turner contributed an opinion piece to the *New York Times* defending affirmative action remedies. On 16 April 1995 in "The Fairest Cure We Have," he criticized the political parties for their participation in creating oddly shaped districts and stated: "The Administration is now trying to defend them all, including some plainly indefensible gerrymanders." This rather moderate view, while conflicting with the line out of the Department, comported with the findings of numerous courts, including the Supreme Court. Turner's views were not especially welcome by his former colleagues who were attempting to defend those indefensible districts. The Division, under both Dunne and Patrick, chose to hunker down.

CONCLUSION

The Voting Rights Act is an essential piece of legislation, and a strong case can be made for the case-specific approach of administrative enforcement. While the case-specific approach has engendered some disputes over the years, on the whole it has operated effectively. A similar case cannot be made for redefining voting opportunity as proportional representation. It cannot be found within Section Five, the enforcement authority at the Department's command. The courts are also making it clear that it cannot be found in Section Two.

Leadership appointed by the sitting administration and careerists drawn to its civil rights mission affect the CRD's performance. Voting Section attorneys are guaranteed to face contentious judgments in deciding upon redistricting submissions. The interest group environment that surrounds those decisions assures that whatever decision is made, criticism will be engendered. Legal challenges from unhappy interests have become common, as well.

The difficulty of arriving at a decision is exacerbated by the shifting interpretations of discriminatory purpose or racial fairness, though the Division must have definitional flexibility to respond to emerging methods of limiting minority electoral strength. The public law attorneys who came to the Division to push for civil rights saw the changed definition as a natural evolution in the law, not the sweeping alteration it was. In some cases, they ignored the guideline that they should not intrude into state line drawing.

Voting Section attorneys are recruited from successful legal and academic backgrounds, elite law schools, and prestigious firms. Their worldview frequently reflects a conscious sensitivity to racism in society, as befits their role in the Justice Department. The Voting Section's policy function places them at an intersection of law and politics; while they excel at one, many have little feel for the other. Their legal experience has not confronted them with the political choices made by state legislators in redistricting. State officials are conscious of racial concerns of course—but also of committee responsibilities, leadership struggles, imprecations from colleagues, and partisan motivations. While praising the legal abilities of Voting Section attorneys, Dunne points out that some lack the political sensitivity that can be helpful in navigating such a politically pregnant area as legislative redistricting.[58] This can certainly help explain the lead-footed approach taken by the Section in redistricting. While the attorneys of the Division are well suited to case-by-case legal inquiry, they are ill suited to broad policy determinations. The imperative of increasing minority representation required a substantive change in policy. How that policy alteration was achieved, masked as a shift in legal interpretation, is the subject of the next chapter.

NOTES

1. James P. Turner, "Case-Specific Implementation of the Voting Rights Act," in Bernard Grofman and Chandler Davidson, eds., *Controversies in Minority Voting: The Voting Rights Act in Perspective* (Washington, DC: Brookings Institution, 1992).

2. James Q. Wilson explains that the critical task concerns "those behaviors which, if successfully performed by key organizational members, would enable the organization to manage its critical environmental problem." James Q. Wilson, *Bureaucracy: What Government Agencies Do and Why They Do It* (New York: Basic Books, 1989), 25–26.

3. Wilson, *Bureaucracy*, 26.

4. Howard Ball, Dale Krane, and Thomas P. Lauth, *Compromised Compliance: Implementation of the 1965 Voting Rights Act* (Westport, Conn.: Greenwood Press, 1982), 133–136.

5. James P. Turner, interview by author, tape recording, Accokeek, Md., 27 August 1997.

6. Wilson, *Bureaucracy*, 26.

7. John R. Dunne, "Law Day USA," (Speech at Fordham Law School, 1 May 1990); John R. Dunne, telephone conversation with author, 20 January 1998; Turner interview; David Johnston, "Justice Department's Civil Rights Chief Is Sitting on Sidelines of Main Battle," *New York Times*, 10 January 1991.

8. Paul M. Sniderman and Edward G. Carmines, *Reaching Beyond Race* (Cambridge, Mass.: Harvard University Press, 1997); "Social Audit: Black/White Relations in the U.S." (Princeton, N.J.: Gallup Organization, 10 June 1997). See <http://www.gallup.com/poll/socialaudits/sa970610.asp>.

9. Brian K. Landsberg, *Enforcing Civil Rights: Race Discrimination and the Department of Justice* (Lawrence, Kans.: University Press of Kansas, 1997), 163.

10. Joan Biskupic, "Questions, Criticism Surround Apparent Choice of Lucas," *Congressional Quarterly*, 15 April 1989, 830–831.

11. Joan Biskupic, "Panel Delays Vote on Lucas at Sen. Heflin's Urging," *Congressional Quarterly*, vol. 47, no. 30, 29 July 1989, p. 1964.

12. Ethan Bronner, "Bush Nominates Ex-NY Legislator for Rights Post; Reaction Is Cool," *Boston Globe*, 26 January 1990; Michael Isikoff, "Civil Rights Nominee Defuses Criticism," *Washington Post*, 8 March 1990; Joan Biskupic, "Bush's Civil Rights Nominee Wins Senate Confirmation," *Congressional Quarterly*, Vol. 48, no. 10, 10 March 1990, 754; Sam Howe Verhovek, " 'Sensitive' but Untested," *New York Times*, 27 January 1990.

13. Clint Bolick, "The Legal Philosophy That Produced Lani Guinier," *Wall Street Journal*, 2 June 1993; Neil A Lewis, "Aides Say Clinton Will Drop Nominee for Post on Rights," *New York Times*, 3 June 1993; Lyle Denniston, "Black Caucus Is Wary on Choice for Rights Post," *Chicago Sun-Times* 17 November 1993.

14. Lynne Duke, "Attorney Named to Rights Post," *Washington Post*, 2 February 1994; "A Chief for Civil Rights" (editorial), 3 February 1994.

15. George Stephanopoulos, *All Too Human: A Political Education* (Boston: Little, Brown & Co., 1999), 360–375; Deval L. Patrick telephone conversation with author, 20 January 1998; *Louisiana v Hays*, 862 F. Supp. 119 (W.D. La. 1994).

16. Dunne, "Law Day USA."

17. David Johnston, "Justice Department's Civil Rights Chief Is Sitting on Sidelines of Main Battle," *New York Times*, 10 January 1991.

18. Richard A. Bloom, "Justice's Dunne and the Voting Rights Act," *National Journal*, 4 May 1991; Dunne telephone conversation.

19. Robert Pear, "Citing Race Bias, U.S. Vetoes 2 States' Redistricting," *New York Times*, 3 July 1991; Robert Pear, "U.S. Rejects New York Plan for City Council Districts; Finds Hispanic Voters Hurt," *New York Times*, 20 July 1991. Bronx County, Kings County, and New York County, New York, are covered under Section Five.

20. In Beth Donovan, "Nation Watches as Texas Struggles to Create Minority Districts," *Congressional Quarterly*, vol. 49, No. 33, 17 August 1991, 2293–2295.

21. Ellen Spears, "The Republicans Go to Court: A Review of Republican Legal Strategies on Minority Rights in the Area of the Voting Rights Act" (Atlanta, Ga.: Southern Regional Council, April 1992).

22. Dunne telephone conversation; Patrick telephone conversation.

23. Brian K. Landsberg, "The Role of Civil Service Attorneys and Political Appointees in Making Policy in the Civil Rights Division of the United States Department of Justice," *Journal of Law and Politics* 9 (1993), 275, 277; Turner interview.

24. Suzanne Weaver, *Decision to Prosecute: Organization and Public Policy in the Antitrust Division* (Cambridge, Mass.: MIT Press, 1977).

25. Turner interview.

26. Landsberg, "The Role of Civil Service Attorneys," 277.

27. Dunne telephone conversation.

28. Wilson, *Bureaucracy*, 48, 58; Landsberg, "The Role of Civil Service Attorneys," 277; Joel Selig, "The Reagan Justice Department and Civil Rights: What Went Wrong," *University of Illinois Law Review* 4 (1985), 785.

29. U.S. House, Hearing before the Subcommittee on Civil and Constitutional Rights of the Committee on the Judiciary, *Authorization Request of the Civil Rights Division of the Department of Justice for Fiscal Year 1991*, 101st Cong.

30. Turner interview.

31. Civil Rights Division, *Authorization Request for Fiscal Year 1991.*

32. Landsberg, "The Role of Civil Service Attorneys," 278–279.

33. Dunne telephone conversation; David Simon, telephone conversation with author, 9 January 1998; Brenda Wright, telephone conversation with author, 13 January 1998.

34. Dunne telephone conversation; Patrick telephone conversation.

35. Turner interview.

36. Civil Rights Division, http://www.usdoj.gov/crt/voting/noticepg.html.

37. Ball, Krane, and Lauth, *Compromised Compliance*, 86–91; *Johnson v Miller*, 864 F. Supp. 1354 (S.D. Ga. 1994); *Smith v Beasley*, 946 F. Supp. 1174 (D. S.C. 1996).

38. Selig, "What Went Wrong," 788; Landsberg, *Enforcing Civil Rights*, 120–122.

39. Nelson Hermilla, letter to author, 30 December 1997.

40. Dunne telephone conversation.

41. Dunne telephone conversation.

42. *Brief for the Appellees,* submitted to the Supreme Court in *Miller v Johnson*, Nos. 94-929 and 94-797 (1994).

43. *Johnson v Miller*, 864 F. Supp. 1365.

44. Turner interview.

45. Dunne telephone conversation; Patrick telephone conversation.

46. Dunne telephone conversation; Wright telephone conversation.

47. Simon telephone conversation.

48. *Johnson v Miller*, 864 F. Supp. 1368; *Smith v Beasley*, 1208.

49. Angie LaPlace, telephone conversation with author, 30 December 1997.

50. Bernard Grofman and Chandler Davidson, "The Enforcement of the Voting Rights Act by the U.S. Department of Justice: Compromised Compliance? Republican Plot? Or Great American Success Story?" (paper presented at the annual meeting of the American Political Science Association, 1992).

51. *Garza v County of Los Angeles*, 918 F. 2d 763 (9th Cir. 1990).

52. Turner interview.

53. Wilson, *Bureaucracy*, 93.

54. John R. Dunne, "Remarks before the Cardozo Law School Symposium on Districting Issues," New York, 6 April 1992; Dunne telephone conversation.

55. Deval L. Patrick, "Remarks at the NAACP National Convention," Chicago, Illinois, 12 July 1994; Deval L. Patrick, "Remarks before the Town Hall, Los Angeles," 4 October 1994; Deval L. Patrick, "Remarks for Fall 1994 Rubin Lecture," Columbia School of Law, New York, 2 November 1994; Deval L. Patrick, "Remarks before the National Conference of State Legislators," St. Louis, Missouri, 29 July 1996; Bernard Grofman and Lisa Handley, "1990s Issues in Voting Rights," *Mississippi Law Journal* 65, no.2 (winter 1995), 205.

56. *Smith v Beasley*, 1183–1193; Patrick telephone conversation.

57. *Johnson v Mortham*, 926 F. Supp. 1460 (N.D. Fla. 1996).

58. Dunne telephone conversation.

4

The Department's New Interpretation of the Voting Rights Act

> The Voting Rights Act was aimed to the subtle, as well as the obvious, state regulations which have the effect of denying citizens their right to vote because of their race.
>
> *Allen v State Board of Elections* (1969)

> The Voting Rights Act is not an all purpose anti-discrimination statute.
>
> *Presley v Etowah County Commission* (1992)

The Justice Department has distinct but overlapping functions under the VRA: to follow judicial precedent in its quasi-judicial Section Five preclearance powers and to urge its own interpretations upon the courts through litigation. The turf on which interpretative battles are fought contrasts a traditionalist approach with a modern one. Traditionalists seek to closely examine textual expression, the better to defer to and enforce the will of the democratically elected legislature. Modernists regard law as a progressive science, with interpreters permitted to look not only to plain meaning but also to other sources that may assist in arriving at sound legal policy.

The choice of method matters. In 1969 in *Allen v State Board of Elections* the Supreme Court emphasized the legislative history and congressional intent to defeat a racially discriminatory Mississippi districting change. But in *Presley v Etowah County Commission* (1992) a more restrained Court hewed carefully to statutory language and denied a remedy for an Alabama county's alteration to the powers of its first black elected county commissioner. In both *Allen* and *Presley*, dissenting Justices analyzed the cases differently, providing stark examples of how conflicting methods of legal interpretation can lead to opposite results. In the nineties the Department's desired voting rights policy results were temporarily achieved through the service of the modern, results-driven mode of interpretation. Whereas the DOJ had a history of seeking moderately progressive legal interpretations, in the nineties it transformed purpose and *Gingles* in order to push and defend maximization.

TRADITIONAL AND MODERN APPROACHES IN THE SUPREME COURT

In *Allen,* Chief Justice Warren, writing for the majority, based his analysis upon "the weight of the legislative history and an analysis of the basic purposes of the Act." The right to vote should be broadly interpreted, because "the right to vote can be affected by a dilution of voting power as well as by an absolute prohibition on casting a ballot." The Court took note of testimony before Congress that seemed to indicate a limited scope was intended for the Act. In response to a congressman's question whether the Act would reach issues concerning qualifications for potential candidates, Assistant Attorney General for Civil Rights Burke Marshall stated: "The problem that the bill was aimed at was the problem of registration, congressman. If there is a problem of another sort, I would like to see it corrected, but that is not what we were trying to deal with in the bill." Attorney General Katzenbach testified, however, that "Our experience in the areas that would be covered by this bill has been such as to indicate frequently on the part of State legislatures a desire in a sense to outguess the courts of the United States or even to outguess the Congress of the United States." He also remarked "there are an awful lot of things that could be started for purposes of evading the Fifteenth Amendment if there is a desire to do so." The Court read Katzenbach's testimony and the "mass of legislative history" to outweigh the testimony of Assistant Attorney General Marshall and ruled for an expansive interpretation of the Act.[1]

Justice Harlan wrote a partial concurrence and dissent in which he objected to the "Court's extremely broad construction of Section Five." He seemed conscious of Justice Frankfurter's warning in his *Baker v Carr* dissent that "What is actually asked of the Court in this case is to choose among competing bases of representation—ultimately, really, among competing theories of political philosophy."[2] Harlan argued that the Court had ignored the role of Section Five within the Act, that it was untrue to the statutory language, and that it misused and mistook legislative history.

Harlan first examined the role of Section Five within the Act's complex structure. He believed that the heart of the Act was contained in Section Four, which prohibited all literacy tests and similar devices for five years. Harlan regarded Section Five as "designed to march in lockstep with Section 4. . . . Section 5, moreover, reveals that it was not designed to implement new substantive policies but that it was structured to assure the effectiveness of the dramatic step that Congress had taken in Section 4." Harlan asserted that Section Four was designed to see that black citizens would have equal access to the ballot box, assuring state responsiveness to their interests. The Court's decision would mean that federal intervention "is no longer limited to examining any new state statute that may tend to deny Negroes their right to vote" but instead it would encompass a revolutionary new sphere of federal intrusion into state decision making. Harlan's review of the legislative history led him to conclude "that the history the Court has garnered undermines its case, insofar as it is entitled to any weight at all."[3]

This thirty-year-old dispute about the meaning of the Act and how to interpret it still animates debate about the Act today. In his concurrence in *Holder v Hall*, Justice Thomas critiqued the broad approach used by the Court to arrive at its result in *Allen*, arguing, as had Harlan, that interpretation should be anchored in the statutory text. Thomas called for a "systematic reassessment" of the Court's interpretation of the Act. His reading would not support the idea that courts might intervene to remedy dilutive districting plans—an effort by past Court majorities that Thomas likened to a "conjurer's trick." Abigail Thernstrom argues that Section Five was a minor issue at the 1965 hearings and that most remarks concerning the scope of the Act indicate that registration and voting were the limited aims. To her, Burke Marshall's remark would encapsulate the Act's intent. Historian J. Morgan Kousser has attacked Thomas and Thernstrom for what he terms their radical revisionism. Kousser returns to the legislative history for a number of expansive remarks from the period, indicating that Chief Justice Warren had correctly applied legislative history in *Allen*. Kousser prefers testimony such as that of Attorney General Katzenbach when he indicated that "an awful lot of things" could be devised by the states to evade the Fifteenth Amendment unless prevented by Section Five. If these examples are probative of anything, it is probably that legislative history commonly presents conflicting views that can be used to support varying positions.[4]

Traditional textual analysis and modern legal realism have both been applied in efforts to extend or limit the reach of the Act. Since 1965, the Department has had a central role arguing before the Supreme Court in key cases interpreting the VRA. It has usually staked out a position favorable to the policy ends of the civil rights community, but has almost always seemed mindful of how far the Court might go. The Court has commonly granted the positions taken by the Department a great deal of respect. A brief review of important cases shows the Department's successes and failures and how they have helped to shape understandings of the Act through the years.

NUDGING THE COURT DOWN A PROGRESSIVE PATH

The facts in *Allen* made it quite apparent that some jurisdictions would continue efforts to limit black voting power. The DOJ encouraged the result in *Allen* in its brief to the Supreme Court. The Department prodded the Court toward a broad interpretation of textual language and legislative history. The DOJ's brief did "recognize, of course, that the instant cases do not involve statutory changes which, in so many words, alter the existing rules governing the casting of individual ballots." Nonetheless, "the right to vote can be curtailed as effectively by an impermissible demarcation of an elected official's constituency as by the destruction of ballots or the refusal to permit access to the voting booth."[5]

In *Gaston County v United States* the majority accepted the Department's argument that because Gaston County had historically provided inferior education to its African-American citizens, they would be unfairly disadvantaged in meeting a literacy test. The United States relied upon the legislative history of Attorney General Katzenbach's remarks about the unfairness of literacy tests, as well as upon the argument that Congress "was well aware" in 1965 that the tests had been unfairly administered. The Department staked out a position that would animate much of its policy in ensuing years: "In sum, the Voting Rights Act is result-oriented."[6]

The Department also sought a progressive ruling from the Supreme Court in *Beer v United States*. *Beer* was the New Orleans case in which the Department denied preclearance for discriminatory effect to a city council redistricting because the city, while offering some improvements in recognizing concentrations of black citizens, had not done as much as the DOJ deemed feasible. The Department argued that a mere determination that the change would be no worse than the pre-existing plan would defeat the congressional purpose to enforce the Fifteenth Amendment. What is required, argued the government, is a "realistic inquiry into the effects the proposed plan would have in actual operation." The Court should balance dilution against any non-racial justification offered and reject the plan if the justification did not outweigh the dilution. The Department contended that New Orleans's submission could not meet that standard because less dilutive alternative plans were available to the city. In this case, however, the Court rejected the Department's reasoning, holding that Section Five's effects test applies only to retrogression in minority voting strength.[7]

The DOJ supported the effort of plaintiffs' challenge to Mobile, Alabama's, at-large system for electing city commissioners in the 1980 case of *City of Mobile v Bolden*. The Department acknowledged that a recent Court decision emphasized that a Fourteenth Amendment challenge must be based on a claim of purposeful discrimination, not merely disparate impact. (The Department applied similar reasoning to its legal position on the Fourteenth and Fifteenth Amendments and Section Two of the VRA.) In *Bolden*, evidence that the at-large system had been interposed for a racial purpose was not well developed on the record. The city asserted that no formal barriers to political participation existed, but the Department argued that "The immediate instrumentality by which whites assure that blacks will be denied representation is racially polarized voting in Mobile" and that at-large voting enhanced that practice. Moreover, the Department contended that the Court should infer discriminatory purpose when racially disparate representation exists where a less dilutive electoral system is feasible.[8] The Court, however, rejected the DOJ's position.

The Court also ruled against the Department's position in 1986's defining Section Two case of *Thornburg v Gingles*—but in *Gingles*, under the direction of Reagan appointees Solicitor General Charles Fried and CRD chief Reynolds, the DOJ sided with North Carolina. The Department's brief (which was heavily dependent on legislative history) argued that recent electoral success by African-American candidates in state legislative races was adequate proof that the state's use of multimember districts did not impair the ability of blacks to participate in electoral politics and elect candidates of their choice. The Department's position drew a critical response in a brief filed by congressional supporters of the Act including Senator Dole, author of the compromise that was crucial to the amendment's passage. Their *amicus* brief (which also argued from an understanding of legislative history, as well as statutory meaning) contended that recent and limited success of African-American candidates is not enough to establish equal opportunity.[9] The Court divided five to four in favor of a decision written by Justice William Brennan upholding the plaintiff's challenge to the multimember plan.

Traditional and modern methods may be regarded as tools in the lawyer's kit, to be wielded in pursuing the desired result. Contrary to what might be the popular impression, the conservative advocates of the Reagan administration were not less hesitant to argue from matter extraneous to statutory text than were those criticized as unfettered legal realists. Nonetheless, in applying a jurisprudential method, it is important to keep in mind that while traditional interpretation is indeed difficult, it expresses a judgment to anchor construction to a text approved by the people (as in the Constitution), or through the people's representatives (as in the passage of a statute). The modern approach's reliance upon a creative judiciary dislodges this democratic connection and countenances the judiciary to uphold elite values rather than public policy.[10] The modern approach places more faith in appeals to elite institutions—the judiciary foremost among them, or, in the preclearance context, the quasi-judicial deciders of the CRD.

THE SECTION TWO RESULTS TEST, *GINGLES*, AND INCORPORATION

The results test was added to Section Two of the Act to address the Court's decision in *City of Mobile v Bolden*, which held that claims of vote dilution must be based upon an allegation of intentional discrimination. Civil rights advocates believed that the intent standard was so difficult to prove as to emasculate the concept of vote dilution. They thus successfully sought to amend Section Two to cover election practices that result in a denial or abridgement of the right to vote on account of race or color.

An important issue under Section Two's results test is the statutory definition establishing a violation. Section 2(b) states that the results test is violated if "based on the totality of the circumstances, it is shown that the political processes leading to nomination or election in the State or political subdivision are not equally open to participation [to members of a protected class] in that its members have less opportunity than other members of the electorate to participate in the political process and to elect representatives of their choice." In short, the court should attempt to determine whether a jurisdiction's practices somehow result in the political process being less open to minority citizens' ability to participate and to elect favored candidates than it is to white citizens. The Senate Report on the legislation provided a nonexclusive list of factors for consideration. The Senate factors include the extent of official discrimination that has affected the right to vote; racially polarized voting; use of dilutive schemes such as at-large voting and candidate slating; effects of historical discrimination on housing, employment, health, and education; racial appeals in campaigns; and numbers of minority groups elected to office. Lesser considerations include responsiveness of officials to minority concerns and state rationale for the questioned electoral procedure.[11]

Yet the statute leaves open to interpretation the meaning and interaction of terms such as "less opportunity to participate" and "to elect representatives of their choice." These terms are subject to differing meanings of equal opportunity; some have questioned whether a white person, a black Republican, or a candidate who caters to business interests can be a representative of choice.

The Supreme Court rejected the Reagan administration's position in *Gingles*. It is important to give some attention to majority and concurring opinions because *Gingles* molded expectations for enforcement in the nineties.

Justice Brennan, writing for the Court, focused upon a reading of the legislative history, law-review articles, and social science literature; little regard was given to a textual analysis. He wrote that before assessing the Senate Report factors, a challenge to multimember districts requires that three preconditions be met. The preconditions seek to establish that a Section Two violation may only be found if the minority group can establish that it is sufficiently numerous and geographically compact to form a majority in a single-member district, that the minority group votes cohesively and that voting is so racially polarized that the majority would usually defeat the candidate favored by the minority group. The preconditions are largely drawn from Justice Brennan's reading of the social science literature; they are only marginally part of the then existing case law and the Court cites no consideration of them within the legislative history.[12]

Justice Brennan wrote that "the essence of a Section Two claim is that a certain electoral law, practice, or structure interacts with social and historical conditions to cause an inequality in the opportunity enjoyed by black and white voters to elect their preferred candidates." The essence of the interaction he speaks of, however, is not expressed in the text.[13] Moreover, Justice Brennan's singular focus upon the election of a candidate of choice ignores the statutory requirement that the minority must also suffer an inequality in the ability to participate in the political process. In another section of the decision that gained only plurality approval, Justice Brennan found that only the correlation between the race of the voter and the selection of a candidate, not the causes of the correlation, matter to a Section Two inquiry. Justice White responded: "This is interest-group politics rather than a rule hedging against racial discrimination."[14] The majority reviewed an ambiguous statute that manifested some differing values, including a results test versus a proviso against proportional representation, and interpreted it as if no compromises or trade-offs had been expressed.

Justice O'Connor filed an opinion concurring in the judgment but cautioning that the Court should attempt to address the balance struck by Congress. She argued that the legislature intended to allow vote-dilution tests to proceed under the results standard but did not intend to create a right to proportional representation. O'Connor asserted that the Court had combined its definition of minority voting strength and vote dilution in a manner that would result in proportional representation. She explained that in order to determine when voting strength is diluted, a court must have some benchmark in mind. The approach the Court had adopted, O'Connor argued, was that "undiluted minority voting strength means the maximum feasible minority voting strength." She asserted that Congress had not intended a single, universal standard for local jurisdictions without regard to local conditions or history of discrimination in voting. The proper evaluation would focus upon access to the political process generally, not solely to a consideration of whether a group's favored candidates had been elected. Justice O'Connor—as a former majority leader of the Arizona state senate, the only sitting Justice to have served in a legislature—pointed out why courts should defer to congressional intent, rather than seek what the Court might regard as a just result: "Compromise is essential to much if not most major federal legislation, and confidence that the federal courts will enforce such compromises is indispensable to their creation."[15]

The Court's opinion cheered voting rights advocates, who deem proportional representation as synonymous with fair districting. The Section Two process, however, is expensive and time consuming, and the burden of proof is on the complainant to prove discriminatory results, not on the state to prove absence of discrimination. Activists therefore sought to insert the broader results standard into the preclearance procedure by arguing for full incorporation of Section Two into the Section Five review process. Their consistent ally Representative Don Edwards used hearings into pending Section Five regulations to pressure the Department to include an incorporation provision. The effort was successful. In a subsequent defense of incorporation, the Department relied upon a footnote to the 1982 Senate Report that stated that "In light of the amendment to Section Two, it is intended that a Section Five objection also follow if a new voting procedure so discriminates as to violate Section Two."[16] There is also some administrative efficiency to incorporation because the Voting Section might review a Section Five submission and find no retrogression or purposeful discrimination, but a clear display of a results violation. An objection could help avoid a costly and lengthy Section Two trial. The Section Five process might also alert a jurisdiction to possible liability on a results standard and spur corrective action. The Supreme Court rejected incorporation in the 1997 case of *Reno v Bossier Parish School Board*,[17] but this decision occurred after incorporation had played a critical role in the definitional battle over nineties' enforcement waged by the Division.

A NEW INTERPRETATION OF DISCRIMINATORY PURPOSE

The results test, *Gingles*, and incorporation provided momentum toward proportional representation, but grounding in Section Five's purpose or effects test was lacking. Since *Beer* established effects as being circumscribed to retrogression it has been of limited utility. Purpose as traditionally defined by the CRD encompassed a specific intent to discriminate based on race. The purpose basis would have to become more inclusive. With the progressive impetus of the eighties, urgings by the civil rights advocates, and a creative new interpretation, it did.

John Dunne went into some detail to explain the meaning of discriminatory purpose in his 1991 address to the National Conference of State Legislators (NCSL). He stated:

A discriminatory purpose means a design or desire to restrict a minority group's voting strength, that is, the ability of that group to elect candidates of its choice, below the level which that minority might otherwise have enjoyed.

Discriminatory purpose does not mean racial animus. As Judge Kozinski of the Ninth Circuit noted in the *Garza* case, legislators who harbor no ill will at all towards minorities would nevertheless be engaging in purposeful discrimination if they fragmented a minority community in order to protect incumbents who might be voted out of office if the minority voters were able to elect candidates of their choice.

On the other hand, discriminatory purpose does not mean the intentional adoption of a plan that gives a minority group control of less than a proportional or maximum number of districts. A minority group is not automatically entitled to a proportional redistricting plan. Disparate effects alone, even when they are totally foreseen, do not equal discriminatory purpose under Section Five, although they may be a problem under Section Two.

Disparate effects, however, do need to be explained in a Section Five submission so that we can be sure that the state has satisfied its burden of proving the absence of racially discriminatory purpose.[18]

Garza, a Section Two case, stands out as perhaps the broadest interpretation of intent in the case law. The United States Court of Appeals for the Ninth Circuit found in 1990 that the Los Angeles County Board of Supervisors had drawn lines in 1981 (and prior decades) intended to protect incumbents that had as a by-product also split concentrations of Hispanic voters. Though Hispanics might form a majority in a single-member district in 1990, they could not have done so in 1981. The Court declared the 1981 plan to be intentional discrimination in violation of Section Two, ignoring the Supreme Court's teaching requiring a finding of invidious intent. The Court of Appeals and the Department also ignored the Supreme Court's 1966 decision in *Burns v Richardson* that indicated that line drawing to protect incumbents does not necessarily establish a discriminatory purpose.

Garza greatly distorted the meaning of discriminatory purpose. There was no evidence of intentional discrimination based upon any bias, prejudice, or dislike of Hispanics. The Court of Appeals therefore noted that the county had intentionally protected incumbents, found that incumbent protection is a discriminatory purpose where it splits minority voters, and ruled that when purpose is shown, the *Gingle*s test for geographical compactness and numerosity need not be met.[19]

Dunne's description of purpose to the state legislators and reliance on *Garza* was consistent with the way the Department was to enforce Section Five in its 1991–1992 objections, but it was not consistent with the views of the United States in a brief submitted to the Supreme Court in July of 1992. In *Voinovich v Quilter,* the solicitor general filed an *amicus* brief in a Section Two case in which Ohio Democrats sought to overturn a Republican-conceived state legislative plan that maximized minority districts. The Democratic challenge was premised on the theory that minorities could have been granted more influence if their populations had been spread around in more districts. The claim was one of Republican advantage at the expense of minority influence. Here is how the United States, in a brief signed by Solicitor General Kenneth W. Starr and Civil Rights Division chief John R. Dunne defined purpose:

But evidence of attempted political gerrymandering does not suffice to make out a claim of *racial* gerrymandering; it need hardly be said that racial gerrymandering requires specific intent to discriminate against a particular *racial* group.

To make out a racial vote-dilution claim, plaintiffs must show that the challenged districting scheme was in fact intended to harm voters of a particular racial or ethnic group, and was intended to do so because they are members of that group. . . . " 'Discriminatory purpose' . . . implies more than intent as volition or intent as awareness of consequences. . . . It implies that the decisionmaker . . . selected or reaffirmed a particular course of action at least in part 'because of,' not merely 'in spite of' its adverse effects upon an identifiable group."[20]

How then does one make any sense of Dunne's 1991 advice to the NCSL? In the speech, "Discriminatory purpose does not mean racial animus"; but in the *Voinovich* brief, discriminatory purpose means racial animus. What does the design to restrict minority voting strength below the level the group might otherwise have enjoyed mean if it does not mean maximization, or proportional representation? In practice, no precise demarcation could be drawn.

The portion of the NCSL address concerning substantive standards is confusing, reflecting the attempt to meld disparate sections of the Act. The "below the level" remark implies maximization; then Dunne cautions that proportional representation is not required by the statute; then he reiterates that a very good reason had better exist if proportional representation is not achieved. It is very difficult to determine what exactly is required. According to the NCSL remarks, legislators could expect complaints from participants wherever they drew lines. If minorities were not granted the opportunity to elect candidates of their choice—an opportunity they might otherwise have enjoyed—a valid objection might be lodged, but none of this should be taken to mean that proportional representation is required. State legislators might have reasonably concluded that wisdom lay in watching what the Department does, not what it says, and what it had been doing, as reported in *Congressional Quarterly* in August 1991, was demanding "creation of virtually every minority district that had been proposed to the legislatures."[21]

Congressional Quarterly's judgment was borne out in later decisions of the Supreme Court, and even in Dunne's later reflections. He concedes that "I tried to increase . . . opportunities but in that effort . . . to increase I wandered into maximization in the eyes of the Court. That was really not my policy at the outset."[22] Dunne's effort was dependent upon an expanded interpretation of purpose, as James P. Turner explained when asked if the Department had taken a different approach in the nineties:

Well, I'd have to say there was. And, as you look back over it and describe it, it sounds almost evolutionary but it turned out to be fairly significant in my judgment. We had always taken the position, from the get go, that there was no obligation to maximize minority representation so that the jurisdiction's failure to discover, to look for and find the districts that would give minorities the most control conceivably, or practically conceivably, was not required by the Voting Rights Act. That would not be a violation. That was the standard administrative interpretation. . . . But gradually we began to recognize and accept that turndown of the higher, the broader based, the more minority participation district, turning that down as evidence of purpose. So, once you accept that as evidence of purpose, that has undercut a little bit the position that you're not required to maximize. Because maximizing would be about the only way you could do that.

North Carolina is probably the best example of how accepting this kind of purpose evidence became more and more of a way to decide the cases and I think if you go back we may have gone off the track and lost the thread.[23]

The altered purpose standard was related to the Department's *de facto* incorporation of the Section Two results test into the Section Five purpose objection. The North Carolina objection letter also relied upon cases directly based on Section Two's results test, such as *Hastert v State Board of Elections* and *Jeffers v Clinton*. The Georgia objection letter was quite similar. Dunne recognizes in hindsight that too much regard was given to Section Two in making Section Five decisions. The redefinition of discriminatory purpose as any plan that could have created more minority districts but did not is really a results test founded on proportional representation, not a Section Five purpose finding. While it can be argued that the masked incorporation encompassed a large step toward fulfilling maximization in the early nineties, it did not appear exceptional to many voting rights practitioners at the time. Lawyers' Committee for Civil Rights Under Law counsel Brenda Wright and North Carolina Assistant Attorney General Tiare B. Smiley both recall no surprise at the Department's adoption of the Section Two standard—it seemed an incremental and natural evolution in the law.[24] This is at least in part a tribute to the successful campaign that activists conducted to soften up voting-law decision makers.

PURPOSE AS POLICY—OBJECTION LETTERS

As a result of the 1990 census, the state of North Carolina gained an increase in its congressional seats from eleven to twelve. North Carolina submitted its state house and senate and congressional redistricting plans to the CRD for preclearance. On 18 December 1991 John Dunne objected to all three plans. The objection letter explained that the state carries the burden to show that its plan is free of discriminatory purpose and retrogressive effect and does not constitute a clear violation of Section Two. The letter continued that the DOJ could "not preclear those portions of a plan where the legislature has deferred to the interests of incumbents while refusing to accommodate the community of interests shared by insular minorities," citing *Garza v County of Los Angeles* and *Ketchum v Byrne*. *Garza* and *Ketchum*, both Section Two incumbency cases, conflate Sections Two and Five.[25]

The North Carolina objection letter continued that a submission will not be precleared "where the proposed plan, given the demographics and racial concentrations in the jurisdiction, does not fairly reflect minority voting strength." The introductory portion of the North Carolina letter concludes that "our entire review is guided by the principle that the Act ensures fair election opportunities and does not require that any jurisdiction guarantee minority voters racial or ethnic proportional results." The letter never defines the terms "fairly reflects" or "fair election opportunities"—although as state legislators came to understand and as courts later found, those terms meant "racial or ethnic proportional results" to the Department.

The Department, in its purported quasi-judicial role, was instead applying the tools of advocacy by selecting favorable precedent and ignoring contradictory authority.[26]

North Carolina's submission created the first district in which a black could win since Reconstruction, so no claim of retrogression existed. The Department objected because it contended that the state could have created another black-majority district. The CRD's objection letter language is curiously murky. It asserts that the lines in the south-central to southeastern part of the state "appear to minimize voting strength. . . . it appears that the state chose not to give effect to black and Native American voting strength in this area, even though it seems that boundary lines that were no more irregular than found elsewhere in the proposed plan could have been drawn to recognize such minority concentration in this part of the state." The letter continues that North Carolina was "well aware" of alternative plans, including a second black district, that would "appear to provide the minority community with an opportunity to elect a second member of congress of their choice to office." The alternative was rejected, however, "for what appears to be pretextual reasons. Indeed, some commentators have alleged that the state's decision to" draw its lines was an attempt to protect white incumbents while "minimizing minority electoral strength." Since the burden is on the states to prove nondiscrimination, the DOJ need not be more specific, but courts later found many of the rationales offered by the Department to be weak, and some courts recognized the DOJ had masked the results test in the Section Five objections.

Founded on the misplaced certitude of *Garza* and not carrying the burden of proving discrimination, the letter is nonetheless cast in timidity. The CRD strikes down state policy here for what "appears" or "seems" to violate the Act and where "some commentators have alleged" incumbency protection. What commentators, of credibility, are the allegations sufficiently weighty? The CRD sets up a Section Two dilution standard, but in stating that North Carolina "chose not to give effect" to minority voting strength, offered "pretextual reasons" for the submission, and made a "decision" to draw the lines as it had, the Department shifts to a purpose argument. The conflation of Sections Two and Five is near total. The letter never explicitly states the basis of the objection. (The Department argued the purpose basis before the Supreme Court.)

Moreover, the CRD found that the minority community was denied an "opportunity to elect," but Section Two speaks to "the opportunity . . . to participate in the political process and to elect representatives of their choice"—as the Supreme Court had indicated only five months earlier in *Chisom v Roemer*. Such terms as "the opportunity . . . to participate . . . and to elect," "result," "effect," "purpose," and "minimize" are legal terms of art. Traditionalists teach that terms of art must be interpreted in accordance with their accepted meaning among the learned.[27] The Department's letter does not offer such clarity.

There was no retrogression in North Carolina's plan, nor was there any evidence of a racially invidious intent. *Beer* held that a nonretrogressive plan could not draw an objection unless it violated Section Five's purpose basis. *Burns* indicated that incumbency protection is not sufficient to show invidious intent. Former Assistant Attorney General for Civil Rights Drew S. Days III testified in 1982 that "[A]meliorative changes, even if they fall short of what might be accomplished in terms of increasing minority representation, cannot be found to violate section 5 unless they so discriminate on the basis of race or color as to violate the constitution." The CRD argues to this day that it continues to adhere to that standard and that mere evidence of incumbent protection is not enough to establish discriminatory intent.[28] But that understanding of purpose would not support the result of forcing more minority districts, and so the Division relied upon *Garza* and implicit incorporation.

Dunne's letters objecting to Georgia's state legislative and congressional plans were similar in tone. The 21 January 1992 letter objecting to Georgia's first submission also cited *Garza* and *Ketchum*. As an introductory matter, the letter asserted that elections in Georgia are racially polarized, "which appears to be exacerbated by the requirement that state legislative and congressional positions be elected by majority vote." The Georgia letter was also replete with such phrases as "appears," "it was charged," and "a concern was raised," but no finding was provided that the appearance was borne out or that the charges and concerns came from credible sources and were valid. The CRD took note of available alternative plans it deemed superior and criticized the Georgia legislature for rejecting them. The letter claimed that in two areas minority votes were minimized by the line drawing, splitting the "community of interest" shared by black voters—but as in the North Carolina letter, there was no identification of what that interest might be, other than color.

The Department's letters honor the value of increasing black officeholding to the exclusion of competing federalism concerns, and they shroud the objections in uncertain authority. The objections based avowedly on purpose grounds but reliant upon a results standard shielded the Department from having to comply with Section Two analysis: to meet the three *Gingles* preconditions and then undergo a totality-of-the-circumstances test.[29] The irresolute expressions of "it appears" that the state chose to minimize black voting strength or "some commentators have alleged" that the state had a discriminatory purpose could not meet the Section Two burden placed upon the complainant, so the CRD couched the objection under Section Five, where the burden is on the state. Even here though, the objections were not lodged under the Department's regulation authorizing an objection for a clear finding of a Section Two violation. The Department chose to regard nearly any showing that additional districts could be drawn as proof of discriminatory purpose and dismissed any state rationale as pretextual. It is almost as if the blatantly racist techniques rejected in *Allen* are held to taint state decision making forever. The Voting Section is charged with assuring the right to vote, but also with intervening minimally in state decision making. Faced with an ambiguous statute that expresses a number of values without precisely stating the trade-offs among them, the Department chose one and disregarded others.

CARRYING THE FIGHT TO THE COURTS

The Department's legal briefs defending the districts may reflect a clearer expression of policy, both because of the gravity of appearing before the Supreme Court and the involvement of the solicitor general. The Division chief can recommend, but the solicitor general decides, what cases should be pursued before the Supreme Court and what position to take. The Bush administration was not noted for racial liberalism generally, a point driven home by examining the Department's position in another contentious racial-preference case.

Metro Broadcasting, Inc. v Federal Communications Commission, decided by the Supreme Court in 1990, involved a challenge to the policy of the Federal Communications Commission (FCC) to grant preference to applicants for broadcast licenses on the basis of race. The Bush administration argued that the governmental preference was unconstitutional. Its brief asserted that since the FCC policy classified persons by reason of race, the program should be subject to strict scrutiny. Therefore, under the Supreme Court's teaching, the racial classification must serve a compelling state interest by narrowly tailored means. The FCC argued that its policy promoted diversity in programming. The solicitor general's brief replied that the FCC's rationale "appears to require official identification and labelling of, among other things, 'Black,' 'Hispanic,' and 'Aleutian' programming and viewpoints, and indulging in the assumption that we can tell how someone will *think* and *act* based solely on the color of his skin. This type of racial stereotyping is anathema to fundamental constitutional principles."

The brief further argued that nothing in the statute showed that Congress had identified a compelling state interest and commanded the FCC to award a racial preference. To claims that some congressmen had argued in favor of programming diversity, the brief responded that "Congress may work its will only by enacting legislation . . . and general statements contained in the legislative history—which were not voted on by the Congress, perhaps not even seen by many of its members, and certainly not presented to the President—cannot substitute for an express statutory provision mandating the use of preferences."[30] The Supreme Court ruled against the Department's position and in favor of the FCC's policy as a proper expression of congressional intent.

There are conflicts in Bush Department legal policy between the objection letters and the *Metro* brief. What was the "community of interest" asserted in the North Carolina and Georgia letters if not an indulgence "in the assumption that we can tell how someone will *think* and *act* based solely on the color of his skin?" The *Metro* brief is almost a perfect predictor of *Shaw v Reno*, where Justice O'Connor wrote for the Court that racial gerrymandering "reinforces the perception that members of the same racial group—regardless of their age, education, economic status, or the community in which they live—think alike, share the same political interests, and will prefer the same candidates at the polls."[31]

In *Presley v Etowah County Commission* in 1992 the DOJ attempted to aid African-American elected officials in an egregious example of Southern inventiveness to diminish black power over government functions. Etowah County, Alabama, had elected four district commissioners voted upon by all county voters and a county chairman since 1964. Following a consent decree in a VRA case, the county's electoral system was changed to a system in which an African-American commissioner could be elected. Following the election of the county's first black commissioner, the holdover officials voted to alter the powers of all commissioners, removing authority over road maintenance and expenditures in their districts. In a companion case, plaintiffs complained that Russell County's system of road maintenance discriminated against two recently elected black commissioners (although the Russell County system had been in place years before their election and was a response to corruption, not to black officeholding). The petitioners in both cases argued that neither county had sought preclearance when they altered the distribution of power among commissioners. Joined by the Department, they argued that the adjustments were "changes with respect to voting" within the meaning of Section Five and required preclearance.

The Department argued that it had long treated certain transfers of decision-making authority as changes with respect to voting. It contended that changes to an official's decision-making authority—such as the power to tax and spend or to approve road or bridge projects—directly implicate the citizen's voting power.[32] The Bush administration argued for a vast extension of federal authority into local decision making in order to assure fair results. A similar position was asserted shortly thereafter by voting rights scholar Lani Guinier, who contended that under Section Two a court might maintain jurisdiction over legislative decision making in order to assure a "meaningful vote." She also argued that Section Five protects minority voters from having their representatives' votes diluted in the legislative process.[33] But a cutting-edge legal theorist such as Professor Guinier did not author the Department's brief; conservative Solicitor General Kenneth W. Starr signed it.

The Court rejected the Department's position, finding that Congress did not intend to subject all or most decisions of covered jurisdictions to federal supervision. It observed that the interpretation offered by the United States could require a covered jurisdiction to obtain preclearance for each budget that differed from that of a previous year. Moreover, the Court found that the Department's construction would leave "federalism . . . a mere poetic ideal."[34]

Presley is an example of a case in which a naked usurpation of black governmental authority inspired the Department to wield the VRA as "an all-purpose antidiscrimination statute"—which, some argue, it appeared to be in the wake of cases such as *Allen* and *Gingles*. As Justice Stevens wrote in dissent, "this is a case in which a few pages of history are far more illuminating than volumes of logic and hours of speculation about hypothetical line-drawing problems." In *Presley*, the Court found that the VRA does not exist to remedy all forms of discrimination in political participation, historical or present day, and it is not the job of the CRD to correct deficiencies that Congress has not addressed.

While examining the positions taken by the Bush administration in racial-preference and VRA cases illuminates inconsistencies in approach to statutory interpretation, one of the most critical interpretations by the DOJ was its explication of *Gingles*. The first *Gingles* precondition, requiring that a minority group be "sufficiently large and geographically compact to constitute a majority in a single-member district," was to play a significant role in post-*Shaw v Reno* law because the Clinton administration was left to defend Bush administration actions forcing states to create crazy-quilt districts. The Clinton DOJ would find it necessary to try to modify, or even abandon, the first precondition. The Bush administration never had to defend its objection letters, but it did address and defend the necessity of the first precondition on several occasions, with one notable exception.

In *Growe v Emison* the United States District Court for the District of Minnesota had decided in a Section Two challenge that the first *Gingles* precondition need not be applied to a single-member state legislative districting plan. The Department defended the first precondition because otherwise, as *Gingles* found, minority voters would lack the potential to elect representatives of their choice. Moreover, "by requiring plaintiffs to satisfy the first *Gingles* precondition, the Court merely assures that relief under Section 2 will be limited to those minority groups that have actually been injured by the challenged structures or practices." A unanimous Court upheld the Department's position, noting that proof of a Section Two violation presumably requires the same standard that measures whether a violation has been remedied. [35]

The Bush Department also held fast to defending the first *Gingles* precondition in *Voinovich v Quilter*. The Ohio apportionment board, consisting of three Republicans and two Democrats, redistricted the state's legislative seats in 1991. The board voted along party lines for a plan that included eight majority-minority districts. The Democrats sued, asserting that the plan diluted minority voting strength by packing African Americans into eight districts when they could have had "influence" in many more, and claiming that the Republicans had intentionally diluted minority voting strength for partisan reasons. The district court sided with the Democrats, but the Department pointed out in its Supreme Court brief that the legal theory accepted by the lower court was directly at odds with the first precondition and asserted that the Supreme Court should side with other district courts that had rejected such reasoning. The Department also argued that discriminatory purpose requires animus based upon race. The solicitor general's argument again carried the day.[36]

The Bush Department curiously abandoned its defense of *Gingles* in a Florida case. *Johnson v DeGrandy* involved a challenge by Hispanics to Florida's state senate and house plans. The state argued that its plan achieved substantial proportionality for Hispanics in Dade County, the locus of contention, but the Department asserted that the plan diluted Hispanic voting strength statewide. The Department contended that by considering Hispanics living outside of Dade County, the plan was not proportional, and that statewide dilution could be remedied by drawing additional minority districts in Dade County.[37]

In *DeGrandy* the Department read the first *Gingles* precondition out of consideration, because there was no proving that the dispersed Hispanic populations outside of Dade County were sufficiently numerous and geographically compact to form a majority in a single-member district. A traditional approach to interpretation, which the Department had followed in *Growe* and *Voinovich*, would have recognized that dispersed Hispanic populations throughout Florida could not meet the first *Gingles* precondition. In effect, the Department was arguing that the state's proportional representation defense was inadequate because Florida could have gone further and maximized Hispanic seats by drawing a disproportionate number of seats in Dade County. The Department and plaintiffs were successful in persuading the district court that Hispanic (and black) voting strength had been diluted by the failure to maximize. The Supreme Court in its 1994 decision eventually affirmed in part and reversed in part but, most importantly, found that "reading Section 2 to define dilution as any failure to maximize tends to obscure the very object of the statute and to run counter to its textually stated purpose."[38]

The Department also pushed a theory of virtual representation in *DeGrandy*, though it never quite admitted that virtual representation was the aim. The DOJ argued that Florida's plan had deprived Hispanics in Florida of the equal opportunity to elect candidates of their choice to the state legislature. The Department asserted that in dilution cases minority voters often reside outside of the remedial districts, but that those cases are brought not simply to benefit those who live inside the boundaries. The remedy covers the political unit—not the district as a political unit, but the racial or ethnic minority unit. A court plan may thus include voters (of a particular race) whose votes have not been diluted in order to remedy the harm to unincluded voters (of the same race) whose votes have been diluted. The Department adopted the language of a 1988 Fourth Circuit case: "That not all can be given the remedy of assured direct representation, does not . . . mean that the remedy is wholly ineffectual as to those not included in 'safe' districts. Rather, it must in logic be assumed that the special interests of minority voters not included in safe districts will nevertheless be 'represented' albeit less directly, by those minority candidates elected from 'safe' districts."[39]

The Department thus does not rest its propagation of virtual representation wholly on descriptive representation. The implication is not only that Hispanics must be granted additional safe districts to elect candidates of their choice who are descriptive, but that by virtue of shared characteristics the officials will be substantively representative in some regard. But under what assumption do we draw districts that we expect to elect Hispanic candidates? The Department answers: "The theory is not that House members elected by Hispanic majorities will represent the interests of Hispanics outside their districts on all issues. Rather, it is that they will tend to do so on those issues that are of special concern to Hispanics, such as English-only initiatives and language-based employment discrimination." The Court rejected the Department's foray into political theory, noting that it reflected a serious departure from past dilution claims but that the argument had not been properly asserted in the litigation.[40] Thus, the limits of the litigation process aborted this venture into competing theories of representation.

The Department continued to push virtual representation, however. In *Shaw v Hunt*, it contended that North Carolina was not foreclosed from drawing what it termed "black opportunity districts" in locations different from the areas in which alleged Section Two violations occurred.[41] In *Bush v Vera*, it argued that the victims of dilution include not only persons in geographically compact areas, but "all members of the politically cohesive minority group."[42] But the Court rejected the Department's theory in *Shaw v Hunt*:

> If a Section 2 violation is proven for a particular area, it flows from the fact that individuals in this area "have less opportunity than other members of the electorate to participate in the political process and to elect representatives of their choice." The vote dilution injuries suffered by these persons are not remedied by creating a safe majority-black district somewhere else in the State.

For example, if a geographically compact, cohesive minority population lives in south-central to southeastern North Carolina, as the Justice Department's objection letter suggested, District 12 which spans the Piedmont Crescent would not address that Section 2 violation. The black voters of the south-central to southeastern region would still be suffering precisely the same injury that they suffered before District 12 was drawn.

To accept that the district may be placed anywhere implies that the claim, and hence the co-ordinate right to an undiluted vote (to cast a ballot equal among voters), belongs to the minority as a group and not to its individual members. It does not.[43]

Shaw v Hunt neatly illustrates the logical progression adopted by the Department. The Department sees the equal right to vote as a group right; as the group is injured, the remedy need not alleviate the harm to the individuals actually wronged by dilution of their votes. Therefore, a district may be drawn removed from the locus of the harm, and the injury of an ineffective vote suffered by certain voters will be remedied because they will be virtually represented by an official of a distant locality, but of the same race or ethnicity.

The Bush Department's theories as presented to the Supreme Court are both more clearly stated and less consistent than the objection letters. The position taken in the *Metro* brief is not consistent with the voting cases—unless there is something in voting cases that requires a different Equal Protection analysis (a contention later unsuccessfully urged by the Clinton administration). The *Metro* disparagement of legislative history as method is abandoned in several cases. The definition of purpose relied upon in the objection letters is different than that expressed in the *Voinovich* brief. *Presley* involved blatantly discriminatory conduct by white officials, reminiscent of the bad old days of *Allen*. Yet it is at least ironic that the Bush administration would urge a theory endorsed by Lani Guinier, later to be derided by Republicans as a "quota queen." In *Growe* and *Voinovich* the Department supported the sanctity of *Gingles*. In *DeGrandy* it attempted to redefine the first *Gingles* precondition in order to require maximization.

The Bush administration was at least mildly attentive to textual interpretation in Supreme Court briefs. Nonetheless, the traditional method was deemed expendable when the administration wished to pursue a certain result. The Clinton administration continued to defend the preclearance decisions of the Bush administration by adopting and expanding methods of modern interpretation. As early as February 1993 Clinton administration Acting Solicitor General William Bryson submitted a brief to the Supreme Court in support of the *DeGrandy* position devaluing the importance of the first *Gingles* precondition.[44]

The Clinton Department also acted quickly to reverse the Department's position in a Georgia case. The reversal of an established legal position following a change in administration is regarded warily by DOJ professionals because it opens the Department to charges that it succumbs to political meddling. That perception is at odds with the professionals' self-image of a highly professional law office. The case position reversed by the new administration was *Holder v Hall*. Black residents of Bleckley County, Georgia, had filed suit alleging that the county's long-standing practice of electing a single county commissioner diluted black voting strength in violation of Section Two. The plaintiffs argued that under a hypothetical five-member commission, African

Americans would be able to elect a candidate of their choice. In a preliminary brief, the Bush Department stated that Section Two is not violated by a county's well-settled usage of a single-office form of government. The brief argued that plaintiffs' theory would permit challenges to any size governmental board, on the theory that the body could be enlarged to permit more minority candidates to win. Once again, the Bush Department came to the rescue of *Gingles*: "If the first *Gingles* precondition could be automatically evaded in that manner, it would cease to have any meaning at all."[45]

The Clinton administration abandoned the defense. In an *amicus* brief, it acknowledged that the first precondition requires that the minority group prove geographic compactness and numerosity—which the *Holder v. Hall* plaintiffs could show, if Bleckley had a five-member commission. The brief completely distorted *Gingles*, which was a suit seeking to alter a multimember district plan, and *Growe,* which held *Gingles* applicable to a single-member plan. None of the Court's decisions had indicated that an existing plan such as that of Bleckley County could be manipulated in that fashion. The Department also unpersuasively dismissed the argument *Holder's* plaintiffs' proposal would bring on proportional representation. The Supreme Court decided in favor of the county because Section Two lacks any benchmark for what a reasonable size of an elective body might be.[46]

In 1993 the Supreme Court decided in *Shaw v Reno* that an Equal Protection claim could go forward against districts so bizarre in design that they could only be understood as racially gerrymandered. *Shaw* involved a challenge to North Carolina's Twelfth Congressional District by individual white citizens. They asserted that the oddly configured district constituted an unconstitutional racial gerrymander, in violation of the Equal Protection Clause of the Fourteenth Amendment. The *Almanac of American Politics* described North Carolina's Twelfth Congressional District as:

> the most egregious example in the nation of the application, urged by blacks and Republicans, that the 1982 revisions of the Voting Rights Act require the maximization of black percentages in certain districts. It is called the I-85 district, because it consists of a series of urban black areas, many of them poor, mostly connected by a line sometimes no wider than I-85, splitting adjacent districts in two.... There is an argument for connecting together voters with some sense of affinity and common interest. But there is also an argument that such districts amount to a form of apartheid, and their shape eerily resembles those of some of South Africa's homelands.[47]

The Department joined in defense of the constitutionality of the plan. It finally explicitly asserted that its North Carolina objection was grounded on a purpose basis. The objection letter had been so unclear that both the state and the *amicus* American Jewish Congress had assumed the Department had lodged its objection at least partially on Section Two grounds. The new administration sought to distinguish the Court's 1989 decision in *City of Richmond v Croson* that held that racial classifications by state and local governments must be subjected to strict scrutiny regardless of the race of those benefited or disadvantaged. The Department asserted that race-conscious districting is sometimes necessary in order to fulfill the mandate of the VRA.[48]

The *Shaw* Court ruled that the challenge could go forward and carried the apartheid analogy even further than had the *Almanac of American Politics*. The Court stated that such a plan could promote the racial stereotype that all members of a racial group think alike and vote alike and could encourage elected officials to believe that they are racial, not district, representatives. *Shaw* was followed by decisions such as *Miller v Johnson,* which found that courts could rely not only upon odd shape but upon direct proof that race was the predominant motivating factor in a legislature's decision to classify voters by race.[49]

One post-*Shaw v Reno* problem for the Department was that it had to defend districts drawn by Southern states under federal compulsion that were undeniably misshapen. In defense of these odd districts the Department systematically repudiated the devotion it had expressed for the first *Gingles* precondition in its *Growe* and *Voinovich* briefs. For example, when *Shaw* was remanded to the district court, the United States asserted that a community of interest for *Gingles* purposes may be other than geographic, such as socioeconomic, or shared values and traditions. (Section Two became a factor because the United States argued that North Carolina had a compelling state interest in avoiding potential Section Two liability.) In its post-trial brief in *Shaw*, the Department simply excised the word "geographically" from many of its expressions of *Gingles*'s preconditions.[50] The Department, civil rights litigation activists, and the states were never able to argue persuasively that their use of community of interest was anything but a proxy for race. Several courts recognized the argument as pretextual.

The Department also dropped the geographical element in advocating for misshapen districts in Louisiana, Georgia, and Texas. In *United States v Hays* the Department contended that although the district court had found Louisiana's District Four to be not geographically compact, "The *Gingles* compactness requirement . . . does not demand compactness in any absolute sense. Rather, the question . . . is whether the proposed majority-minority district is reasonably compact in light of a State's traditional redistricting practices." Thus, the Department adopted an interpretation urged by civil rights advocacy groups that sought to extend minority districts beyond geographical limits: that compactness should be understood as "functional," not geographical. Yet the Department argued that even its own elastic definition of compactness might not be required in certain circumstances. In *Bush v Vera*, the Department contended that Texas had a strong foundation for believing that the Act required it to draw both black and Hispanic congressional districts in Harris County, which would support only one compact minority district. Since the Act gave no basis for preferring one group over another, "the State reasonably concluded that its Section 2 responsibilities required it to provide both black and Hispanic voters an opportunity to elect their preferred candidates—even if that required a departure from compactness."[51]

Thus, to the Department, neither geography nor compactness was essential to the Court's required precondition of geographic compactness. Yet the Department is "obliged to do more than to define compactness simply in terms of whatever majority-minority district it is willing to approve."[52] Otherwise, the door is open to abolition of geographic representation in the United States, a result surely never contemplated by the Congress.

The policy choice made by the Division was to force Southern states to maximize minority districts. The result (aided by Democratic state legislatures seeking to preserve incumbency as a secondary concern to federal coercion) was intentionally drawn, bizarrely-shaped congressional districts. A literature was engendered in which various attempts were made by social scientists to measure compactness (also expressed as meanderingness).[53] These studies were consulted, if not always relied upon, by the courts. The studies generally found the districts under attack to be among the nation's most misshapen. The Clinton administration therefore had to adopt a legal policy of interpreting the geographical compactness element in a manner that negated the *Gingles* precondition. The Department also had to proffer an explanation of communities of interest that did not seem to rely predominately upon race, but the Department never persuasively asserted that black citizens in North Carolina had anything in common other than skin color. In Georgia the district court found that the state defendants, while making some valid points regarding shared concerns among black residents, were nonetheless "traffick[ing] in racial stereotypes."[54]

In North Carolina, the Supreme Court noted that in presenting evidence of past discrimination, the Department and defendants were relying upon evidence not even considered by the North Carolina state legislature when it drew the Twelfth Congressional District. In Louisiana, the state and Department attempted to defend the bizarrely shaped Fourth Congressional District. An expert witness testified that as the Fourth District followed the Red River, its residents shared a commonality of interest. Additional witnesses testified that the new Fourth was similar to the old Eighth District. The district court dismissed the "Red River valley theory" as "clearly a *post hoc* rationalization" and "unbelievable." It conceded that the old Eighth was bizarre but noted that it was drawn to protect an incumbent and was never challenged; the new Fourth was driven by race. Reliance upon similarity to the old Eighth was "mere pretext."[55]

The Department also displayed little fidelity to the Section Two requirement that minority voters be able to show they have "less opportunity . . . to participate in the political process and to elect candidates of their choice." In its brief in *Bush*, the Department combined its reading of *Gingles* and *DeGrandy* to construct a new set of preconditions that might justify a state in creating minority districts. The revised first precondition would be that "members of the minority group are sufficiently numerous and concentrated to have the 'potential to elect' candidates of their choice in a reasonably compact district (even if they would not constitute an absolute voting majority), *Gingles*, 478 US at 50 n 17."[56]

But the footnote the Department cites explains that the reason a minority must "show . . . that it is sufficiently large and geographically compact to constitute a majority in a single-member district is this: Unless minority voters possess the *potential* to elect representatives in the absence of the challenged structure or practice, they cannot claim to have been injured by that structure or practice."[57] So the Department in *Bush* attempted to read "geographically compact" out of *Gingles* and "concentrated" in; attempted to substitute "less opportunity . . . to elect" for "less opportunity . . . to participate . . . and to elect"; and rejected *Gingles* teaching that the minority be able to form a majority in a single-member district. The thrust of the Department's position in these cases was proportional representation, indicated by the election of minority candidates. The Department's choice to focus only upon the election of minority candidates as a candidate of choice undermined the requirement that there be shown a diminished opportunity to participate. It also ignored the proviso to Section Two that cautions against a requirement of proportional representation. As the Court explained the Dole Amendment in *Johnson v DeGrandy*, "the proviso also confirms what is otherwise clear from the text of the statute, namely that the ultimate right of Section Two is equality of opportunity, not a guarantee of electoral success for minority preferred candidates of whatever race."[58]

The Supreme Court's *DeGrandy* finding reflects classical liberal nondiscrimination: equality of opportunity. The Department's position was that of post-sixties civil rights orthodoxy: proportional representation in compensation for historical wrongs. In fact, the Department's stand in the nineties was in contrast with its own historical position of reliance upon minority organizations to register and mobilize minority voters. That earlier understanding recognized that even in a society in which racial discrimination sometimes requires majority-minority districts to assure equal opportunity, there are many opportunities for minority voters to forge coalitions with other citizens. Far from a conferral of proportional representation, that conception, as the Court stated in *DeGrandy*, recognized that the VRA contemplates that minority citizens will participate in the rough-and-tumble of redistricting politics.[59] The older understanding was based upon the exercise of opportunity and depended upon citizen action, not federal fiat.

The Department also fought to limit the Equal Protection reach of *Shaw v Reno* to districts that were bizarre looking on their face. A more traditional Equal Protection jurisprudence would permit a searching inquiry into legislative purpose. In *Hays*, the government proposed four principles for assessing an Equal Protection claim. First, the court should look to the manner by which the state has drawn and continues to draw districts as the most important benchmark. Districts drawn in accordance with a state's traditional practices do not raise the perception of excessive consideration of race. For example, in *Hays* the Department argued that District Four had been modeled on the old District Eight, which was oddly shaped in order to protect an incumbent. Second, *Shaw* is violated only where a district departs dramatically from traditional state practices. Third, *Shaw* means an objective assessment of the district only, not an examination of legislative intent. Fourth, the court should look to whether the district as a whole is bizarre, not just segments of it. The Department interpreted *Shaw* to limit Equal Protection analysis to district shape because a bizarre configuration would indicate to citizens that the state had taken action not available to other interest groups. Where traditional redistricting principles are followed, no such inference could be made.[60]

Several problems present themselves concerning the proposed measures. Appellees in *Miller* asserted that the government's proposed benchmark was "almost Kafkaesque" because where the Department forces the state to draw a "bizarre" minority district, the state's other districts would almost necessarily be misshapen themselves. The Kafkaesque analogy might be carried further by noting that the Southern states' tradition included drawing contorted districts precisely for the purpose of minimizing black voting strength. For example, in Mississippi some supervisor districts in 1973 were drawn intentionally to dilute black votes and resembled a "turkey" and a "baby elephant." The Court in *Shaw v Reno* noted that antiblack gerrymandering occurred in Mississippi as early as the 1870s. Moreover, it is doubtful that the citizenry's deductive abilities are so discrete as to infer racial purpose from district shape but draw no such conclusion on a direct expression of legislative intent. Justice Voorhees made the point in his dissent to the district court's decision in *Shaw v Hunt*. He wrote: "A citizenry's perceptions of its political process can be as critical in a democracy as the process itself, and factors that can adversely affect such perceptions should not be dismissed. . . . [Racial gerrymandering] seriously underestimates the intellectual grasp of those voters. . . . [T]hey know when race is energizing the affairs of state."[61]

The DOJ also argued that in redistricting cases, states must treat citizens as members of groups and not as individuals. So in *Hays*, the Department asserted that if racially gerrymandered districts were subject to strict scrutiny, the central purpose of the Equal Protection Clause—"to insure equal treatment regardless of race"—would be defeated,[62] but the Court rejected the Department's group-based conception of the Fourteenth Amendment. In *Miller v Johnson* the Court reminded us that "At the heart of the Constitution's guarantee of equal protection lies the simple command that the Government must treat citizens 'as individuals, not as simply components of a racial, religious, sexual or national class.' "[63]

The Department also tried to avoid the term "majority-minority district" in the post-*Shaw v Reno* era. In *Shaw v Hunt*, it argued that North Carolina had created "black opportunity districts." The Department's new definition states these districts occur where the minority group "has a meaningful opportunity to elect the representative of its choice, despite racial discrimination in voting, either because the group constitutes a voting majority in the district or because it constitutes a sizeable minority that can elect its preferred candidate because some non-minority voters will be willing to vote for the minority-preferred candidate."[64]

The Department's creative effort only raised more questions. What is a "meaningful opportunity to elect the representative of its choice?" What has happened to the statute's opportunity to participate? How does the Department define "racial discrimination?" How big must a nonmajority-minority voting bloc be, and what does it say for the racially polarized voting prong of *Gingles* if the minority might combine with white voters to elect a candidate? None of these issues were addressed.

CONCLUSION

Timothy G. O'Rourke contends that in 1991 the Department adopted a hybrid objection theory in which a finding of discriminatory purpose masks an underlying rationale of failure to maximize. This shifts the burden of proof in the results test from the complaining party to the state. A tradition of uninformative objection letters emerges as a tactic to force maximization. Placing the burden on the states to show nondiscrimination in Section Five reviews is a hard fought for, valuable component of the preclearance process, but in the nineties, the Division used the placement of the burden as a shield against close examination of its new maximization agenda.

O'Rourke suggests that the Department's cloaking of the results test in the raiment of purpose offers several advantages. It presents a more effective tool than the limited *Beer* nonretrogression measure. The purpose prong has a traditional significance for preclearance decisions that is lacking in a results objection. It sidesteps a true results objection, in which the Department might have to specify what Section Two requires in a given case. For example, under Section Two analysis, the Department would be expected to establish the *Gingles* preconditions as a predicate to showing a Section Two violation by the "totality of the circumstances." So the Department bypasses these difficulties by objecting that a discriminatory purpose is shown when a state does not draw all possible majority-minority districts. Finally, the hybrid approach permits the Department to seek maximization without addressing the question of incorporation. Katharine Butler adds that the Department's reasoning may be understood as follows: "The Act requires that states take every opportunity to create majority black districts; every opportunity means any opportunity not expressly disallowed by federal law; a state could have gerrymandered; failure to gerrymander means the state intentionally chose a plan knowing it did not contain as many minority districts as could have been created; thus, the state must have intended to discriminate against blacks." [65]

O'Rourke and Butler are right. The Justice Department forced states covered under Section Five to maximize majority-minority districts. In the years since, under the imperative of *Shaw v Reno* and subsequent cases, the Department has searched unsuccessfully for a principled legal justification that did not exist in the objection letters. Instead of relying upon text, it has sought some means to attract Court agreement to the Department's policy judgment. The DOJ wedded itself to the notion of group rights under the Equal Protection Clause. It promoted the theory that racial classifications may be maintained under the Equal Protection Clause when they are imposed by the state for benign purposes.

When the text of a statute, the Constitution, or Supreme Court precedent interfered with the desired result, the Department read language out of the provision, recast its definition, or ignored it. The text was a vehicle to serve the desired result of increasing minority representation in Congress. Faced with circumstances in which no racial purpose was evident, the Department nevertheless proceeded as if it were setting out to rectify egregious acts of discrimination. Where once (as in cases such as *Allen*) loose method served as a reaction to negate blatantly discriminatory conduct, in the nineties it served to promote a system of representation thought to favor African-American interests. As *Presley* shows, some jurisdictions do continue to devise creative schemes to keep blacks down (though there are far fewer attempts and far fewer methods). But a *Presley* or *Allen* wickedness does not exist in each redistricting submission that fails to maximize. There are limits to the statute, restraints ignored by the Department in its preclearance decisions.

The structure of the VRA embellishes the Department's power while adding to the confusion. As an advocate, the Department should be free to argue the legal policy positions of the administration when they can be founded on sound legal principles. But under Section Five, the Department is also to be something other than a partisan for minority interests. It is to decide as would a court. The requirement is to be fair to both minority interests and to the submitting jurisdiction. The Department's approach has not been to apply the law but to pursue its definition of justice through creativity. By application of a precedent like *Garza* while ignoring contrary rulings, by developing hybrid theories of the Act and coercing states to maximize majority-minority districts without foundation in law, the Department repudiated its quasi-judicial role in favor of its advocacy function.

NOTES

1. *Allen v State Board of Elections*, 393 U.S. 544 564–572 (1969).
2. *Allen*, 393 U.S. 583; *Baker v Carr*, 369 U.S. 186, 300 (1962).
3. *Allen*, 393 U.S. 583–591.
4. *Holder v Hall*, 512 U.S. 874, 891–945 (1994); Abigail M. Thernstrom, *Whose Votes Count? Affirmative Action and Minority Voting Rights* (Cambridge, Mass.: Harvard University Press, 1987), 20–27; J. Morgan Kousser, *Colorblind Injustice: Minority Voting Rights and the Undoing of the Second Reconstruction* (Chapel Hill, N.C.: University of North Carolina Press, 1999), 60–61; R. Shep Melnick, *Between the Lines: Interpreting Welfare Rights* (Washington, DC: Brookings Institution, 1994), 34–35, 52–53.
5. U.S. Department of Justice, *Memorandum for the United States as Amicus Curiae*, submitted to Supreme Court in *Allen v State Board of Elections*, Nos. 3, 25, 26, 36 (1969), 12–13.
6. U.S. Department of Justice, *Brief for the United States*, submitted to Supreme Court in *Gaston County, North Carolina v United States*, No. 701 (1969), 20–23.
7. U.S. Department of Justice, *Brief for the United States*, submitted to Supreme Court in *Beer v United States*, No. 73-1869 (1976).
8. U.S. Department of Justice, *Brief for the United States as Amicus Curiae*, submitted to Supreme Court in *City of Mobile v Bolden*, No. 77-1844 (1980).
9. *Brief for the United States as Amicus Curiae Supporting Appellants* and *Brief of Senators DeConcini, et al., in Support of Appellees*, in *Thornburg v Gingles*, No. 83-1968 (1986).
10. Jeremy Rabkin, *Judicial Compulsions: How Public Law Distorts Public Policy* (New York: Basic Books, 1989), 139.
11. *Voting Rights Act, Section Two*; Senate Committee on the Judiciary, *Report of the Committee on the Judiciary on S. 1992*, 97th Cong., 2d sess., 1982, S. Rept. 97-417, 28–29.
12. *Thornburg v Gingles*, 478 U.S. 30, 50–51 (1986). The *Gingles* preconditions were found to cover single-member districts in *Growe v Emison*, 507 U.S. 25 (1993).
13. *Gingles*, 478 U.S. 47, *Turner v Arkansas*, 784 F. Supp. 553 (E.D. Ark. 1991).
14. *Gingles*, 478 U.S. 61–74, 83.
15. *Gingles*, 478 U.S. 83–105.
16. *Report of the Committee on the Judiciary on Sec. 1992*, 12 note 31.
17. *Reno v Bossier Parish School Board*, 520 U.S. 471 (1997).
18. John R. Dunne, "Remarks before the National Conference of State Legislators," Orlando, Fla., 13 August 1991.
19. *Garza v County of Los Angeles*, 918 F.2d 736 (9th Cir. 1990); *Burns v Richardson*, 384 U.S. 73, 89 note 16 (1966).
20. U.S. Department of Justice, *Brief for the United States as Amicus Curiae Supporting Appellants*, submitted to the Supreme Court in *Voinovich v Quilter*, No. 91-1618 (1992) (emphasis in original, citation omitted).

21. Beth Donovan, "Nation Watches as Texas Struggles to Create Minority Districts," *Congressional Quarterly*, vol. 49, no. 33, 17 August 1991, 2293.

22. John R. Dunne, telephone conversation with author, 20 January 1998.

23. James P. Turner, interview by author, tape recording, Accokeek, Md., 27 August 1997.

24. Dunne telephone conversation; Brenda Wright, telephone conversation with author, 13 January 1998; Tiare B. Smiley, telephone conversation with author, 31 December 1997.

25. John R. Dunne, letter to Tiare B. Smiley, 18 October 1991; *Garza v County of Los Angeles*, 918 F.2d 763 (9th Cir. 1990); *Ketchum v Byrne*, 740 F.2d 1398 (7th Cir. 1984).

26. Dunne to Smiley, 18 October 1991.

27. William Blackstone, *Commentaries on the Laws of England, Introduction*, Sec. 2, 59–62 (1765).

28. Drew S. Days III, "Section 5 Enforcement and the Role of the Justice Department," in Bernard Grofman and Chandler Davidson, eds., *Controversies in Minority Voting: The Voting Rights Act in Perspective* (Washington, DC: Brookings Institution, 1992), 56; Mark A. Posner, "Post-1990 Redistrictings and the Preclearance Requirement of Section 5 of the Voting Rights Act," in Bernard Grofman, ed., *Race and Redistricting in the 1990s* (New York: Agathon Press, 1998), 100.

29. Timothy G. O'Rourke, "*Shaw v Reno*: The Shape of Things to Come," *Rutgers Law Review* 26 (1995), 723, 752.

30. U.S. Department of Justice, *Brief for the United States as Amicus Curiae Supporting Petitioner*, submitted to Supreme Court in *Metro Broadcasting, Inc. v Federal Communications Commission*, No. 89-453 (1990), 25–26.

31. *Shaw v Reno*, 509 U.S. 630, 647 (1993).

32. U.S. Department of Justice, *Brief for the United States as Amicus Curiae Supporting Appellants*, submitted to the Supreme Court in *Presley v Etowah County Commission*, Nos. 90-711, 90-712 (1991), 14, 18.

33. Lani Guinier, "No Two Seats: The Elusive Quest for Political Equality," *Virginia Law Review* 77 (November 1991), 1413, 1493–1508.

34. *Presley v Etowah County Commission*, 502 U.S. 491, 510 (1992).

35. U.S. Department of Justice, *Brief for the United States as Amicus Curiae Supporting Appellants*, submitted to the Supreme Court in *Growe v Emison*, No. 91-1420 (1992); *Growe*, 507 U.S. 25.

36. U.S. Department of Justice, *Brief for the United States as Amicus Curiae Supporting Appellants*, submitted to the Supreme Court in *Voinovich v Quilter*, No. 91-1618 (1992), 11; *Voinovich v Quilter*, 507 U.S. 146 (1993).

37. U.S. Department of Justice, *Motion to Affirm in Part and Vacate in Part*, submitted to Supreme Court in *Johnson v DeGrandy*, No. 92-519 (1992).

38. *Johnson v DeGrandy*, 512 U.S. 997, 1016–17 (1994).

39. U.S. Department of Justice, *Brief for the United States in Opposition to Motion to Dismiss or Affirm*, submitted to the Supreme Court in *United States v Florida*, No. 92-767 (1993); *Brief for the United States as Appellee*, submitted to the Supreme Court in *Johnson v DeGrandy*, citing *McGhee v Granville County*, 860 F.2d 110, 118 n. 9 (4th Cir. 1988) (citations omitted).

40. *Brief for the United States as Appellee, Johnson v DeGrandy; DeGrandy*, 512 U.S. 997.

41. *Brief for the United States as Amicus Curiae Supporting Appellees, Shaw v Hunt*, No. 94-923 (1995).

42. *Reply Brief for the United States, Bush v Vera*, No. 94-805 (1996).

43. *Shaw v Hunt*, 517 U.S. 899, 917 (1996).

44. *Brief for the United States in Opposition to Motion to Dismiss or Affirm*, submitted to the Supreme Court in *United States of America v Florida*, No. 92-767 (1993).

45. U.S. Department of Justice, *Brief for the United States as Amicus Curiae*, submitted to the Supreme Court on petition for a writ of *certiorari* in *Holder v Hall*, No. 91–2012 (1993).

46. U.S. Department of Justice, *Brief for the United States as Amicus Curiae Supporting Respondents*, submitted to the Supreme Court in *Holder v Hall*, No. 91-2012 (1993); *Holder v Hall*, 512 U.S. 874 (1994).

47. Michael Barone and Grant Ujifusa, *Almanac of American Politics, 1994* (Washington, DC: National Journal, 1993), 969.

48. U.S. Department of Justice, *Brief for the Federal Appellees*, submitted to the Supreme Court in *Shaw v Gerson*, No. 92-357 (1992), 25–26.

49. *Shaw v Reno*, 509 U.S. 647–648, *Miller v Johnson*, 515 U.S. 900 (1995).

50. U.S. Department of Justice, *Brief for the United States in Opposition to Plaintiff-Intervenors Motion for a Preliminary Injunction*, and *Post-Trial Brief for the United States*, submitted to the district court in *Shaw v Hunt*, No. 92-CV-202 (E.D. N.C., 1994).

51. U.S. Department of Justice, *Brief for the United States*, submitted to the Supreme Court in *Louisiana v Hays*, 94–558 (1995); U.S. Department of Justice, *Brief for the United States*, submitted to the Supreme Court in *Miller v Johnson*, 94-929, 94-631, 94-797 (1995); U.S. Department of Justice, *Brief for the United States*, submitted to the Supreme Court in *Bush v Vera*, 94-805, 94-806, 94-988 (1995).

52. O'Rourke, "Shape of Things to Come," 754.

53. *Johnson v Miller*, 864 F. Supp. 1388, note 42.

54. *Johnson v Miller*, 864 F. Supp. 1376.

55. *Hays v State of Louisiana*, 862 F. Supp. 119, 122 (W.D. La. 1994).

56. U.S. Department of Justice, *Brief for the United States*, submitted to the Supreme Court in *Bush v Vera*, 25.

57. *Gingles*, 478 U.S. 50 note 17.

58. *DeGrandy*, 512 U.S. 1014, note 11.

59. *DeGrandy*, 512 U.S. 1020.

60. U.S. Department of Justice, *Brief for the United States*, submitted to the Supreme Court in *Louisiana v Hays*, No. 91-1539, 21–22. The same arguments were presented in *Brief for the United States*, submitted to the Supreme Court in *Miller v Johnson.*

61. Davida Johnson et al., Appellees, *Brief for Appellees*, submitted to the Supreme Court in *Miller v Johnson;* Frank R. Parker, *Black Votes Count: Political Empowerment in Mississippi After 1965* (Chapel Hill, N.C.: University of North Carolina Press, 1990); *Shaw v Reno*, 509 U.S. 640, citing Eric Foner, *Reconstruction: America's Unfinished Revolution, 1863–1877* (New York: Harper & Row, 1988); *Shaw v Hunt*, 861 F. Supp. 408, 494 (E.D. N.C. 1994). Chief Justice Voorhees was speaking of a "bizarre" district, but his observation has broader applicability.

62. U.S. Department of Justice, *Brief for the United States*, submitted to the Supreme Court in *Louisiana v Hays*, 15.

63. *Miller v Johnson*, 515 U.S. 911. (The Court cites several precedents, which are omitted here.)

64. U.S. Department of Justice, *Brief for the United States as Amicus Curiae Supporting Appellees*, submitted to the Supreme Court in *Shaw v Hunt*, Nos. 94-293 and 94-924 (1995), 4–5, note 2.

65. O'Rourke, "Shape of Things to Come," 752–53; Katharine Inglis Butler, "Affirmative Racial Gerrymandering: Rhetoric and Reality," *Cumberland Law Review* 26 (1995), 313.

5

External Influences on the Department's Decision Making

> The direct association between the preclearance powers under Section 5 of the Voting Rights Act, the "max-black" plan of the ACLU, and the black caucus of the Georgia legislature served to turn the Justice Department into a suspect interest group advocate. . . . (T)here is more than a touch of irony in the Justice Department under President Bush being depicted as a "captured" agent of the ACLU.
>
> Samuel Issacharoff,
> "Constitutional Contours of Race and Politics"

There is perhaps no task undertaken by state and local governments with greater political overtones than that of redistricting. A redistricting plan generally stays in effect for ten years. How the plan turns out will affect partisan alignments, minority membership, and organized interests representing virtually the entire range of actors who have a concern with government action: business, labor, environmentalists, election reformers, human service providers, and others. Of most immediate interest to those state legislators who must draw the plans, redistricting may affect the seat they presently hold, or the one they hope to move up to, or the seats of their allies or enemies.

State legislators must be mindful of a range of interests as they approach redistricting, but judicial decisions and the VRA have circumscribed them over the past several decades. The Supreme Court in its one-person, one-vote decisions has required that congressional seats within a state be drawn to have the least numerical deviation possible, down to the last person. Covered jurisdictions have had each election-law change examined to root out retrogression or discriminatory purpose. The Division's nineties' interpretation of discriminatory purpose pushed covered jurisdictions to draw as many minority districts as possible. State legislatures that failed to maximize, even if they received preclearance or were not subject to Section Five, still faced the threat of Section Two lawsuits by disappointed civil rights advocates. Indeed, a major concern of covered states is that even if their Section Five submissions are precleared, the process provides ammunition for a subsequent Section Two challenge by civil rights litigators and activists seeking more minority districts.

Into this political maelstrom is cast the Voting Section of the Department's Civil Rights Division. Department attorneys are very wary of external influences and believe any political influence, even well intentioned, is wrong.[1] But in the nineties civil rights petitioners were clearly favored and the states were regarded with suspicion by the Division. Thus was wrought a regime of winners and losers in the redistricting battles (until the courts overturned much of what the advocates and Division had accomplished). The Division quite naturally has a history and mission of serving the cause of civil rights; in nineties' voting rights enforcement, it was in thrall to the theories and policy choices of their civil rights clients.

ORGANIZED INTERESTS IN THE VOTING RIGHTS ARENA

The constellation of interests that surround an agency affects the way it goes about its business. For most of the VRA's life the Division's enforcement record placed it in a context of interest group politics, balancing the concerns of the states and civil rights groups. In the nineties the Division responded to the political arrangement around it by functioning in a client relationship with civil rights groups.

Interest group politics exists when agency action produces both high costs and high benefits to rival interest groups. So long as the interests are able to mount effective campaigns to favor their own positions, they tend to offset each other. The usual understanding of client politics is that most or all of the benefits of agency action go to a single, concentrated interest, while the costs are dispersed widely. Because the benefits are great to the small group, its incentives are high to press for implementation; but dispersed costs fail to attract intense organized opposition.[2] But in the nineties' voting rights enforcement, however, there were deviations in these models. The voting rights advocacy groups and the CRD entered into a client relationship, but not in the classical sense. The relationship came about because the Southern states, though several of them fought to do so, were unable to mount effective campaigns for their positions. Suspicions born of the legacy of racism, the new definition of purpose, the Division's practice of terming Southern rationale's as pretextual, and the mighty hammer of preclearance drove the states into acquiescence. The field was left to the advocacy groups.

Client politics is associated with iron triangles. In the iron-triangle model a congressional committee, an executive agency, and regulated industry set the boundaries for policy entry. The historian Hugh Davis Graham argues that in the civil rights arena the role of the regulated industry has been assumed by the domination of civil rights "victims." Moreover, he asserts that the triangle has been reshaped into a quadrangle to allow for the involvement of the courts.[3] The quadrangle metaphor holds up for voting rights enforcement, with the significant alteration that the Division stands as both executive and court surrogate under the Voting Rights Act.

The Division began its stewardship of the Act with the moderate and limited goals of ensuring African-American citizens the right to register to vote and to have a fair ballot count. The Division acted appropriately and with great skill to defeat new roadblocks thrown in the path of minority voting power, such as those in evidence in *Allen*. Yet the Division did not take the vast new responsibilities conferred by *Allen* and *Gaston* as an invitation to wholesale intrusion into state decision making. Under Carter administration chief Drew S. Days III, a former LDF litigator, the Division resisted calls to promote maximization through racial gerrymanders. When Reagan appointee William Bradford Reynolds drove policy on the 1982 amendment, regulatory proposals, and the *Gingles* brief, the professionals were nonetheless able to maintain control over much of the Section Five program. Through a good number of controversies the careerists have generally been moderate in their approach, fulfilling their responsibilities to the disenfranchised while respecting legitimate interests of the states.

Up until the nineties' round, an interest group model of politics existed in Department enforcement. The primary contending interests of the states and the civil rights advocates had entry to the decision-making process and their positions were listened to and often heeded. The Department brokered the interests of the states and advocates. The interest group model was at work.

Things changed in the nineties. The civil rights groups were rewarded and the states were routed. The Department used its preclearance powers to coerce covered states to create as many minority districts as possible. The district court in Georgia found that the Department was almost entirely beholden to civil rights interest groups. Courts in other states reached a similar conclusion. In the nineties round of redistricting, the interest group model, after over twenty-five years of usage, was discarded. In its place rose a client model in which the concerns of civil rights advocacy groups were heeded and those of the states were discounted. A closer look at the organized interests involved reveals their concerns, impact, and interaction with the Department.

CIVIL RIGHTS INTEREST GROUPS

Minority positions in the preclearance process are represented by public interest legal advocacy organizations, such as the ACLU, LDF, Lawyers' Committee for Civil Rights Under Law, and MALDEF. Such groups can provide access to courts and regulatory agencies, communications to the media, and outreach to sympathizers in government. These organizations often subsist on funding raised from foundations or from direct mail; they may have no mass membership, or a membership that exists mostly in name only.[4]

The LDF and MALDEF exist as organizations without mass memberships. The LDF is a centralized organization, with key direction coming from the director-counsel. There are approximately 28 staff attorneys in Washington and some 400 cooperating attorneys nationwide. The LDF thus has an easier time controlling its litigation than a more broadly democratic organization might. The Lawyers' Committee, which has a Voting Rights Project, is also not a democratic mass-membership organization. It grew out of President Kennedy's 1963 call for the legal community to help in the South. Law firms are the Committee's constituent units. The ACLU has a mass membership and does draw upon the membership for policy positions, though the organization is not democratically arranged internally. Headquarters are in New York, and there are state affiliates. Much litigation activity is decentralized, with state and local affiliates deciding how to proceed within broad national parameters.[5]

Many of the active litigation organizations that attempt to influence voting rights policy are public interest law firms, answerable to no democratic structure. Even membership-based organizations in the voting rights bar fall prey to oligarchical tendencies and representational failures. Staff may develop interests and ideologies different from those of the people they ostensibly represent. The more extreme views of the activists and staff, not the more moderate views of the represented, are likely to dominate the organization's activities. In the case of the public interest law firms, the constituency most likely to be heard by the organization's leadership may be the foundation that provides money and resources for advocacy.[6]

While active membership involvement can fetter staff policy dominance, it can also provide credibility and insight into the local legal and political arenas. In the absence of these advantages it is up to local cooperating attorneys of the public interest litigating organizations to build relationships with community leaders. The prominence of the public interest law firms in voting rights raises some representational issues because of their elite nature and distance from grassroots influence.[7]

The relationship between an organized interest's legal arm and a government agency such as the Civil Rights Division can be one of shared aims (including shared resources) or conflict. Either the advocacy organizations or the Department may enter a case from concern that the other will not seek all possible remedies or will settle the case prematurely.[8] During the Reagan and Bush administrations, the advocacy organizations and the Justice Department faced off against each other in a number of cases. Although most of these conflicts occurred in such areas as education and housing, the Division took positions contrary to those of the voting advocates in cases such as *Holder v Hall*, in which the Department opposed plaintiffs' Section Two challenge to a Georgia county's single-commissioner form of government.

Civil rights litigation organizations, even the relatively well funded LDF, are usually short on resources such as money, local counsel, and access to factual materials and experts. Voting rights cases can be onerous. Department resources and Department credibility are valuable. For example, in the Section Two litigation in *Garza v County of Los Angeles*, the trial lasted for forty-two days and there were fifteen expert witnesses, resulting in several thousand pages of transcripts. The Department's intervention was essential to the civil rights groups' victory. Bernard Grofman, who served as an expert witness for the Department in the case, states that Los Angeles County spent $6 million defending the suit. Without the Department's help "minority litigants simply did not have the resources to cope with the mounds of paper, computer printouts, and expert witness affidavits" presented. The civil rights organizations are thus constantly petitioning the Department because government assistance is regarded as a resource, freeing the civil rights organizations for other tasks.[9] Moreover, the courts have often granted the Department greater credibility than the interest groups.

The civil rights community was well positioned by the early nineties to exercise litigation and lobbying expertise. The civil rights establishment had become political insiders in Washington by 1970. The umbrella Leadership Conference on Civil Rights utilized a formidable coalition and sophisticated lobbying skills to shepherd the 1982 renewal and results test amendment through the Congress.[10] The civil rights groups had ready access to Voting Section staff in the nineties, and unlike the Reagan years, when they were unwelcome in the office of Civil Rights chief William Bradford Reynolds, the activists and their legal representatives were able to advocate directly to Bush administration chief Dunne. In voting rights enforcement the litigation organizations were a constant presence in the Department's environment, repeat players in the preclearance process.

In the late eighties and early nineties the advocates went to work to soften up how the Department, state legislators, and courts would regard the first *Gingles* precondition, that the minority group must be "sufficiently large and geographically compact to constitute a majority in a single member district." The advocates were able to persuade the Department and many state legislators that geographically compact should not be taken in its natural meaning; that if any possible contortion could produce a majority-minority district, then functional compactness would be served.[11]

All interested parties, and especially the advocacy groups, eagerly anticipated the Department's early actions in the nineties' round of redistricting. John Dunne took office in March of 1990 and issued moderate statements on voting rights and affirmative action. In one address, he remarked that affirmative action properly understood should contemplate opportunity, not preference, and called for a return to this interpretation. As Dunne became more knowledgeable on issues such as Southern intransigence and racially polarized voting, however, he became determined to take a more aggressive path in voting rights. In early July of 1991 he released an objection letter to Mississippi's state house and senate plans. Frank R. Parker, director of the Voting Rights Project of the Lawyers' Committee, hailed the Department's objection: "This suggests that the Justice Department will enforce the Voting Rights Act in a more sweeping fashion than it did during the administration of Ronald Reagan." *Congressional Quarterly* reported in August on the intense interest placed upon interpreting CRD administrative rulings. It noted that when Texas legislators began to meet to redistrict, they had in hand objection letters to five of the first six state legislative maps the CRD had reviewed in 1991. *Congressional Quarterly* interpreted the Justice Department objections to mean that covered jurisdictions must maximize minority districts. The *Voting Rights Review*, a publication of the Southern Regional Council, praised the Department for tracking legislative black caucus plans in their objections. The *Review* praised Dunne for addressing "the central question in redistricting: maximization."[12]

Minority advocates believed that they could leverage a threat of the Department's objection into more seats. In an April legislative hearing on redistricting, the director of litigation for Texas Rural Aid (and former regional director of MALDEF) testified that "unless there is [*sic*] at least two additional Hispanic Congressional districts and one additional Black Congressional district, . . . the reapportionment of Congress is not going to pass the Department of Justice." Hispanic state representative Ramon Martinez, wielding a plan that would favor his desire to run for a congressional seat, declared that "if this district as we envision it is not a product of the legislative process, we will enlist the help of the U.S. Department of Justice and the courts under the jurisdiction of the Voting Rights Act."[13]

In the South Carolina state house redistricting battle, the floor manager for the advocates' maximization plan warned his colleagues that the "Department of Justice is calling the shots." The CRD was in close touch with the ACLU, the South Carolina Black Legislative Caucus and its ally the Statewide Reapportionment Advisory Committee, and the NAACP as they fought for what their expert demographer termed a "dream plan" of legislative seat maximization. After a version of the dream plan for house redistricting passed the legislature, the CRD was advised by the advocates that it should quickly approve the submission to avoid a deadline by which a federal court would impose its own plan. The day before the deadline, Patrick issued a letter preclearing the state's submission. Having observed the process in the house, the South Carolina senate meekly complied with what it perceived to be the CRD's demands.[14]

One of the plans submitted to the Georgia legislature created three minority districts and was developed by the Georgia Legislative Black Caucus, represented by attorney Kathleen Wilde of the ACLU. She argued that the Voting Rights Act requires that black districts be drawn wherever feasible. Ms. Wilde contended that compactness could be divorced from geography; only functional compactness was necessary. State Senator (now Congressman) Sanford Bishop warned of a voting rights lawsuit and the certainty of CRD objection for any plan that preserved incumbency over maximization.[15]

The Georgia court found that Wilde was in "constant contact" with the Voting Section attorneys responsible for reviewing Georgia's plan:

> There were countless communications, including notes, maps, and charts, by phone, mail and facsimile, between Wilde and the DOJ team; those transactions signified close cooperation between Wilde and DOJ during the preclearance process. . . .
>
> Ms. Wilde's relationship with the DOJ Voting Section was informal and familiar; the dynamics were that of peers working together, not of an advocate submitting proposals to higher authorities. DOJ was more accessible—and amenable—to the opinions of the ACLU than to those of the Attorney General of the State of Georgia.[16]

Wilde often forwarded suggestions to the Voting Section "per your request." On one occasion a Department attorney told counsel for the state to work out a state house district with Wilde because she was "still having some problems with it." The court found that throughout the preclearance process the Department relied upon a version of the three-seat max-black plan devised by Wilde as a benchmark. Though the Department protested at trial that it had not suggested an outcome, the court found that the state legislature believed that it was being forced to maximize—a belief the Department and the advocate groups encouraged. When the Department released its objection letter to the state's second submission, it released it first to the ACLU, which immediately provided it to its clients in the Black Caucus. Thus the Caucus leaders were already discussing the ACLU's triumph with the press before Georgia's attorney general or legislative leadership received the letter. The advocates kept the pressure up on the state through the CRD up until the last moment of preclearance.[17]

The court also criticized the Department for permitting politicians and other parties in interest to misuse regulations that honor anonymous comments. Under 28 CFR sec. 51.29, commenters can ask that they not be identified. This provision is meant to protect minorities who might otherwise be subject to intimidation or retaliation. In Georgia, politicians and other commenters used it as a secret back channel to the regulators. These "informants" or "secret agents," as the district court termed them, included at least one state senator who was a candidate for Congress, and an aide to the lieutenant governor, who reported to the Department on the legislature's deliberations. State legislators whose conduct was questioned could not identify their accusers. One African-American state senator, the chair of the Senate Reapportionment Committee, was accused by an informant of being an "Uncle Tom" and "the worst friend of blacks in Georgia."[18]

At every turn, despite defeat in the legislative halls, the advocates seemed certain of final victory. State Representative (now Congresswoman) Cynthia McKinney remarked of committee passage of a two-seat plan in August that "these plans are going through like a bullet train, but they're going to stop at the Justice Department station." The district court ultimately concluded: "Succinctly put, the considerable influence of ACLU advocacy on the voting rights decisions of the United States Attorney General is an embarrassment."[19]

The Georgia state senator accused of being an Uncle Tom was not the only black legislator to have his efforts marginalized by the process. In North Carolina, Wilde represented a number of minority organizations opposed to a plan favored by the North Carolina Legislative Black Caucus. She entered into a bitter feud with black elected officials who produced that state's redistricting plan, including House Speaker Daniel Blue and House Congressional Redistricting Committee co-chair Representative Toby Fitch. Wilde alleged in an interview that the Black Caucus had "sold out" and wrote to the Justice Department that black elected officials had been complicit in purposeful discrimination. Jeremy Rabkin has pointed out that the more government is accountable to private litigants, the less it can be accountable to the public good. Limiting choices of officials limits their responsibility; elected figures cannot be responsible for decisions they are not permitted to make. The Department, on the prodding of the ACLU's Wilde and other interests, rejected North Carolina's first plan, producing a most ironical example of Rabkin's point. For in North Carolina African-American elected officials, many of whom owed their offices in part to past voting rights victories, had the political decision making in redistricting removed from their purview by the advocacy groups. Civil rights litigators have accepted what Stephen L. Wasby calls the "myth of rights." They resort to their specialty, litigation, to produce recognition and implementation of rights. The litigators are unwilling to entrust political decisions to elected officials.[20]

The involvement of Representative Martinez in Texas and state legislators Bishop and McKinney in Georgia illuminates another aspect of the advocacy environment.

Maximization was sought not only by civil rights groups that pursued more minority seats, but also by minority politicians who wished to fill those seats. In Louisiana, the African-American chair of the senate committee charged with redistricting, Senator Cleo Fields, encouraged a plan favorable to his aspirations. Much of the Louisiana debate concerned not whether a second seat was required by the Department, but whether to draw it to include more southern Louisianans partial to Senator Fields's candidacy, or northern Louisianans favorable to Legislative Black Caucus chairman state Senator C.D. Jones's campaign. In Texas, Senator Eddie Bernice Johnson, chair of the state Senate Redistricting Committee, leveraged her position and the threat of Department intervention into a congressional seat. Johnson "had her eye on just about every one of [Congressman Martin Frost's] black and Hispanic areas to create a new district for herself." Johnson communicated with the Department and used the specter of federal intervention to get her way. A Democratic Party strategist remarked that Johnson "knew exactly what cards she had. She played a very tough game and she won."[21]

There is no suggestion that the CRD favored certain candidates, but given other partisan accusations leveled at it, the Division should be wary. An incautious association with political machinations may place the agency in the position of intruding on the composition of the legislative branch. In the words of "Federalist 51," the separation of powers "is admitted on all hands to be essential to the preservation of liberty" and thus "each department should have a will of its own; and consequently should be so constituted that the members of each should have as little agency as possible in the appointment of the members of the others."[22] The Division should be scrupulous to avoid the political thicket that surrounds state politicians and their ascendant ambitions, no matter how well meaning the Department's goals.

An important component of the civil rights organized interest is the voting rights issue network, dominated by partisans of proportional representation. Gregory Caldeira describes a "policy network" of those working on voting rights policy. He includes in this network interest group lawyers and cooperating attorneys, bureaucrats, voting rights projects, think tanks, some members of the judiciary, academics, members of key congressional committees, officeholders and potential officeholders who might gain or lose from voting rights litigation, the Ford and Rockefeller foundations as sponsors, "and officials and rank-and-file lawyers in the voting rights section of the Department of Justice." Grofman and Davidson, occasional consultants to the CRD, characterize the Department as "a vital component of the voting rights bar."[23]

The issue network has found the Voting Section to be a hospitable forum. There is frequent contact between the voting rights bar and the Section's attorneys, a common pattern where an attorney's practice coincides with that of a regulatory agency. Voting Section professionals and advocates share an interest in promoting minority voting power. This does not mean that interests and strategies and passions are always identical. Deval L. Patrick reports frequent and acrimonious reactions to his decisions from activists; voting rights litigator Brenda Wright expresses dismay at the Department's unwillingness to push enforcement far enough. Marching in lockstep, then, is not a necessary attribute of issue-network membership. Entry is governed by the willingness to closely monitor and attempt to act on certain issues. In the voting rights area, the network has been limited to a one-sided representation. Critics of the established views of the VRA have been under attack from network members.[24]

Timothy G. O'Rourke has accused the elite partisans in the issue network of "constant tinkering" with the messy results of democracy. "Precisely because they are not politicians, the Guardians are, indeed, more concerned with fixing the results than with improving the politics that gives rise to the results." O'Rourke thus noted that a Brookings conference on voting rights had included "no elected officials, no registrars, no party leaders; there were many lawyers and social science experts. There was much talk about lawsuits, but virtually no discussion of ways to increase voter turnout, to build biracial coalitions during political campaigns, or to energize the political parties at the grass roots."[25]

The issue-network members share an endemic distrust and disdain for state legislatures. One can pore through the literature and find little commentary from those elected officials whose responsibility it is to draw districts. The marginalization of elected officials is a relief to the experts. They believe (not without merit) that many elected officials do not like the Act. Grofman and Davidson observe that "officials—the only people, really, who understand much about the act and have an opinion one way or the other—are fortunately simply a small, small percentage of the electorate."[26] The low salience of voting rights to the general public permits experts to pursue their vision of proportional representation more freely than other civil rights policies with acute effects, such as preferential hiring or school admissions.

In the 1980s a vigorous challenge to the prevailing view developed. Such critics as Charles S. Bullock III, Katharine Inglis Butler, and Timothy G. O'Rourke had raised questions concerning enforcement for some time, but the 1987 publication of Abigail Thernstrom's revisionist account of the history of the Voting Rights Act, *Whose Votes Count? Affirmative Action and Minority Voting Rights*, set off a true firestorm within the issue network. The attacks on Thernstrom were not just immediate, but persistent; they began upon her book's publication and continue to this day.[27] Graham attributes the venomous response to challengers of the dominant account to the fact that students of voting rights have been predominantly partisans of the Act. Critics have been unwelcome. By the early nineties, voting rights conferences had become so acrimonious that some potential participants simply stayed home.[28]

The two former Division chiefs most responsible for Division strategy during the nineties' redistricting cycle offer somewhat different views of the Voting Section within the issue network. Dunne states the careerists and advocates "had a good working, professional and personal relationship. Some of them [the advocates] had been in the Voting Section at one time. They were out there on the cutting edge trying to advance what the average person would think was a common cause." Patrick stresses the independence and professionalism of the staff and cites the many "angry phone calls, disappointed letters . . . from the advocacy groups . . . [as indicating] that we weren't working in lock step with them."[29] There is little question of the quality and professionalism brought to the job by career attorneys. Nonetheless, their professional concerns and relationships dovetail enough with those of the advocates to place the Voting Section within the issue network.

The network has been relentless and successful at law review lobbying—advocacy for a certain mode of preferred analysis. Litigators such as Laughlin McDonald and Lani Guinier and social science experts such as Bernard Grofman have contributed numerous law review articles, academic pieces, and newspaper commentaries. The effectiveness of law review lobbying was on display in *Growe v Emison*. In that case, the Supreme Court chastised a federal district court in Minnesota for relying not on evidence of racial bloc voting, but upon a law review article that proclaimed racial bloc voting a pervasive national phenomenon.[30]

Social scientists justifiably lay claim to nudging the courts in the issue network's preferred direction. Grofman and Davidson write of the critical role of social science experts that:

> Because the Voting Rights Act does not formulate specific tests for vote dilution, the meaning of that concept has been the topic of continuous case-by-case adjudication, while at the same time there has been an ongoing evolution of administrative standards within the Voting Rights Section of the Justice Department. The interpretation of the Act has involved a remarkable sequence of interactions, leading perhaps to a kind of "reflective equilibrium" in which social scientists' courtroom testimony in voting rights cases in the 70s and the late 60s influences judicial interpretation of the statute, which in turn set the stage for law review articles and further social science testimony in the 1980s on the proper interpretation of terms such as "racially polarized voting" culminating in [*Thornburg v Gingles*], which in turn becomes the basis for subsequent lower court decisions.[31]

A proportional representation policy appeals to the rational thinkers of the voting rights issue network as being dependent on verifiable scientific terms—representation based upon racial percentage of the population. This equation has the added benefit of removing decision making from state legislatures, institutions that the network members regard with suspicion. The preferred avenue for the advocates, lawyers, and social scientists has been not the legislatures but the courts—or their issue-network associates and quasi-judicial preclearance arbiters in the Voting Section.

Distrust of state legislators is often reflected in calls for redistricting to be removed from the responsibility of elected officials. Common Cause has proposed the establishment of an independent redistricting commission in order to shift the process away from incumbent or partisan interests. Samuel Issacharoff has speculated that the Supreme Court may have been using its 1994 Term to signal that redistricting should be consigned to nonpartisan commissions. He applauded the use of a team of Special Masters appointed pursuant to state law to produce a redistricting plan in California. Former Civil Rights Division counsel Turner has invited partisan players to absent themselves from the debate on affirmative action policies. Arguing for a measured approach to affirmative action under court guidance, Turner wrote that "we can trust the law-enforcement professionals at the Justice Department and elsewhere to get on with the business of enforcing the civil rights laws."[32]

With a few exceptions, there has been muffled criticism of the easy movement of social scientists from the pages of academic journals to the adversary setting of the courtroom. Graham suggests that the literature has taken on a tone of advocacy because it is being supplied by those with a stake in outcomes, who wish to push legal decision making toward their policy preferences. The less ubiquitous critics of the established voting rights regime have also lent themselves to the advocate's cause. Even the commentary on the role of the expert witness can sometimes be partisan. A Voting Section counsel and social scientist coauthored a law review article pondering whether academicians had been sacrificing their truth-seeking function to a cause. They concluded that "experts serving the defendant's side in these cases are more likely to fall from professional grace than are plaintiff's experts."[33]

Up until the nineties there was little effective opposition to the voting rights issue network; no one had a direct and sustainable interest in dueling the voting rights elite. The network has been adept in framing issues and assuming the moral high ground, and it possesses advantages over "one-shotter" opponents.[34] But again, things changed in the early nineties. As dissatisfaction with racial and incumbent gerrymandering spread across the South, sophisticated attorneys brought legal challenges. Robinson O. Everett of North Carolina, a Duke Law School professor, and A. Rowland Dye, Larry H. Chesin, and A. Lee Parks of Georgia have spearheaded the effort to contest the DOJ's decisions. Challengers in South Carolina have retained Parks, and attorney Paul Loy Hurd of Louisiana has lent his talents to challenges in Louisiana, Virginia, and Texas. The rise of these skillful practitioners, who collectively have won many of the victories of the decade, has countered the previous advantage held by the talented attorneys and social scientists associated with the public interest law firms and DOJ.

The attorneys have been assisted by social science witnesses, including Ronald Weber of the University of Wisconsin and Charles S. Bullock III of the University of Georgia, who have questioned the interpretations that have prevailed among the issue-network experts. For example, in Texas Dr. Allan J. Lichtman and Dr. Chandler Davidson, authors of many articles on voting rights, testified in support of the state's plan. Several experts who testified for intervenors supplemented their testimony. The United States submitted reports of four experts, including Dr. J. Morgan Kousser, who reviewed the motivations behind recent redistricting efforts in Texas. United States witness Dr. Lisa Handley concluded that the districts at issue in Texas were "reasonably compact." The district court rejected her conclusion. The Texas court gave greater deference to the opinion of plaintiffs' main expert witness Dr. Weber, who testified that race was the overriding factor in drawing the districts and that the districts were wildly noncompact.[35]

Courts hear a dizzying amount of testimony from experts on topics such as racial polarization and the "meanderingness" of districts. Yet some members of the judiciary lament that clarity has been sacrificed. In *Johnson v Miller*, the district court complained that the experts in favor of maintaining the max-black plan had "launched conflicting assumptions, databases, and bases of assumption, only to be trounced by Dr. Katz, who impugned [their testimony]," leaving the court with "little of use." The court complained of being "subjected to especially mind-numbing and contradictory statistical data." Also, recent voting rights cases have shifted decisional rules. In Justice Brennan's formulation in *Gingles*, nothing matters but the correlation of race and voting preference. Since the Court's decision in *DeGrandy*, however, lower courts look to evidence that whites vote as a bloc for reasons unrelated to racial animus, such as party or issue positions.[36] But the Court's "predominant racial motive" standard announced in *Miller* is difficult to apply. The Court acknowledges that race plays a role in redistricting, but it is unclear how much is permissible. This leaves expert witnesses scrambling and formerly useful formulas under question.

The recently emergent challengers to racial districting are far less organized than the civil rights establishment groups and public interest law firms. It is a matter of decades of cooperation versus just a few years. So far there has been only a small amount of joint action among the attorneys and social science experts who have so successfully challenged the status quo. There have been some personal contacts, but no formal gatherings; certainly nothing like the conferences and training sessions that assist the activists and public interest law firms. Funding sources have been limited and alliances with other interests (including the Republican Party) sporadic. Robinson O. Everett, for example, has conducted much of the *Shaw* litigation on a *pro bono* basis, having relied on young volunteer attorneys to assist, as well as some fees recovered upon successful completion of *Shaw v Reno*. The challenger's motivations have not been uniform either; some have been impelled forward by opposition to racial preferences, some by local or regional political considerations, some by partisan concerns. In certain areas, Democrats have joined in challenges to districting plans. At the end of the decade, there had been an emerging institutional effort to assist plaintiffs. The Campaign for a Color-Blind America has assisted in finding legal representation and expert witnesses for challengers.[37]

The current disarray hampers the progress of the voting rights issue network, but its work goes on. The Department cooperates with many of the attorneys who bring voting suits and employs many of the social scientists who provide academic commentary as expert witnesses. At least when the presidency is in the hands of the Democrats, the issue network provides candidates for head of the Civil Rights Division; the last four Democratic nominees have been alumni of the LDF. Some Voting Section attorneys depart only to resurface as counsel for one of the public interest law firms.

THE REPUBLICAN PARTY AS VOTING RIGHTS ADVOCATE

When Turner invited partisans to stay out of voting rights policy, he did so in the wake of concerted efforts by Republicans to influence redistricting in the states and Division decision making on state submissions. Democrats also focused intensively on redistricting but had less involvement in attempting to influence Department policy making because they were hamstrung by the need to mollify minority interests. It was an explicit Republican strategy to create more minority districts to "bleach" other districts; it was a Republican Department of Justice that had a maximization policy; and the relationship of those two facts caused a swirl of speculation concerning whether the Division hierarchy acted in concert with GOP political strategists—a "Republican Plot."

Republican Party operatives acknowledge that minority voters reliably vote in overwhelming numbers for Democratic candidates; some black precincts exceed 90 percent Democratic voting. Republicans therefore believe that if minority voters can be packed into a number of districts at percentages high enough to guarantee a minority candidate will be elected, the consistently Democratic voters will not be available to surrounding districts. This can make other Democratic candidates less competitive, since white voters tend to be more conservative and more Republican than do minority voters. This is not a recent finding. Sixties studies by the Republican National Committee, *Congressional Quarterly*, and the Library of Congress showed that creation of new black districts would benefit Republicans. Republican strategist Kevin Phillips made the same connection in his 1970 book *The Emerging Republican Majority*: "[M]aintenance of Negro voting rights is essential to the GOP. Unless Negroes continue to displace White Democratic organizations, the latter may remain viable as spokesmen for Deep Southern conservatism."[38]

Such lessons were hardly lost upon Republican strategists in the nineties. Republican National Committee chairman Lee Atwater, in his own effort at law review lobbying, wrote that the 1982 results test amendment and the 1986 Supreme Court decision in *Gingles* meant that minority seats must be maximized. Wherever minority seats can be created, Atwater argued, they must be created. He suggested that the confluence of the Section Two results test and Section Five's prohibition against retrogressive effect or discriminatory purpose had two consequences. First, all existing minority districts must be maintained. Second, all possible new minority districts must be created. Atwater supported his arguments with claims that rested flatly on proportional representation: since minority groups are approximately 20 percent of the population, they deserve a like number of seats.[39]

The Republicans moved early and aggressively in the 1990 redistricting cycle. The Republican National Committee provided $50,000 in start-up funding to Lawyers for the Republic, Inc. This organization was created as a tax-exempt operation to provide districting data to interested parties. It offered free software called "Fairness for the Nineties" to participants in the redistricting process. A display of the software's capabilities in June of 1990 attracted the NAACP, MALDEF, the Lawyers' Committee, Southwest Voter Education Project, Civil Rights Division officials—and even suspicious representatives of the Democratic Party, who could hardly be denied a display by a tax-exempt organization. The software was offered to minority groups at no cost and with no strings attached. The executive director of Lawyers for the Republic even offered to try and arrange for foundations to donate computer hardware. Nonetheless, civil rights strategists regarded Republican overtures with a great deal of suspicion. A formal alliance never developed, because of the advocates' distrust of the Republicans and desire not to be drawn into a partisan battle. Many of the civil rights groups instead availed themselves of software developed by the ACLU of Virginia.[40]

The Republican Party was also heavily involved in the redistricting submission process under the Department's preclearance authority. Republican activists, state party officials, and attorneys filed Section Five comments urging maximization in a number of states. In Georgia, Republican attorneys filed their comments under the name "Georgians for Fair Redistricting." Party operatives sought to use 28 CFR sec. 51.29, the regulation intended to provide confidentiality to minority commenters who might face intimidation and harassment, to hide their own identities.[41]

In a 1992 briefing paper entitled "The Republicans Go to Court," the Southern Regional Council observed that the Republican Party had filed a number of lawsuits early in the process, even before state legislatures had had an opportunity to act. The paper found that whereas in past years the initiative had rested with civil rights groups, the Republican Party's tactics had shifted the terms of the process. If successful, the Republicans' strategy would move redistricting from Democratic-dominated legislatures to Republican-dominated federal courts. While Republican plans might benefit minority districts, the report warned that the tactic would bypass the more favorable Department. The report continued that "these increased standards [referring to the 1982 amendment's results test], community vigilance and, in most cases, vigorous enforcement have led to substantial gains, making the Justice Department the preferred route for winning fair representation." Moreover, "the federal courts are not acting as a consistent protector of minority voting rights, especially in comparison with the institution's role in much of the 1980s and the Justice Department's current aggressive rulings."[42]

Minority advocacy groups were suspicious of the Republicans, but joined with them when circumstances were propitious. Courts came to recognize the unusual alliance of Republicans and African-American advocacy groups in seeking an affirmative action remedy. In the Louisiana congressional redistricting litigation, the trial testimony showed that the max-black plan adopted by the legislature owed its passage to an alliance of the black and Republican caucuses, "historically uncommon bed fellows," but nonetheless part of an increasing pattern across the country.[43]

The Democrats were hardly defenseless. The tortured twists and turns of partisan advantage seeking were on display in North Carolina. The state, supported by the Legislative Black Caucus, submitted a congressional plan with one black district to the Voting Section. The Republican Party, however, had offered an alternative plan with two black seats. The ACLU, representing a number of minority advocacy organizations including the NAACP, argued for a two-seat plan. The Department objected to the state plan on the basis that the refusal to adopt the Republican plan constituted evidence of a discriminatory purpose.

Following the Department's rejection of the first North Carolina submission, the Democrat-dominated legislature devised a plan that continued to protect incumbents while creating a tortuous looking black-majority Twelfth Congressional District. The Twelfth became known as the "I-85" district because it meandered in search of black enclaves in a band no wider in places than Interstate Highway 85. The Division approved the plan. Both Dunne and David Simon point out that the Department had no authority to object to plans that drew odd-looking districts; they could only object to plans that harmed minority voting power. Simon protests, quite correctly, that the Democratic legislature did not heed Dunne's objection letter. The letter suggested concentrations of voters in south-central to south-eastern North Carolina could have formed a new district. The legislature drew a different district in order to protect incumbents. Nonetheless, Dunne later regretted that the Division could be considered to have some responsibility because it had underemphasized compactness. James P. Turner lamented that "it seems to me that we lost our polar star there somewhere. . . . dragging that district all the way across the state, no wider than the interstate at times, was too much."[44]

Checked by the Democratic legislature's ability to evade its successful influence upon the Division's preclearance powers, North Carolina Republicans filed suit complaining of a partisan gerrymander. That suit was dismissed but individual Republican voters soon filed another suit challenging the state's plan on statutory and constitutional grounds, in what eventuated in the Supreme Court's landmark decision in *Shaw v Reno*. After the decision in *Reno* caused the matter to be sent back to the federal district court in North Carolina for trial, the Republicans were open about their calculations in both testimony and closing arguments. Many members of the North Carolina legislature believed that the Department of Justice was acting out of partisan motives. Among the twists and turns that characterized voting rights in the nineties is that the *Shaw* litigation was commenced by Republican voters after the Party was frustrated that its successful efforts to induce DOJ intervention had been thwarted by Democratic racial gerrymandering. The individual challengers, however, received only sporadic assistance from formal Republican Party channels.[45]

Many suspected, and continue to suspect, that the Division was used as part of a Republican Plot. The debate began almost as soon as the Voting Section's review of submissions commenced. In an op-ed piece in the *Washington Post* on 23 September 1991, Abigail Thernstrom accused the Justice Department of complicity in a Republican-civil rights group alliance to maximize minority legislative seats. Thernstrom wrote that Dunne had learned a political lesson: "He can embrace legislative quotas, make civil rights groups happy and line the political pockets of Republicans while hardly making a political ripple." One month later Bernard Grofman fired back in the same pages, terming Thernstrom's charges "nonsense."[46]

Other observers, including Samuel Issacharoff and Timothy G. O'Rourke, have accused the Department of succumbing to partisan political considerations. Grofman has continued to defend the Department from accusations of partisan political interference. Both John Dunne and his Clinton administration successor Deval L. Patrick have denied that the Department rendered decisions based on anything other than the facts and law. Former Department professional J. Gerald Hebert, then special litigation counsel to the Voting Section, complained that accusations of partisan enforcement were "untrue, unfounded, and calculated to undercut the important work of our Voting Rights Section." Turner, who supervised the Voting Section for twenty-five years, likewise rejects partisan involvement.[47]

A number of analysts have remarked upon the success of the Republican Party strategy. David Lublin recounts the spirited academic debate concerning how much of the Republican advances in 1992 and 1994 can be attributed to maximization. Carol Swain contends that the Democrats lost five seats in 1992 and another twelve in 1994; David Bositis of the Joint Center for Political and Economic Studies concurs with Swain's estimate. Lublin believes that Democrats lost five seats due to racial redistricting in 1992. There has been much more contention about the number of seats lost by Democrats in 1994 due to racial redistricting, but Lublin settles definitely upon two, and quite likely four others, so he places the aggregate 1992–1994 loss at from seven to eleven seats.[48] The impact of these numbers is truly significant. In the 105th Congress a shift of only eleven seats would have made Democrat Richard Gephardt the Speaker instead of Republican Newt Gingrich. In the 106th Congress, the Republicans held an even slimmer six-vote margin.

How then do we square the Republican success and accusations of partisan influence in the Division's decision making with the outright and consistent denials of Department personnel? Dunne is certainly central to untangling this puzzle. When he arrived at the CRD post he had little experience with civil rights law and a stock Republican aversion to group preference. Dunne himself explains his education in the voting rights area: "My views changed as I learned more about devices used to diminish voting rights, and I became more determined to promote strong enforcement."[49] Dunne was also a political veteran who had survived several redistricting cycles as a state senator, and if vigorous enforcement of the Voting Rights Act should collaterally benefit Republicans, then so be it. The Division's professionals, who at the least have a strong interest in increasing the efficacy of minority votes and at most a sincere belief in maximization, were little inclined to go to the ramparts against a policy they believed might achieve their policy objectives.

Skepticism inheres because the Bush administration was adamantly opposed to preference or proportional representation remedies in other areas of civil rights policy. There were those in the White House and higher reaches of the Department who did not favor the kind of preference that seemed to be at work in voting rights enforcement, but the administration left Dunne and his staff alone to pursue their best judgment. Dunne recalls that there were "a bunch of people around the President who didn't really care much for civil rights. . . . But in the area of voting rights Dick [Attorney General Thornburgh] pretty much left me on my own. He made that very clear. . . . The Attorney General left me on my own, and I was there to enforce the law the way I thought it was intended to be carried out. . . . I left that office comfortable that in the voting rights area we were very much on our own." The Division had been marginalized by the administration in other aspects of civil rights enforcement. In a *New York Times* article on 10 January 1991 Dunne described himself as "on the bench" on major civil rights issues that were before the administration.[50] But the Division was left unimpeded in voting rights enforcement by administration higher-ups who in all likelihood disagreed with the Division's legal position. It is quite probable that rather than forcing the Division to back off from preferential remedies, Republican superiors in the administration simply left the Voting Section and Dunne alone to pursue their policy preferences—that not too coincidentally would serve partisan interests.

David Simon, Dunne's legal counsel, confirms this atmosphere. The Republican National Committee placed a number of calls to Dunne's staff concerning preclearance decisions. The RNC, though, was not the boss of John Dunne. The Bush White House was. And in Simon's words, "No one will ever believe how hands off the Republicans were. No one in the White House or the Attorney General ever told us how a case should come out. . . . We kept waiting for those calls, it never happened. . . . Probably everyone was too afraid it would come out. . . . No one higher up than John ever got involved, and no one said this is what you have to do."[51]

It is also true that exerting political pressure on the Voting Section could be counterproductive. The Division careerists disdain partisan interference and know how to fight bureaucratic battles. In his op-ed article in the *New York Times*, Turner attacked the political parties for intervening in voting rights enforcement for their own partisan purposes. Turner never detected any partisan machination on the part of Dunne: "John Dunne believed more black districts were better for blacks, the standard liberal line, and he saw an opportunity to achieve that result, and he took it."[52] Dunne made his most partisan remark of which I am aware in an interview with the *National Journal*:

I know what it's like, and I urge people, "Bare knuckles, the toughest hardball politics you can practice, do it in the state capitols and the country (*sic*) courthouses." But when it comes here, . . . you call it according to what the law says, and that's the way it's going to be called. Now if it falls [that] there are some happy alliances made between Republicans and minorities, as a Republican I'm not going to jump up and down and say, "Hey, you can't do that." But I will if it violates the Voting Rights Act.[53]

I have reviewed the texts of many of Dunne's speeches on redistricting, including a February 1991 address to the Republican National Committee Seminar on Redistricting, and I have found no other partisan tilt in any of his remarks. (By contrast, in an address to the NAACP National Convention in 1994, Deval Patrick complained about the lack of Section Two litigation initiated in recent years and stated "There were a number of reasons for this but they can be summed up in one word, 'Republicans.'")[54]

Simon makes another good point that belies Republican intervention in the Division's decision making. In Texas, the Division did not object to a Democratic Party racial gerrymander opposed by Republicans. The Republican Party sued over the redistricting, which Simon argues proves the Division's independence:

Texas was a key, pivotal state, and one that at least one member of the Bush family has an interest in. . . . Nevertheless, we did not do what the Republicans wanted in Texas, we did not require additional minority seats in Texas, even if they could have been drawn. . . . That disproves both the maximization policy and the theory that we were doing the bidding of the Republican Party, because that was the most important state to the Republicans in the entire redistricting, and we didn't do what the Republicans wanted.[55]

Simon suggests that there was a kind of schizophrenia within the administration. They wanted to help Republicans, but on the other hand many were die-hard conservatives who did not support any of the tactics of the Voting Section. "They liked the political result, but objected to the legal analysis, so they didn't want to get involved because it was a no-win situation for them. I think if the White House had gotten involved in voting rights, they would have told us to stop objecting, but that would have been bad for Republicans, so they didn't get involved."[56]

Proving a negative is a difficult task, and proving that the Division did not act out of partisan interest is proving a negative. While such speculation fits a neat theory, there is little hard evidence that Dunne acted to effect a Republican Plot. Dunne, Simon, and the Division professionals were acting out of a sincere belief in increasing minority descriptive representation. In doing so, they were proceeding in an arena in which Dunne was permitted license to follow his judgment. Their genuine policy objective coincided with the political interest of a president and a political party that had no sincere interest in increasing minority descriptive representation for its own sake. Had Bush administration higher-ups including the attorney general wished to put the brakes on, they could have done so. President Bush had vehemently opposed quotas, yet here was an enforcement strategy that moved toward proportional representation by race. The partisan implications were overt and pursued doggedly by the Republican National Committee and state parties. The Division was permitted to pursue a policy avenue in conflict with the administration's civil rights policy agenda because of partisan political judgments made by higher-ups in the administration. There is no smoking gun because none was ever required. Permitting the Voting Section to act on its own legal judgment and policy wishes could achieve the desired result.

THE STATES

The covered states are also interests external to the Department with crucial concerns about Voting Section decision making. The states have always preferred submitting to the Department because it could be lobbied in ways that the district court could not. The federal district court in Washington has been regarded as a liberal bastion hostile to Southern ways. Ball, Krane, and Lauth argued in *Compromised Compliance* that the Department's practice of seeking negotiated settlements with local officials had conferred upon the states the condition of client, contrary to the statute's intent. Quite the opposite relationship developed in the nineties.

John Dunne had put the states on notice early in the nineties' redistricting cycle. In a 13 August 1991 speech to the National Conference of State Legislators he stressed the Department's oversight powers. Dunne noted that no jurisdiction had ever been successful in a declaratory judgment action in district court when a plan had already been disapproved by the CRD. Therefore, the covered jurisdictions would have to satisfy the CRD that their plans could meet the Division's test for racial fairness. Dunne remarked that any effort to submit directly to the court would be met with the full adversarial resources of the Department.

On a certain level, the chief was only explaining the Department's procedures when a case proceeds to declaratory judgment. State legislators, though, might well understand the remarks as an admonition that the CRD's judgment was inviolable. Moreover, they could interpret the chief to be warning that if a state should avoid CRD's preclearance process (if for example, a state should believe it was not being treated fairly by the DOJ, as some states did come to conclude), then CRD would use its powers to pursue the state through the more expensive and time-consuming declaratory judgment process. So the states would be better off submitting to the Department. The Department is in a strong bargaining position to force corrections. The chief of the Civil Rights Division here seems to say that opposition to the Department is all but hopeless.

Dunne also provided the legislators with several examples of submissions in which the Department had exercised its judgment. In Louisiana, for instance, he described an objection where a plan seemed to protect incumbents over minority interests. In the same plan in another part of the state, however, Dunne noted that the Department had not objected to a failure to draw a minority seat where the resulting district would have split a community that wished to remain in a single district, and the proposed alteration would "have had an odd, somewhat tortured shape." The Mississippi plan had a host of problems, including some overt racial politics.

Dunne indicated that skepticism would be applied to efforts of minority legislators to support plans that were unacceptable to civil rights interest groups. For example, Dunne recounted that a Virginia state house plan drafted by the state's legislative black caucus was objected to because the NAACP, Republican Party, and ACLU had drawn an alternative plan with two additional black seats. Virginia's plan raised an alarm because it seemed to protect incumbents (including an African-American office-holder) at the expense of the additional seats. In a 1992 address Dunne was more explicit in indicating that minority support would carry weight but not be dispositive. Minority legislators, he asserted, might offer support in exchange for a committee assignment or leadership position or out of party loyalty. Their backing might therefore be discounted. "On the other hand, we pay close attention to the positions of such advocacy groups as MALDEF, the ACLU, LULAC and the NAACP."[57]

The practical application of Dunne's suspicion was most evident in North Carolina. The Department objected to the state's plan, which had been crafted with the assistance of Representative Toby Fitch, the African-American co-chair of the House Congressional Redistricting Committee, and the African-American Speaker of the House, Daniel Blue. Every racial minority member of the house voted for the plan. The Department instead backed the objections of the ACLU, representing several minority interest groups. An acrid exchange took place between Representative Fitch and ACLU attorney Kathleen Wilde. Blue and Fitch were both respected legislators. Yet the Department's siding with the ACLU threatened the biracial coalition that brought them to power in the house.[58]

In the *Shaw* litigation, North Carolina state Senator Dennis Winner testified about a meeting that North Carolina officials attended with Dunne on 17 December 1991, the day before the Department issued its objection letter. Senator Winner's interpretation of the meeting was that Dunne had his mind made up to require proportional representation. Dunne recalls that he continued to hold the position that proportional representation was not required, but he also remembers his concern that minority representation would include consideration of the minority percentage in the population—a wholly understandable benchmark.[59] This overlap of benchmark with Section Two's proviso against the requirement of proportional representation leads to a definitional dance on the head of a pin, and state legislators faced with Department objections rightly saw attainment of the benchmark as their ticket to preclearance.

The Democratic-dominated state legislatures fought to protect incumbents in the face of the Department's mandates. The North Carolina legislature proved especially inventive, drawing a second black district to satisfy the CRD. But the new Twelfth Congressional District ignored the area where Dunne's objection letter indicated a violation existed in favor of a bizarre looking map that would preserve Democratic incumbents.

Texas's redistricting was a true political minefield. Advocates for maximization declared a direct line to the DOJ and proclaimed the willingness of the CRD to object if their wishes were not heeded. Democratic Congressman Martin Frost faced the danger of losing minority voters to state Senator Eddie Bernice Johnson's demands for more minority districts. Frost, a deft line drawer and the chair of the House Democratic redistricting committee know as IMPAC 2000, was able to create a plan that protected nearly every Democratic incumbent and rewarded Johnson and other minority aspirants. The result was a plan that was so unusual that John R. Dunne wrote in his preclearance letter: "While we are preclearing this plan under Section Five, the extraordinarily convoluted nature of some of the districts compels me to disclaim any implication that the proposed plan is otherwise lawful or constitutional."[60]

The suspicion with which the Department regarded the state's submissions is also evident in its dismissal of state rationales as "pretextual." This claim harmonized with the position that a failure to adopt a proposal with a greater number of minority seats indicated discriminatory purpose. In *Shaw v Hunt,* the Court recounted some of the factors asserted by North Carolina and rejected by the Department as pretextual. North Carolina had explained that it did not maximize in its original plan because it did not wish to split precincts or counties; the state plan would create one majority-black district and a substantial number of other districts in which African Americans would have a significant amount of influence. The submission also demonstrated the disadvantages of plans proposed by the Republicans, and on which the Department had relied. The Court rejected the Department's characterization of pretext in North Carolina as insupportable.[61]

In Georgia, the district court criticized the Department for failing to recognize that the legislature was concerned with racial, political, economic, and personal factors affecting all Georgians in drawing its plan. The alternative offered by the ACLU that the Department relied upon was concerned only with racial percentages. The Supreme Court upheld the lower court's ruling that the Department's characterizations of pretext were insupportable. The Court found that a state's adherence to districting principles other than those necessary to create maximization does not support an inference of discriminatory purpose.[62]

To reflect upon the difficulty of the decisions the CRD must make, it can hardly be gainsaid that the states facing Section Five reviews have richly earned suspicion over the years. Georgia in particular had established a record in the seventies and eighties of trying to undermine the prospects of an African-American congressperson. The Louisiana legislature heedlessly jettisoned an African-American majority district in the eighties in a dispute with the governor. The 1992 North Carolina two-seat plan was not drawn where Dunne had indicated the violation existed. The Democratic legislature drew the map in a contorted fashion to protect white Democratic incumbents while providing two black districts. The CRD leadership believed that some states would claim they could not draw black districts without splitting traditional political districts; then the Voting Section would find numerous instances in which boundaries were obliterated to protect white incumbents. Some officials have found it frustrating that after over 100 years of permitting racial gerrymanders to disenfranchise African

Americans, the courts now find plans that increase the number of African-American representatives to be unconstitutional.[63] It is against this background that the Division must render its decisions.

The crisis of redistricting in the nineties was nonetheless avoidable. Perhaps conditioned by the states' history of mistreatment of minority citizens, the CRD did an inadequate job of examining the intent of the state legislatures. Not every failure to maximize shows discriminatory intent. North Carolina produced its first plan that could elect a black congressperson this century, directed by African-American house leadership. The CRD's objection to that plan threw the legislature into turmoil and opened old wounds. The state was still litigating its redistricting plan in 1999. The Georgia legislature produced a one-seat plan that was objected to, then a two-seat plan that was objected to, then a three-seat plan that was precleared. But in subsequent court battles the state was restored to a one-seat plan, only after three African-American candidates had been elected under the three-seat plan. Amid great concern that at least two of them would lose in nonmajority-black districts, they have each scored impressive victories. The toll on the Georgia legislature and citizenry has been great. In Louisiana, as elsewhere, the legislature has had its deliberations interrupted by signals sent by the DOJ or allies purporting to speak for it. The CRD was still filing objections in Louisiana in 1996 to a plan that had gained court approval. In each of these states, legislators accused the CRD of engaging in partisan machinations in favor of the Republican Party. The damage has been considerable.

In North Carolina, Georgia, Louisiana, Texas, and other states, legislators came to believe that the Department wanted maximization. The states were reduced to "abject surrender [to the Department's] maximization agenda."[64]

CONCLUSION

The vast political implications of decennial redistricting are bound to attract intense interest from those with a stake in the proceedings. These groups include civil rights groups, the political parties, the states, and the voting rights issue network—including the Department, a network participant and decider of submissions.

Something different happened in the nineties' round of redistricting. The kind of politics surrounding the preclearance process changed. In prior rounds of redistricting, there was the kind of balance described by the interest group model. From its earliest period, the Department was wary of using its intrusive power to invalidate state enactments; it preferred to rely upon negotiation and voluntary compromise, and the efforts of minority organizations to mobilize registrants and voters. The states and civil rights groups asserted their concerns, with neither interest dominating. The parties always fight over redistricting, but the nineties introduced the Republicans as staunch advocates of proportional representation.

Once again the ways established after the 1965 enactment and nurtured through the years fell. In the nineties' round of redistricting, balance was sacrificed. The civil rights groups were triumphant; the state legislators felt bludgeoned into submission. The alternative plans that Dunne's objection letters posited were constructions of the public interest law firms and their peculiar comrades, the Republicans. Certainly, the Department has discretion in preclearance; its evenhanded historical approach confirms it. How an agency will exercise that discretion can be influenced by the constellation of interests groups that surround it. Dunne indicated that the Department would respect the positions of the advocates over those of the states, and that is what happened. In the nineties round, interest group politics was dead; client politics overwhelmed the states.

Justice Brennan described the CRD as the "champion of the interests of minority voters" under Section Five.[65] This is a powerful argument: no one disagrees that the Act was intended by Congress to fulfill the necessary function of assuring black suffrage. But the CRD also has a substantial degree of discretion in utilizing its powers. The statute is molded in compromise, including the Section Two proviso that attempts to assure the results test will not be used to require proportional representation. Congress surely must have contemplated that both state and civil rights interests would be considered in the preclearance process.

Given the history of disenfranchisement by the states and the need for federal intervention, the champion-of-minority-interests role has forceful appeal, but the Justice Department is also a part of the government entrusted with making quasi-judicial decisions on submissions, just as would the federal district court. There is an inherent conflict in the role of the Department as a surrogate for the federal district court and as an agency with a mandate to promote minority voting rights through litigation. This is a difficult balance under any circumstance.

There is little question that the Department has an indispensable role to play in securing minority voting rights. But Justice Brennan was wrong. The problem concerns the power arrangement the DOJ has been given, and how it uses its powers. An agency entrusted by statute with quasi-judicial powers and whose regulations require it to decide submissions as would a court should not have a client. There is a duty of fairness to all interested parties—to the states, as well as to the advocacy groups.

NOTES

1. Michael W. Dolan, "Political Influence on the Department of Justice: Are the Pressures Only External?," *Journal of Law and Politics* 9 (1993), 309.

2. James Q. Wilson, *Bureaucracy: What Government Agencies Do and Why They Do It* (New York: Basic Books, 1989), 76.

3. Hugh Davis Graham, "Voting Rights and the American Regulatory State," in Bernard Grofman and Chandler Davidson, eds., *Controversies in Minority Voting: The Voting Rights Act in Perspective* (Washington, DC: Brookings Institution, 1992), 190–193.

4. James Q. Wilson, ed., *The Politics of Regulation* (New York: Basic Books, 1980), 385–386.

5. Stephen L. Wasby, *Race Relations Litigation in an Age of Complexity* (Charlottesville, Va.: University Press of Virginia, 1995), 51–52, 63–67.

6. Gregory A. Caldeira, "Litigation, Lobbying and The Voting Rights Bar," in Grofman and Davidson, *Controversies in Minority Voting*, 246–250.

7. Caldeira, "Voting Rights Bar," 246–250.

8. Wasby, *Race Relations Litigation*, 21–23.

9. Wasby, *Race Relations Litigation*, 78–80, 88–89; Bernard Grofman, "Would Vince Lombardi Have Been Right If He Had Said: 'When It Comes to Redistricting, Race Isn't Everything, It's the Only Thing?'" *Cardozo Law Review* 14 (1993), 1237, 1255, note 72, 168.

10. Hugh Davis Graham, *The Civil Rights Era: Origins and Development of National Policy, 1960–1972* (New York: Oxford University Press, 1990); Michael Pertschuk, *Giant Killers* (New York: W.W. Norton, 1986).

11. Katharine Inglis Butler, "Affirmative Racial Gerrymandering: Rhetoric and Reality," *Cumberland Law Review* 26 (1995), 313, 353.

12. John R. Dunne, "Law Day USA," (Speech at Fordham Law School, 1 May 1990); John R. Dunne, telephone conversation with author, 20 January 1998; Thomas B. Edsall, "Sending Signal, Justice Rejects Mississippi Redistricting Plan," *Washington Post*, 3 July 1991; Beth Donovan, "Nation Watches as Texas Struggles to Create Minority Districts," *Congressional Quarterly*, 17 August 1991, 2293–2295, Southern Regional Council, "Substantial Gains Are Seen in State Legislative Redistricting," *Voting Rights Review* (Atlanta, Ga.: Southern Regional Council, fall 1991).

13. *Vera v Richards*, 861 F. Supp. 1304, 1315, 1324 (S.D. Tex. 1994).

14. *Smith v Beasley*, 946 F. Supp. 1174 (D. S.C. 1996).

15. Darren Hamilton, "Senate Reapportionment Committee Examines Second Black District," *Decatur-DeKalb News Era*, 15 August 1991; Frank LoMonte, "Senators Approve Overhaul," *Augusta Chronicle*, 13 August 1991; *Johnson v Miller*, 864 F. Supp. 1354, 1361 (S.D. Ga. 1994).

16. *Johnson v Miller*, 864 F. Supp. 1362 (citation omitted).

17. *Johnson v Miller*, 864 F. Supp. 1361–68.

18. *Johnson v Miller*, 864 F. Supp. 1367.

19. James Salzer, "Third Black District for Richmond Killed," *Augusta Herald*, 9 August 1991; *Johnson v Miller*, 864 F. Supp. 1368.

20. Thomas B. Edsall, "North Carolina Voting Plan Rejected," *Washington Post*, 20 December 1991; Jeremy Rabkin, *Judicial Compulsions: How Public Law Distorts Public Policy* (New York: Basic Books, 1989), 248; Wasby, *Race Relations Litigation*, 107.

21. "Republicans Paired Off in Remap Plan," *Monroe-West Monroe La. News Star*, 2 April 1992; Michael Barone and Grant Ujifusa, *Almanac of American Politics, 1994* (Washington, DC: National Journal, 1993), 545, 1209; Richard S. Dunham, "Johnson Wins Big for Blacks: Senator's Tactics Pay Off in Congressional District," *Times Herald*, 1 September 1991; *Vera v Richards*, 861 F. Supp. 1322.

22. James Madison, "Federalist 51," in Alexander Hamilton, James Madison, and John Jay, *The Federalist Papers* (New York: Mentor, 1961), 321.

23. Caldeira, "Litigation, Lobbying and the Voting Rights Bar," 273; Bernard Grofman and Chandler Davidson, "The Enforcement of the Voting Rights Act by the U.S. Department of Justice: Compromised Compliance? Republican Plot? or Great American Success Story?" note 17 (paper presented at the annual meeting of the American Political Science Association, 1992).

24. Huge Heclo, "Issue Networks and the Executive Establishment," in Anthony King, ed., *The New American Political System* (Washington, DC: American Enterprise Institute, 1978), 102–103; Deval L. Patrick, telephone conversation with author, 20 January 1998; Brenda Wright, telephone conversation with author, 13 January 1998.

25. Timothy G. O'Rourke, "The Voting Rights Paradox," in Grofman and Davidson, *Controversies in Minority Voting*, 112–113.

26. Grofman and Davidson, "The Enforcement of the Voting Rights Act by the U.S. Department of Justice," note 11.

27. For an early challenge to Thernstrom's book, see Pamela S. Karlan and Peyton McCrary, Book Review: "Without Fear and Without Research: Abigail Thernstrom on the Voting Rights Act," *Journal of Law and Politics* 4 (spring 1988), 751–77. A recent critique of Thernstrom is offered in J. Morgan Kousser, *Colorblind Injustice: Minority Voting Rights and the Undoing of the Second Reconstruction* (Chapel Hill, N.C.: University of North Carolina Press, 1998).

28. Graham, "Voting Rights and the American Regulatory State," 178.

29. Dunne telephone conversation; Patrick telephone conversation.

30. Kay Lehman Schlozman and John T. Tierney, *Organized Interests and American Democracy* (New York: Harper & Row, 1986), 363; *Growe v Emison*, 507 U.S. 25, 42 (1993).

31. Grofman and Davidson, "The Enforcement of the Voting Rights Act by the U.S. Department of Justice," 12 (citations omitted). See also Grofman, "Expert Witness Testimony and the Evolution of the Voting Rights Act" in Grofman and Davidson, *Controversies in Minority Voting*, 218–219.

32. "Common Cause Issue: Reapportionment and Redistricting," www.ccsi.com/^comcause/position/pp_rr.html; Samuel Issacharoff, "The Constitutional Contours of Race and Politics," in Dennis J. Hutchinson, David A. Strauss, and Geoffrey R. Stone, eds., *The Supreme Court Review 1995* (Chicago: University of Chicago Press, 1996), 67–68; James P. Turner, "The Fairest Cure We Have," *New York Times*, 16 April 1995.

33. Peyton McCrary and J. Gerald Hebert, "Keeping the Courts Honest: The Role of Historians as Expert Witnesses in Southern Voting Rights Cases," *Southern University Law Review* 16 (1989), *101*.

34. Caldeira, "Litigation, Lobbying, and the Voting Rights Bar," 239–242; Grofman and Davidson, "The Enforcement of the Voting Rights Act by the U.S. Department of Justice," 12.

35. *Vera v Richards*, 861 F. Supp. 1329–30.

36. *Johnson v Miller*, 864 F. Supp. 1388; *Johnson v DeGrandy*, 512 U.S. 997 (1994); *Vecinos De Barrio Uno v City of Holyoke*, 72 F.3d 973 (1st Cir., 1995).

37. Robinson O. Everett, telephone conversation with author, 23 November 1999; Douglas Markham, telephone conversation with author, 23 November 1999; Campaign for a Color-Blind America, www.equalrights.com.

38. Ward E.Y. Elliott, *The Rise of Guardian Democracy: The Supreme Court's Role in Voting Rights Disputes, 1845–1969* (Cambridge, Mass.: Harvard University Press, 1974), 228 and note 54; Kevin P. Phillips, *The Emerging Republican Majority* (Garden City, N.Y.: Anchor Books, 1970), 287.

39. Lee Atwater, "Altered States: Redistricting Law and Politics in the Nineties," *Journal of Law and Politics* 6 (1990), 661.

40. Richard E. Cohen and Carol Matlack, "All Purpose Loophole," *National Journal*, 9 December 1989; Carol Matlack, "Questioning Minority-Aid Software," *National Journal*, 23 June 1990; James P. Turner, interview with author, tape recording, Accokeek, Md., 27 August 1997; Richard E. Cohen and Carol Matlack, "For the Republic or for the Republicans?," *National Journal*, 9 December 1989, 2986; Wright telephone conversation; J. Gerald Hebert, telephone conversation with author, 7 January 1998.

41. *Joint Appendix* submitted to the Supreme Court in *Miller v Johnson*, Nos. 94-631, 94-797, 94-929 (1995).

42. Ellen Spears, "The Republicans Go to Court: A Review of Republican Legal Strategies on Minority Rights in the Area of the Voting Rights Act" (Atlanta, Ga.: Southern Regional Council, April 1992).

43. *Hays v State of Louisiana*, 839 F. Supp. 1188, 1205 (W.D. La., 1993).

44. Barone and Ujifusa, *Almanac of American Politics, 1994*, 969; David Simon, telephone conversation with author, 9 January 1998; Dunne telephone conversation; Turner interview.

45. Everett telephone conversation.

46. Abigail M. Thernstrom, "A Republican-Civil Rights Conspiracy," *Washington Post,* 23 September 1991; Bernard Grofman, "Race and Redistricting," *Washington Post,* 21 October 1991.

47. Issacharoff, "Constitutional Contours," 54–55 and note 37; Timothy G. O'Rourke, "*Shaw v Reno*: The Shape of Things to Come," *Rutgers Law Review*" 26 (1995), 723, 725–728; Grofman and Davidson, "The Enforcement of the Voting Rights Act by the U.S. Department of Justice"; Grofman, "Vince Lombardi," 1255, note 72; J. Gerald Hebert, quoted in Thomas Longoria, "Redefining Representation: The Politics of the Voting Rights Act of 1965" (Ph.D. diss., Texas A&M, 1994), 105; Turner interview.

48. David Lublin, *The Paradox of Representation: Racial Gerrymandering and Minority Rights in Congress* (Princeton, N.J.: Princeton University Press, 1997), 111–114.

49. Dunne telephone conversation.

50. Dunne telephone conversation; David Johnston, "Justice Department's Civil Rights Chief Is Sitting on Sidelines of Main Battle," *New York Times*, 10 January 1991.

51. Simon telephone conversation.

52. Turner, "Fairest Cure"; Turner interview.

53. Richard A. Bloom, "Justice's Dunne and the Voting Rights Act," *National Journal,* 4 May 1991.

54. Deval L. Patrick, "Remarks at the NAACP National Convention," Chicago, Ill. 12 July 1994.

55. Simon telephone conversation.

56. Simon telephone conversation.

57. John R. Dunne, "Remarks before the National Conference of State Legislators," Orlando, Fla., 13 August 1991; John R. Dunne, "Remarks before the Cardozo Law School Symposium on Redistricting Issues." New York, 6 April 1992.

58. Thomas B. Edsall, "North Carolina Voting Plan Rejected," *Washington Post*, 20 December 1991.

59. *Shaw v Hunt,* 861 F. Supp. 408, 484, note 16 (E.D. N.C. 1994); Dunne telephone conversation.

60. Barone and Ujifusa, *Almanac of American Politics, 1994*, 1265; *Vera v Richards*, 861 F. Supp. 1309.

61. *Shaw v Hunt,* 517 U.S. 912.

62. *Johnson v Miller,* 864 F. Supp. 1368; *Miller v Johnson*, 515 U.S. 924.

63. Simon telephone conversation.

64. *Miller v Johnson*, 515 U.S. 917; *Shaw v Hunt*, 517 U.S. 913.

65. *United Jewish Organizations v Carey*, 430 U.S. 144, 175 (1977) (Brennan, concurring).

6

From Compromised Compliance to Conquered Provinces

> I cannot help but believe that the inevitable effect of any such law which forces any one of the States to entreat federal authorities in faraway places for approval of local laws before they can become effective is to create the impression that the State or States treated in this way are little more than conquered provinces.
>
> Justice Hugo Black,
> dissenting in *South Carolina v Katzenbach*

Much of the debate in voting rights enforcement has concerned the appropriate level of federal intervention into state decision making in order to assure minority citizens a fair opportunity to participate in the political life of the nation. Liberal critics of the Department of Justice's enforcement program, at least prior to the nineties' redistricting cycle, have seen a modest federal response to an overwhelming problem. They argue that the Department's timid implementation has resulted in "compromised compliance." Conservative critics have long feared that the Department's intervention would render the states nothing more than "conquered provinces."

In the nineties the Department intervened forcefully to seek more minority districts. The Department was praised by many voting rights advocates, who commended it for using maximization plans developed by public interest law firms and the Republican Party as benchmarks for fair redistricting. State legislatures, though, chafed under the Department's demands for maximization and several states fought back before succumbing to the Department's overwhelming advantage: without preclearance the states could not hold elections. State legislatures approved plans, some of which were oddly configured, designed to meet the Department's objections and to protect incumbents. Frustrated Republicans and opponents of racial preference brought suit against these gerrymanders and the Supreme Court proclaimed that the Department had followed an unconstitutional maximization policy. Some critics contended not only that there was a maximization policy, but that it was wielded by a Republican administration seeking partisan advantage.

This chapter will weave much of my previous discussion into case studies of states that acted under DOJ pressure to maximize minority districts. The Department did not require maximization in each locale it reviewed; but on the congressional level there was a patterned and systematic effort to maximize. I will recount the machinations in North Carolina, Georgia, and Louisiana in some detail. The evidence shows that the Department did conquer the provinces in the nineties.

NORTH CAROLINA

The voting rights upheaval was triggered in North Carolina. Important members of the state legislative leadership including Speaker of the House Daniel Blue and House Congressional Redistricting Committee co-chair Representative Milton "Toby" Fitch, were African American. Under their leadership, North Carolina presented a congressional redistricting submission to the Department that included the first district in North Carolina that would favor a minority candidate since the last black Reconstruction congressman, George White, who retired in 1901. The ACLU and Republicans argued that two districts could have been created. The Department sided with the critics and objected to the plan.

On 28 August 1991 North Carolina submitted materials to the Department in support of Chapter 601 of the 1991 Session Laws, a plan for congressional redistricting. The explanatory materials consisted of a set of notebooks with tabs 27A-R and 28A-H, correlating with the required contents and supplemental contents set forth in the Department's regulations concerning redistricting submissions. Two copies of all maps were also provided.

The submission described North Carolina's redistricting process. In February 1991, the senate appointed a Redistricting Committee and Congressional Redistricting Subcommittee. The full committee consisted of twenty-four members, three of whom were African American, in addition to the chairman. The subcommittee consisted of twelve members, one of whom was African American. In February and March, Speaker Blue appointed a House Congressional Redistricting Committee chaired by Representative Fitch and two white co-chairs and consisting of twenty-five additional members, five of whom were black. The senate scheduled a total of six regional public meetings and the house scheduled nine such meetings. These meetings occurred in March and April of 1991. In March, the leadership of both houses developed a Joint Redistricting Computer and Public Access Plan that opened up availability to the public and provided training for legislators and staff. Senate chair Dennis Winner consulted with members of the North Carolina congressional delegation. On 17 April, joint criteria for congressional redistricting were adopted.

The committees agreed to accept submissions from the public up until 9 June 1991, but no plans were forthcoming. On 29 May 1991 the house and senate chairs presented the proposed Congressional Base Plan #1 at a joint committee meeting. It included one minority district. The senate members voted to present the plan at an upcoming public meeting. The next day, the house committee met and adopted its own version and rejected a two-majority-minority district plan proposal by Republican Representative David Balmer. On 18 June the senate committee adopted an amended plan and sent it to the full senate, which approved it on 20 June. The house approved its own plan, rejecting alternatives offered by Republican members. All minority members in the house backed the committee plan. A house-senate conference committee developed a compromise between the two versions that was approved by each house of the legislature. All minority members present in the senate and house voted in favor of the conference committee report. On 9 July 1991, Senate Bill 16 was passed as Chapter 601 of the 1991 Session Laws.

The state's submission pointed out that the congressional plan created the state's first majority-black district, while endowing eight of the other eleven districts with at least 15 percent African-American population; six of those were at least 20 percent black. The submission argued that these districts would permit African-American voters significant influence over the choice of candidates. The plan also attempted to keep precincts whole and to avoid dividing counties into more than two districts. Representative Balmer had offered two plans, Balmer 6.2 and Balmer 7.8. The state explained why the alternative plans were not suitable. Balmer 6.2 purported to include two minority districts, but the second one meandered over 200 miles and was just over 45 percent black; it depended on adding Native American voters to achieve majority-minority status, but the state provided election analyses showing that Native American voters do not cast ballots cohesively with blacks. Balmer 6.2 also decreased minority influence in four districts. No black or Native American legislator supported it. Balmer 7.8 was presented too late for legislative consideration, but the state noted that it too had a second district that was noncompact, making it difficult to campaign. Balmer 7.8 also decreased minority influence in three districts and gained no minority support.

The Republican Party and the ACLU both lodged protests with the Department. They argued that a second minority district could be drawn. The state replied that even under the North Carolina plan, minority voters would have an equal opportunity to elect candidates of their choice in the Fourth District, where African-American 1990 U.S. Senate candidate Harvey Gantt had received over 58 percent of the vote, despite a black voter registration of just over 16 percent. North Carolina argued that it had not packed blacks into districts as other plans proposed, but instead created the majority-minority district required by the Act and then enhanced minority voting strength by developing minority influence districts. The state also asserted that packing minority voters into two districts at the cost of influence districts might be interpreted as a discriminatory purpose, because moderate white Democrats represented black voters better than Republicans. In support, the state provided analyses of the Civil Rights Voting Record for the 100th Congress by the Leadership Conference on Civil Rights, which indicated greater responsiveness by North Carolina Democratic congressmen than Republicans.[1]

The ACLU, which represented a number of minority interest groups who wished to see a second minority district, stated that the African-American incumbents in the legislature had "supported and enabled the intentional discrimination . . . in the name of protecting the Democratic Party. . . . Rep. Fitch knew that additional black districts could be drawn, and deliberately chose not to draw them." The ACLU accused black legislators of siding with Democratic incumbents because white Democrats had helped them get legislation passed. The state replied that trying to enhance black influence by combining African-American legislators with white officials from minority influence districts does not constitute a discriminatory purpose, even if one disagrees with the strategy.[2]

Both racial and partisan politics were occurring. There was concern with incumbency. At a later trial, Representative Fitch conceded that he had hoped in his heart that Justice might intervene to require another black district. Yet he never wavered in his support for the legislative product. Speaker Blue and Representative Fitch had risen to their positions by doing the hard work of legislating and had earned the trust of their colleagues. Only four years after *Gingles* opened up the political process in North Carolina to elect more black state representatives, Blue had been chosen the first African-American Speaker in this century. As Tiare B. Smiley, an assistant attorney general responsible for representing the state remarked:

> Blue and Fitch were not token legislators. They had good coalitions; they had good working relationships. They are minorities, they know the history of the state and they wanted to see the election of more minorities. . . . Part of the importance to minorities of the Voting Rights Act was getting their foot in the door so that the white public would see . . . that they could legislate and operate government in the same way as white legislators, and that whites could be comfortable in voting for blacks.
>
> Toby Fitch and Dan Blue were respected legislators. They had coalitions with white legislators and they did not mind protecting certain legislators who they felt had done well by them and worked with them, and that's politics. . . . They kept the trust of the white Democrats because they were willing to compromise. And [they] fought hard with Justice for the plan.[3]

During the time leading up to the deadline for the Department to decide whether to preclear or object, the Republicans in the state legislature, North Carolina Republican Party, and Republican National Committee (RNC) attempted to convince the Department to object to Chapter 601. The RNC had an attorney on retainer to assist with redistricting, and the North Carolina Republican Party employed his services as well. The attorney arranged a meeting in Washington with Voting Section staff and attorneys. The leader of the Republican Caucus, Representative Arthur Pope, encouraged caucus members to write their objections to the Department. Pope expressed the Republicans' aim: "The purpose was to assign voters, by race, to two black majority districts in order to have the consequences of electing African-Americans to congress."[4]

The North Carolina plan was thus under assault from a strange alliance of the Republican Party and the ACLU. The effort concentrated on the challengers' strengths. The ACLU and North Carolina minorities had a relationship with Voting Section staffers; the Republicans were more comfortable with the party appointees at the head of the Civil Rights Division. Both met with Justice Department officials. Dunne was available to meet with all parties where circumstances warranted.

On 17 December 1991, leading North Carolina legislators met with Justice Department officials, including Dunne. Representative Fitch later testified that nothing was said about increasing the number of black congressional districts to comport with the percentage of North Carolina's black citizens. In fact, Representative Fitch left the meeting believing that the plan would be precleared. However, other attendees recall Dunne raising the issue of proportionality, and the courts credited this testimony.[5] Senator Dennis Winner recalled:

> Most of it had to do with the congressional plan. And Mr. Dunne did most of the talking . . . and most of it got down to sort of that we ought to have a quota system with respect to minority seats. You had 22 percent blacks in this state. Therefore, you ought to have as close to that as you could have of congressional districts.
>
> I think his substance was really that you had—if you had 22 percent blacks in North Carolina, then you ought to have 22 percent minority congressional seats. Whatever shape didn't matter.[6]

Gerry Cohen, the legislature's chief redistricting draftsman, had a similar recollection. He testified that Dunne had posed as a question that since North Carolina had about 23 or 24 percent black population, "Don't you think it would be more fair to have two [congressional districts]?" The accounts of Cohen and Winner seem in accord with the recollection of Dunne, who indicates that he was, in general, concerned with the number of representatives as reflective of population.[7]

On 18 December 1991, the Department of Justice sent out an objection letter to the North Carolina house, senate, and congressional redistricting plans. The Department indicated that it would find objectionable any attempt to protect incumbents at the expense of a possible minority seat. The letter found that "the district boundary lines in the south-central to southeastern part of the state appear to minimize minority voting strength given the significant minority population in this area of the state. In general, it appears that the state chose not to give effect to black and Native American voting strength in this area." The letter also contended that the state was "well aware" of minority interest in another seat and cognizant of alternative plans that might have been adopted, including alternatives supported by the NAACP and the ACLU. These plans might have given minorities "an opportunity to elect a second member of their choice to office" but were apparently dismissed for "pretextual reasons." [8] The letter was premised upon the notion that failure to maximize is consonant with discriminatory purpose.

There were immediate consequences to Dunne's objection letter. North Carolina had to pass a new plan, and everyone understood it had better include two minority districts. Partisan tension grew. Racial conflict grew. The *Washington Post* reported that "the ruling assaults a biracial alliance in the state Democratic Party that in 1990 resulted in the election of Daniel T. Blue Jr. as the first black speaker of the state house since Reconstruction." The *Post* reported a bitter exchange in which white ACLU attorney Kathleen Wilde accused the North Carolina Legislative Black Caucus of having "sold out." Representative Fitch retorted that "I've been black all my life, I've fought for black causes, and I don't need some white woman from Atlanta telling me what to do."[9] Herein lies an irony of the Department's enforcement. Many of the black legislators in North Carolina owed their positions to past Voting Rights Act enforcement actions, but the Department was now telling them that they could not be trusted to exercise their legislative powers.

The legislature went back to work on a two-seat plan, but the leadership did not give up on its design to protect incumbents, and it did not draw the second district where the Department had suggested, in the south-central to southeastern part of the state.

Senator Winner later explained that he had understood the objection as a partisan shot from the Bush administration, which hoped that a second minority district would help Republicans by draining black Democratic voters from moderate Democratic districts. This worry (and Senator Winner admitted he was relying upon conjecture) was widespread as the second North Carolina plan was being developed. John D. Merritt, an aide to Democratic Congressman Charlie Rose who was endangered by the Balmer plans, explained his view of the two-seat Republican plan: "It would have carved it [Representative Rose's district] into pieces, as well as Mr. Hefner's [another Democratic congressman]." Merritt saw the plan "As a premeditated attempt to affect his [Rose's] election . . . they wanted to affect the election prospects of Mr. Hefner and Mr. Rose."[10]

The leadership's concern that incumbent Democrats be protected and the need for a second minority district presented an opportunity for the state to match its challengers' ingenious use of computer technology. The district court that considered the second plan passed by the legislature took note of the "dramatic new capabilities" that permitted manipulation of total population and voting-age population—all down to the census-block level. In addition, North Carolina merged election statistics and voter registration data into its software package. These materials could be moved instantaneously on or off district maps—as Ms. Smiley indicates, you could simply "mouse click" or "lasso" census blocks into districts.[11]

In North Carolina, mapmakers worked with approximately 229,000 census blocks statewide. In addition to the demographic and geographic information at the census-block level provided by the TIGER and census files, North Carolina's legislative staff included precinct election results, available from the database, for a number of recent elections. Digital mapping capability provided for quick call-up and visual display of demographic and statistical data along with geographic characteristics such as highways, streets, rivers, and railroads, as well as existing political boundaries. The district court in *Shaw v Hunt* found that the technology permitted redistricters to draw lines meeting certain criteria but with far more irregular shapes than had been possible when technicians had been limited to existing political boundaries. Thus, requests for special treatment or small shifts of certain types of voters were possible. Since census-block boundaries were either existing political lines or readily identifiable physical features, it was much easier to split existing governmental units such as counties or precincts to satisfy demands of numbers, incumbency protection, or racial characteristics.[12]

The legislature considered a number of plans, including several proposed by Representative Balmer. During 1991, he had offered a plan titled Balmer 8.1 that created a second district by linking black neighborhoods in a narrow band that ran throughout the Piedmont region. It had been dismissed by the legislature originally, but now Democratic redistricters saw it as a way to draw a second African-American district and preserve incumbents. John Merritt, the aide to Congressman Rose, saw the potential as did Mary Peeler, executive director of the North Carolina NAACP. More public meetings were held, and Ms. Peeler presented a plan similar to Balmer 8.1. More Republican plans were considered and rejected. Each house eventually adopted plans based upon the Merritt/Peeler design. All black legislators again supported the leadership's plan and rejected those of the Republicans. Representative Fitch spoke in favor of the plan, but another Democratic legislator complained that the bill was necessary because of political decisions made at the Justice Department. Republican Arthur Pope, angry that GOP tactics had failed to produce advantageous districts, argued that the admittedly ugly map was not the fault of the Department or the Voting Rights Act but of "pure partisan gerrymandering." On the senate floor, Senator Winner again stated that Dunne had suggested proportional representation for partisan reasons: "Quotas. Here is the Bush administration who [*sic*] from the very beginning has been screaming about quotas. When it is to their advantage so they can elect some Republican congressmen, all of a sudden they are for quotas."[13]

The plan was ratified as Chapter 7 of the 1991 Extra Session. This plan strengthened District One as a minority district; the Department had already approved it. It also increased black voting power in District Four, which the state contended was an influence district in which blacks might elect a candidate of their choice. And it created a new District Twelve as a majority-minority seat—the ungainly district later described by the Supreme Court as the "I-85" district in *Shaw v Reno* and struck down by the Court in *Shaw v Hunt*. It was an irony that the legislature was able to manipulate the Republican Balmer 8.1 offering into a plan that created two black districts and protected Democratic incumbents. The CRD approved the plan by letter dated 6 February 1992.[14]

Speaker Blue issued an explanatory editorial to the state's voters. He admitted the map was ugly but argued it was the only way to satisfy the DOJ. Speaker Blue still contended that the state's black population was not compact enough to draw two districts. He acknowledged that the Voting Rights Act protects African-American voters but argued that it does not require stringing black voters together in a ribbon-like district. Yet he asserted that because of the Department's partisan politics, Chapter 7 was the best the legislature could do.[15]

Republicans at first sued on grounds of partisan gerrymandering, but that suit, *Pope v Blue*, was dismissed. Individual voters then filed suit under the leadership of Duke University School of Law professor Robinson O. Everett, claiming to have been harmed because the state separated voters by race in violation of the Equal Protection Clause of the Fourteenth Amendment. The plaintiffs were white Republicans, though they did not identify themselves as such in the court pleadings.[16]

The three-judge federal district court in North Carolina originally dismissed the plaintiffs' Equal Protection claim against the state and federal defendants.[17] The case was appealed to the Supreme Court and was decided as *Shaw v Reno*, the case that was to usher in the transformation of redistricting law. Writing for the Court, Justice O'Connor described the contours of the challenged Twelfth Congressional District:

> It is approximately 160 miles long and, for much of its length, no wider than the I-85 corridor. It winds in snake-like fashion through tobacco country, financial centers, and manufacturing areas "until it gobbles in enough enclaves of black neighborhoods." Northbound and southbound drivers on I-85 sometimes find themselves in separate districts in one county, only to "trade" districts when they enter the next county. Of the 10 counties through which District 12 passes, five are cut into three different districts; even towns are divided. At one point the district remains contiguous only because it intersects at a single point with two other districts before crossing over them. One state legislator has remarked that "[i]f you drove down the interstate with both car doors open, you'd kill most of the people in the district."[18]

The Court identified two separate representational harms in such racial gerrymandering. First, it stated that such districting "bears an uncomfortable resemblance to political apartheid. It reinforces the perception that members of the same racial group—regardless of their age, education, economic status, or the community in which they live—think alike, share the same political interests, and will prefer the same candidate at the polls." The second message that concerned the Court was that an obvious racial gerrymander would encourage elected officials to "believe their primary obligation is to represent only the members of that group, rather than the constituency as a whole. This is altogether antithetical to our system of representative democracy."[19]

The Court therefore held that the plaintiffs could proceed to trial in the district court on their claim that Chapter 7 violated the Equal Protection Clause by segregating by race. As racial classifications require strict scrutiny, the lower court would be required to find whether the gerrymander was narrowly tailored to further a compelling state interest.

The case returned to the district court. The court found that District Twelve did constitute a racial gerrymander but that it passed strict scrutiny.[20] The ruling was again appealed to the Supreme Court.

The Clinton Justice Department filed a brief with the Supreme Court in support of the state appellees, arguing that the Twelfth Congressional District met the strict scrutiny test. By the time of the *Hunt* filing, however, the case law had further matured by the Supreme Court's holding in *Miller v Johnson* that a racial gerrymander could be proven not only by bizarre shape but by direct proof of racial motivation. The Court in *Miller* largely approved a lower court's finding that the Department had indulged in a campaign to coerce Georgia to maximize minority districts. The Department had been arguing, in *Miller*, in *Hays v Louisiana*, and in the district court proceedings in *Hunt*, that only a facially bizarre district should be subject to Equal Protection analysis.

In response to these new difficulties, the Department shifted its arguments. There was no longer any reference to majority-minority districts. Instead, the Department argued that North Carolina had created "black opportunity districts," defined as "a district in which the relevant minority group has a meaningful opportunity to elect the representative of its choice, despite racial discrimination in voting, either because the group constitutes a voting majority in the district or because it constitutes a sizable minority that can elect its preferred candidate because some non-minority voters will be willing to vote for the minority-preferred candidate."[21]

Although the Department suggested that the North Carolina legislature in 1991 and 1992 had debated how many black opportunity districts to create, the concept was apparently only given birth in the Department's October 1995 *Hunt* brief. The elements suggested had no existing coherence in the Act or case law. A "meaningful opportunity to elect the representative of its choice" seems to substitute for Section Two's equal "opportunity . . . to participate in the political process and to elect representatives of their choice." "Racial discrimination in voting" is an elastic concept, perhaps grounded in *Gingles* racially polarized voting conditions, but permitting even more flexibility. The ability to elect as a majority or as a sizable minority able to form coalitions seems to contravene the Court's *Voinovich* ruling, where it held that the ability to form coalitions would indicate the absence of white racial bloc voting. In any case, the "opportunity district" concept was an invention of the Department, offered without precedential authority.

The Department also asserted that North Carolina had a compelling state interest in drawing the opportunity districts in order to comply with Section Two and Section Five. In its argument that District Twelve was narrowly tailored, the Department ran head-on into the contorted landscape of the district. The brief argued that one permissible response to a finding of the presence of the *Gingles* preconditions "is to draw geographically compact minority opportunity districts that the district court used in its *Gingles* analysis. But neither *Gingles* nor the Voting Rights Act compels that specific remedy. So long as the State adopts a plan that provides an equal opportunity to elect representatives of choice, Section Two obligations are satisfied."[22] In other words, virtual representation. Moreover, the Department argued, the state's plan did include a sizable portion of the concentrations of black voters whose presence would have given rise to a Section Two claim. The Department thus accepted the concept, developed by the ACLU, LDF, and other voting rights-issue network advocates, of functional compactness.

The Supreme Court rejected the arguments. The Court found that the Twelfth District was not compelled by a correct reading of Section Five nor was it a remedy narrowly tailored to respond to the state's concern with Section Two liability. The Court also found that District Twelve could not be a response to a Section Two violation, because it could not conceivably be described as "geographically compact." It noted that the Department's objection letter had assailed the state for offering pretextual reasons for not drawing a second minority district, but the Court found that the state's explanations were adequate. The Court stated: "It appears that the Justice Department was pursuing in North Carolina the same policy of maximizing the number of majority-black districts that it pursued in Georgia."[23]

Hunt thus responded to some of the major themes of the Department's advocacy in voting cases throughout the Bush and Clinton administrations. The Court found that the Voting Rights Act protects the right of individuals to an undiluted vote, not the right of a group to proportional representation. The Act guarantees opportunity, not results. One must pay attention to the words of the statute and the precedent; advocates may not simply substitute "functional compactness" or "opportunity districts."

The North Carolina case illuminates these legal theories as important components of maximization advocacy.

GEORGIA

In Georgia, the Department's intervention was far more aggressive than it had been in North Carolina. The relationship among the Department, advocates, and the state was set forth in a 1994 opinion entitled *Johnson v Miller* by the United States District Court for the Southern District of Georgia, decided after *Shaw v Reno*. Under *Shaw* the proponents of Georgia's max-black plan were left with several alternative defenses. They could argue that the plan was not a racial gerrymander, because it was not bizarre in shape and that only shape, and not direct evidence of legislative intent, was important. If the plan were found to be a racial gerrymander, the defense would have to pass strict scrutiny: to show that the plan was narrowly tailored to serve a compelling state interest.

Following the 1990 census, Georgia was entitled to eleven congressional seats, an increase of one. Georgia had been forced by a Department of Justice objection after its 1980 redistricting to create the state's first majority-minority district.[24] In February of 1991 the house and senate went to work setting redistricting guidelines, including requirements of public hearings and permission for parties outside of the legislature to submit plans. Redistricting criteria included constitutional one-person, one-vote considerations, contiguity, following precinct lines where possible, and compliance with Sections Two and Five. Secondary considerations included preserving political subdivisions and existing districts and avoiding races between incumbents.

The legal advocacy group promoting a maximization plan before the state legislature was the ACLU, whose attorney Kathleen Wilde represented the Georgia Legislative Black Caucus, including representatives Tyrone Brooks and Cynthia McKinney. Unlike the situation in North Carolina, the ACLU's plans had strong support among minority Georgia legislators. There were, however, significant disagreements in the Black Caucus concerning whether to back a two- or three-seat plan. As in North Carolina, some African-American legislators thought it more important to protect helpful white Democrats than to maximize.[25]

Wilde had drawn a three-seat "max-black" plan and presented it to the Georgia Legislative Black Caucus as early as 26–27 July 1991. Representatives Brooks and McKinney announced the plan at a press conference on 31 July. The Georgia legislature undertook redistricting in late August of 1991 and submitted a congressional plan on 1 October. The plan contained two majority-minority districts and a third district where African Americans could be expected to wield substantial influence. Representative Brooks not only promoted the three-seat plan; he indicated that the Department would require it:

> This plan [the first redistricting proposal to be submitted to the DOJ by the General Assembly] does not come close to the criteria outlined by the Attorney General last summer, when he specifically told the states covered by the Act that wherever possible, you must draw majority black districts, wherever possible.

> . . . Obviously, it's possible to draw three; those of us who have been working on the max plan for over a year have really not been concerned about anything other than maximizing our voting strength.
>
> We've not been really concerned about territory; we've not been concerned about voter registration numbers, we've been concerned about population, and black voting population. When you start playing games with lines and numbers on voter registration and—all of these other things that really don't matter, you are just simply wasting time. . . .
>
> [I]t's not really the appearance of the district; it's the content of the district.[26]

The Georgia legislature was certainly aware of reinvigorated enforcement by the Department. In August of 1990, the Division had filed a Section Two suit against the state, attempting to invalidate Georgia's majority vote requirement as discriminatory against African-American candidates. The media had reported Department objections in Mississippi, Louisiana, Virginia, and New York City that seemed to indicate that jurisdictions must create all possible minority districts. Representative Brooks pushed the idea that the maximization plan was in accord with Department policy. Key state legislators later testified to attending a meeting in Baltimore at which Dunne had spoken and coming away with the impression that they must create at least two majority-minority districts.[27]

On 30 October Wilde forwarded a Comment Under Section Five to the Department, arguing that the congressional plan had a discriminatory purpose and was also a clear violation of Section Two's results test. (The letter also urged the Department to object to Georgia's state house and senate submissions.) Republican activists filed a comment on 25 October, supplemented by materials arguing that racially polarized voting was common in Georgia. The district court found that beginning in October of 1991 and continuing until preclearance of Georgia's third plan in April of 1992, Wilde and Voting Section staff attorneys Keith Borders and Thomas Armstrong joined together to push maximization. The ACLU enjoyed a direct line to the Voting Section decision makers, while the state's attorney general was nearly shut out. Although Armstrong testified that the Wilde max-black plan was but one of many alternatives considered, the court gave his account little credit and found that the ACLU districting scheme drove the Division's decision making throughout the process of objections to two plans and final preclearance of a third.[28]

On 21 January 1992 the Department objected to Georgia's congressional plan in a letter signed by John Dunne. He declined preclearance because of a concern that the legislative leadership had decided to "limit" black voting strength to two seats. The plan did not "recognize" black voting strength in southwest Georgia. As the ACLU comment letter made clear, the key to drawing a third African-American district was to move Bibb County blacks out of Wilde's second black district into the southwest district, then extend her second black district down to Savannah to pick up African-American voters there. A version of that plan would ultimately gain preclearance. The court found that "Ms. Wilde's triumph of demographic manipulation became DOJ's guiding light."[29]

The Department's 21 January letter found that Georgia had not sustained its burden to show that the plan did not have a discriminatory purpose or effect. However, the court found no evidence that any legislator, particularly the redistricting chairmen, had any intent to discriminate on the basis of race. The Senate Reapportionment Committee chair, Senator Eugene Walker, was African American. He favored a two-seat plan because the max-black plan packed African Americans into three districts, depriving them of influence in the other eight districts. The ACLU letter implied that Senator Walker's position indicated a discriminatory purpose. An anonymous commenter to the Department—one of those the district court termed "secret agents"—stated that Senator Walker was a "quintessential Uncle Tom." Either these remarks or some other suggestion so poisoned the atmosphere that following an initial meeting with Voting Section line attorneys, Senator Walker refused to attend further meetings with Voting Section staff.[30]

Following the rejection of its first plan, the legislature returned for a second round of congressional redistricting. The court found that despite DOJ's disclaimers of any influence over line drawing, the legislators understood that Voting Section suggestions were "implicit commands." The senate passed a three-seat plan, dropping the Eleventh District down to Savannah as the Wilde max-black plan required, but the house refused to go along. A two-seat plan was passed, with Fifth and Eleventh Districts with black voting-age population close to 60 percent and a Second District with black voting strength increased to 45 percent. The General Assembly submitted the plan to the Voting Section on 3 March 1992.

The Department objected again despite, as the court found, the fact that the second plan had substantially addressed the problems outlined in Dunne's first objection letter. The second objection letter complained that the revised Second District still excluded large black populations in Bibb County. The court remarked that the Department was aware that the only way to include Bibb in the Second and keep the Eleventh majority black was to extend the Eleventh to Savannah—the key to Wilde's max-black plan. Georgia's attorney general had attempted to explain the undesirability of the Savannah extension in the state's second submission. The attorney general argued that the extension would require a candidate to run in four media markets, which might disadvantage a minority candidate. Also, the Second District still would be no more than an influence district, because of historically low black voter registration. Moreover, the Second District would be wildly noncompact. The Department rejected the state's rationale.

When the legislature returned for a third attempt at congressional redistricting, it did so with the clear understanding that only the three-seat max-black plan would be precleared. The plan was passed, with amendments to account for the other eight districts. The court found that the plan bore all the imprints of the Department's commands. Narrow land bridges were used to connect geographically distant black populations. The plan split twenty-six counties, twenty-three more than the existing plan. "The dense population centers of the approved Eleventh District were all majority-black, all at the periphery of the district, and in the case of Atlanta, Augusta and Savannah, all tied to a sparsely populated rural core by even less populated land bridges. Extending from Atlanta to the Atlantic, the Eleventh covered 6,784.2 square miles, splitting eight counties and five municipalities along the way." The Department approved, but Georgia's assistant attorney general barely escaped with the preclearance letter in hand because Voting Section attorney Borders was still heeding fax transmissions from Wilde and Representative Brooks criticizing the plan. Representative Brooks exulted: "We got 98 percent of what we were fighting for." [31]

The court criticized the Department for the manner in which it used third-party plans as benchmarks for alternative maximization plans. The Department used the suggestion of alternative plans to conclude that Georgia's failure to adopt a max-black plan was a pretext for discriminatory purpose. The court recognized that while the Georgia legislature had to be cognizant of the interests of all Georgians and numerous racial, political, economic, and personal concerns, the authors of the max-black plan were only focused upon creating racial districts. This is confirmed in the ACLU's comment to the Department: it discusses no issue other than maximization, and it even acknowledges that the original Wilde plan presented by Representative McKinney drew only the three black districts, not the remaining eight.[32] With such a plan as a benchmark, adoption of some form of max-black was inevitable.

The court went on to make findings as to whether Georgia had created an intentional racial gerrymander. It held that the land bridges used to connect black communities were indirect evidence of racial purpose. The court also found direct evidence that the Department had spent months demanding race-based revisions and Georgia had complied out of confessedly racial motivations. The search for African-American voters was literally block by block; the state's redistricting technician started with the "blackest" precincts first, then worked back. Moreover, the court found that the *Gingles* conditions of compactness and racial bloc voting were not in evidence. No compelling state interest was served by the racial gerrymander. The court stated that "proportional representation," "maximization" or "quotas" are not required by Section Five. It declared Georgia's Eleventh District unconstitutional in violation of the Equal Protection Clause of the Fourteenth Amendment.[33]

The district court's decision was appealed to the Supreme Court. The Department argued that the state should be permitted to treat racial minorities as it would other interest groups seeking favor in the redistricting process.[34] The DOJ never acknowledged, however, that other interest groups may not appeal to—or ally themselves with—a federal department with the power to negate state election legislation. There was simply no desire on the part of the Georgia General Assembly to create three minority districts, absent federal coercion.

The Department further argued that the Eleventh was not bizarre and thus the representational harms identified by *Shaw*—racial stereotyping and racial representation—would not be apparent to the citizenry. The brief attempted to explain the district's shape in terms of political, not racial interests. The Department also contended that only evidence of bizarre shape should be given Fourteenth Amendment consideration; direct evidence of intent should not be entertained in the strict scrutiny analysis. Its brief contended that if strict scrutiny should apply, the state had a compelling interest in complying with the Department's Section Five objection as an administrative finding of discrimination. The Department asserted that the state also had a compelling interest in avoiding a Section Two suit—although Georgia did not make that argument itself. The Department denied it had a maximization policy or that anyone (such as Representative Brooks) was authorized to suggest so. Even if the plan was somewhat misshapen, the DOJ's brief reasoned, only "reasonably compact" districts were required to satisfy *Gingles*. Contrary to the lower court's finding of a reasonable degree of crossover voting, the Department contended that racially polarized voting existed in amounts sufficient to meet the *Gingles* preconditions and give the state an independent reason for remediation. The United States argued that racially polarized voting virtually precludes a black candidate from winning in a predominantly white Georgia district.[35]

The Supreme Court rejected the arguments of the Department and other appellants. It found that, as in other Equal Protection contexts, direct proof of racial motivation is powerful evidence of state classification by race. The plaintiff's burden is to show that race was the predominant factor motivating the legislature to place voters of a certain race into a district. The Court approved the lower court's finding that the Department required total capitulation from Georgia. It would not accept the Department's objection itself as providing a compelling state interest. To do so would be to surrender to the executive branch the judiciary's role in enforcing constitutional limits on race-based official action. Adherence to traditional districting principles rather than maximization does not constitute a discriminatory purpose. The Court found that government policy was driven by the goal of maximization.[36]

The Supreme Court sent the case back to the district court. On 1 December 1995, the court found that District Two was also unconstitutional as a racial gerrymander. The General Assembly was unable to agree upon a congressional plan, so the district court drew its own plan for the 1996 elections, with only one majority-black district. The court admitted conflicting evidence on the degree of polarization in Georgia voting but concluded that bloc voting exists, although "not in alarming quantities." Therefore, the second and third *Gingles* preconditions could not be met.[37]

The district court's decision was again appealed. The United States argued that the finding that District Two was unconstitutional was wrong, because it met the *Gingles* standards. Here, as elsewhere, the Department attempted to diminish the requirement of geographical compactness, arguing instead for the adequacy of a "sufficiently large and compact" minority community (although the Department argued alternatively for geographical compactness). Moreover, the Department asserted that racially polarized voting would likely foreclose a black from winning in the district court's new Fourth, Tenth, and Eleventh Districts, which were drawn as influence districts.[38]

In response, the appellees provided more evidence that the legislature had never desired to draw even a second district. That decision was driven by the belief (obviously correct) that the Department would not preclear a plan that maintained only one black district. Representative Sonny Dixon testified to hearing Dunne speak in Baltimore and concluded "we were threatened [and] used as an illustration by Mr. Dunne of [all] that was evil in redistricting." Robert Hanner, chair of the House Reapportionment Committee, left Baltimore convinced a second district would be necessary. Linda Meggers, legislative redistricting technician, testified that "The initial response in our office was that's ridiculous. . . . It was said that it doesn't make any sense and I said maybe not, but . . . we may get into trouble with the Justice Department if we don't draw it." The house speaker testified that the initial plan had been adopted on a perception of the "direction and instructions of the Justice Department." The Department responded that Dunne's remarks had simply pointed out the problems of Georgia and other states in the 1980s round of redistricting.[39] In fact, the Department might have been justified in portraying Georgia as emblematic of the evils of redistricting. In both the 1970s and 1980s the state had had its plans denied preclearance for discriminatory purpose, and with good reason. In the 1980s, the chair of the House Reapportionment Committee made particularly heinous racial comments. Nonetheless, my review of Dunne's recorded Baltimore remarks indicates nothing threatening about them.

The Supreme Court again upheld the lower court. The Department produced expert witnesses to argue that African-American candidates could not win in nonmajority-black districts in Georgia. The Supreme Court approved the lower court's finding of "a general willingness of white voters to vote for black candidates." It also noted that the 1996 election, in which all three black Georgia incumbents had been returned to office, portrayed "the weakness of the Justice Department's methodology of calculating the likelihood of a black-preferred candidate winning based on strict racial percentages."[40] That finding served as an indication that the efforts of the voting rights issue network, which had been so influential in cases such as *Gingles*, is attracting continued judicial skepticism. The Supreme Court is showing a willingness to respect and defer to state experts, especially legislators and staff presumed to have intimate practical knowledge of local circumstances.

Finally, damage was done to the Division's credibility by the conduct and testimony of Voting Section careerists. The district court was explicit about the lack of confidence it could place in their testimony: "The Court finds [Voting Section attorneys] Borders' and Armstrong's professed amnesia less than credible." A singular finding of untrustworthiness by a court, especially a Southern court, might be troubling but not a grievous wound; however, this unfortunate finding is consonant with one made by a district court in South Carolina, where the court harshly criticized CRD professionals for "the apparent epidemic of amnesia that has dimmed the memory of many DOJ attorneys who were involved with South Carolina's efforts to produce a [state legislative] reapportionment plan that would pass preclearance." There may be real consequences for the Division in such findings. The Department's integrity has always been a factor in the respect accorded it by the courts. While some express confidence that the Department can withstand the disparagement, others worry that the criticisms may make the Division reticent to push new theories in voting rights cases.[41]

LOUISIANA

The Department was also rebuked for its intervention in Louisiana by a federal district court in that state. Advocates for maximization of congressional districts implied a direct line to the Department, which they charged would only preclear a max-plan. Personal interests of local politicians gave spice to the stew: the African-American chair of the Senate and Governmental Affairs Committee (which had responsibility for redistricting) and another state senator who served as chair of the Louisiana Legislative Black Caucus each hoped to draw a district that would serve his own aspirations. The Clinton administration's Civil Rights Division chief interjected the Division directly into the legislative redistricting deliberations—after the Department had received a judicial warning concerning federal intervention.

The 1990 census cost Louisiana one of its eight congressional seats. The state already had one majority-minority seat, centered in New Orleans. Louisiana's congressional districts had been traditionally fashioned on the state's eight-member Board of Elementary and Secondary Education (BESE) districts. When the Department objected to the state's redistricting for the BESE districts in 1991 for failure to include a second African-American district, many political observers regarded the action as an indication that the Department would not preclear any congressional plan that did not include two majority-minority districts.

The interpretation of the BESE objection was discussed at a 16 March 1991 joint meeting of the House and Senate Governmental Affairs Committees, entrusted with undertaking redistricting. The Department rejected the BESE plan because, although it deviated only slightly from the 1980s plan that had been precleared, an available alternative would have created a second black district. A new plan being presented at the hearing would include two such districts. Senate chair Cleo Fields explained that the committee had come up with a two-seat plan in order to satisfy the Department's concern that black voting strength not be diluted. The state senate's redistricting technician Glenn Koepp explained how the new BESE plan had been developed: "it's drawn for the specific purpose of picking up black communities and leaving out whites."[42]

Given the BESE experience, Chairman Fields announced that his instruction to the staff was to draw congressional districts that would likely gain Department approval and that "simply meant by the creation of two minority districts." When asked by a senator if criteria such as contiguity and community of interest still applied, Koepp answered that the Department had decided that Louisiana blacks constituted a community of interest, no matter where they resided. Senator Fields emphasized the point in a colloquy with house staffer Patricia Lowery. She indicated that she had reviewed the recently precleared North Carolina plan, and it appeared that the Department was not concerned with splitting county lines. Senator Fields stated that if Louisiana could draw two districts, it must, notwithstanding other considerations.[43]

The state's newspapers kept up coverage of the political battle. In late March it was reported that almost all of the legislature's focus was upon two minority districts, even though it was apparent that parishes would have to be split. The *Alexandria Daily Town Talk* reported suspicions that the Bush administration would require two minority seats in order to assist Republicans. On 1 April a Baton Rouge paper described discontent on the committee among senators who felt that Senator Fields was trying to railroad through a plan to serve his own ambitions. The paper reported that Fields had been to Washington several times to lobby the Department for a second black district. Stung by the criticism, Fields withdrew his plan but stated that the Department might still require that his design be adopted.[44] (A version of Fields's plan was ultimately passed, carried by a legislative ally.) The real conflict was shaping up as one between the

Fields proposal that would concentrate African-American votes in his base of southern Louisiana and a proposal by Legislative Black Caucus chair Senator C.D. Jones that would favor his northeast Louisiana appeal.

It was acknowledged that the outcome of the Fields-Jones battle would drive the configurations of the other districts. The state had other concerns, as well. One problem was that a two-seat bill before the senate would so weaken an incumbent Democrat that it might appear to be an open invitation for former Ku Klux Klan leader David Duke to abandon his presidential campaign and run in the district. Another editorial complained that Fort Polk had been removed from the Fourth District home of Republican Congressman Jim McCrery, the state's lone member of the influential House Armed Services Committee.[45]

Despite these and other incumbency concerns, the senate passed a two district majority-minority plan on 30 April. Senator Jones reported he received a call from the Voting Section immediately after the vote, seeking an update. Several days later the state house passed a one-seat plan, though some members argued that the Department would never preclear. Representative Emile "Pepi" Bruneau stated that the senate plan had a horrible effect on everybody, but that based upon his experience with the Department, opposition to a two-seat plan would be futile. Finally, the house saw the writing on the wall and created a two-seat congressional plan. The house and senate plans were reconciled and Governor Edwin Edwards signed a two-seat plan, Act 42, into law on 1 June 1992. Glenn Koepp later described how Act 42 had been drawn: he had "literally gone through every little town, city or village, and if it had more than two precincts, . . . segregate[d] the district by race."[46]

The state's congressional plan was challenged in federal district court in Louisiana on grounds similar to those at issue in *Shaw v Reno.* The court found that the legislature's intent was to create a racial gerrymander and thus Act 42 was subject to strict scrutiny. The judges assumed for the sake of argument that Louisiana had a compelling interest and considered whether it had achieved its goal by narrowly tailored means. The court held that this standard was not met because the plan accomplished more racial segregation than necessary to give African Americans an opportunity to win. Act 42 also portrayed an "excessive disregard" for traditional redistricting criteria, such as compactness.[47]

The court discussed the role of the Department. "[T]he Attorney General's Office (AGO) had let it be known that preclearance would not be forthcoming for any plan that did not include at least *two* 'safe' black districts out of seven. But neither Section 2 nor Section 5 of the Voting Rights Act justifies the AGO's insistence upon two black districts." District Four was not geographically compact and thus could not meet the *Gingles* test. Since Section Two protects the individual, not group, right to vote, it does not authorize the Department to refuse preclearance to submissions that do not "give full effect" to minority votes or do not create proportional representation. As to Section Five, the court held that a one-seat plan would not have been retrogressive. "Yet members of the Legislature uniformly believed that they needed to create such a [two-seat] districting plan to secure preclearance."

The court analyzed communications from the Department and adjudged that the suggestion that Louisiana draw districts "that would more effectively provide to black voters an equal opportunity . . . to elect candidates of their choice" was a "euphemism for black candidates." The court described how the Department in one letter had suggested contours of a district that later served as a basis for the Fourth District: "What was the authority for the AGO's insistence? The answer presents itself: none." The Department had rejected the state's explanations of historical, cultural, political, economic, and religious reasons for proposing a one-seat plan, stating that aggregating together black voters is more important than such considerations. "What was the authority for this judgment: again, none!" The Department argued that creating black districts trumped all other redistricting criteria (save one-person, one-vote). "What was the authority for this decision? Yet again, none!" But "the AGO arrogated the power to use Section 5 preclearance as a sword to implement forcibly its own redistricting policies, rather than as a shield to prevent lamentable historical abuses."[48]

Louisiana attempted to justify the plan on grounds of incumbency protection and socio-economic commonalities. The court spurned these claims. In doing so, the court rejected the testimony of the state's expert Dr. Allan Lichtman concerning socio-economic commonality in District 4 as a "*post hoc* rationalization." Lichtman's correlation of socio-economic characteristics and race was criticized as creating "a classic chicken-or-egg fallacy."[49] The Louisiana court thus struck another blow against the voting rights issue network.

Hays was appealed to the Supreme Court, but before the Court could render a decision, the case became moot because the legislature repealed Act 42 and passed another two-seat plan, Act 1 of the Second Extraordinary Session of the Louisiana Legislature. One of the crucial factors in the passage of Act 1, which created a revised majority-black Fourth Congressional District, was a letter sent during the legislative debate to the Lawyers' Committee for Civil Rights attorneys representing the Legislative Black Caucus from Civil Rights Division chief Deval L. Patrick.

The letter's introductory paragraph expressed the Division's pleasure at being invited to participate with the Lawyers' Committee in assisting the Legislative Black Caucus (the Department was participating as an *amicus* in the Supreme Court docket). Patrick disclaimed any comment on specifics of what the Department might view as a permissible plan, but he offered "some general observations." He repeated the Department's position that the state had a compelling interest in a two-seat plan to meet the requirements of Section Two and Section Five. In the view of the Civil Rights Division:

> The district court's ruling in *Hays* does not alter these judgments. . . . The court's ruling is based on its conclusion that a more compact second black-majority district could be drawn and that a district with a lower percentage of black voting age residents would still provide black voters with a realistic opportunity to elect candidates of their choice.
>
> [I]t remains reasonable to conclude that the Voting Rights Act requires the state to devise a congressional redistricting plan with two black-majority districts.[50]

The *Hays* court had noted that a district with about 58 percent African-American voting age population would have been adequate to ensure that blacks could elect a representative of their choice (District Four was approximately 63 percent black). The court had cited testimony from social science experts that a lower percentage would provide a fair opportunity to elect, and would entail less segregation, assuming for the sake of argument that a second district was required. The court had also mused that a second district could have been drawn that did less violence to traditional redistricting principles. Yet the court had also disclaimed any opinion as to whether or not any plan with two black seats could pass constitutional muster. Patrick ignored this caution. His letter concluded with a reminder of the Division's power in dealing with covered jurisdictions: "Of course, the state must seek preclearance under Section 5, either from the Attorney General or from the District Court for the District of Columbia, of any new plan before it may be implemented in the 1994 elections."

The letter had an immediate effect on the legislature's deliberations. On 20 April the legislature was deadlocked, with the senate having passed a two-seat bill and the house having rejected it and considering a single-seat bill. The letter to the Lawyers' Committee was immediately transmitted to the Legislative Black Caucus, which used it to argue that only another two-seat plan had any hope of preclearance—a fair judgment, given Patrick's command. Upon the circulation of the Patrick letter, the house reversed course and passed a two-seat plan on 21 April. As Louisiana Assistant Attorney General Angie LaPlace, who represented the state described it, the letter seemed to confirm that the Legislative Black Caucus had a "direct line" to the Department. The impression in Louisiana was that the Department could not directly dictate to the legislature, but was using the Lawyers' Committee as a conduit. The *Hays* plaintiffs later accused the Department of "stage managing" the legislative deliberations. The Department claimed that it was only routinely responding to a request for clarification of its position in the wake of the first *Hays* decision.[51]

The plan was again brought before the district court and was again found to be a racial gerrymander. The court complained that the legislature had misinterpreted its earlier decision and had remained swayed by the Department that a second district must be drawn. It dismissed the state's proffer of nonracial reasons for the district as "mere pretext." The court noted that neither the state nor the Department could show that a one-seat plan would have a discriminatory purpose or effect. Nor could the Louisiana plan pass the first *Gingles* precondition of a numerous and geographically compact minority. [52]

Following another trip to the Supreme Court (which sorted out standing issues, not substantive Voting Rights Act matters), the district court again found Act 1 unconstitutional. The tribunal took aim at Patrick's letter informing the legislature that two seats would still be required: "The Department took this action despite language in *Hays I* emphasizing that the Voting Rights Act simply 'does not justify [an] insistence upon two black districts.' " The court expressed its frustration at the legislature for repeatedly succumbing to Department pressure. Therefore, the court imposed its own redistricting plan, including one black seat.[53]

After the third *Hays* decision rejecting the Department's position in January of 1996, the governor called a special session for the sole purpose of passing a plan drawn by the court, without change, as the law of Louisiana. Under these restrictions, the legislature passed the court plan and the governor signed the legislation. The plan was sent to the DOJ for preclearance. The Division, in a 12 August 1996 letter signed by Patrick, objected again. The letter explained that the Department still believed there was no reason to depart from its position that two districts were required. In this letter, the Division based its objection entirely on the claim of a clear violation of Section Two.[54] At the time the Louisiana objection was interposed, all four district court panels that had considered challenges to the Department's incorporation of Section Two into Section Five had found the merger groundless under a proper reading of the Voting Rights Act. (In 1997 the Supreme Court decided against incorporation.)[55]

CONCLUSION

There is not much doubt that the Department pursued a policy under which failure to maximize was commonly regarded as evidence of discriminatory purpose. In each of the states reviewed here, civil rights advocates and Republicans eagerly offered alternatives to state plans that exploited the new definition of purpose. Those interests registered confidence that almost any plan they could offer that showed additional minority districts would be acceptable to the Voting Section. State rationale's for nonmaximization plans were routinely dismissed as pretextual. The Department had a big stick—without its approval, states could not hold elections under new redistricting plans.

It is true that states could bring their plans to the United States District Court for the District of Columbia, but this is more a theoretical than a practical option. Federal litigation in a distant jurisdiction is costly and time consuming. Department opposition would be vigorous, and the Department's objections had never been overturned by the district court in Washington. As the tide began to turn in the mid-nineties, the Division under Deval Patrick hunkered down, even intensifying its opposition to the judiciary's substitution of constitutional and statutory interpretation for what Patrick described as historical reality.

Several of the states defended the maximization plans against constitutional challenges, but these positions reflected a desire to attain stability and put an end to a controversial process more than enthusiasm for the plans themselves. Despite Department arguments that the states had created the districts, and acceptance by several Supreme Court Justices that the states acted to rectify historical discrimination, these plans cannot properly be understood as actions of the states. North Carolina, Georgia, and Louisiana passed the plans to satisfy the Department's policy objective. In this fashion, at least, the covered states became "conquered provinces."

NOTES

1. Gerry F. Cohen, Director of Legislative Drafting, to the United States Department of Justice, memorandum, Atlanta, Ga., 14 October 1991.
2. Cohen to Department of Justice, memorandum, 14 October 1991.
3. Tiare B. Smiley, telephone conversation with author, 31 December 1997.
4. Rep. Arthur Pope, deposition testimony, in *Shaw v Hunt*, 92-CV-202 (E.D. N.C. 1994), reprinted in "Joint Appendix," submitted to Supreme Court in *Shaw v Hunt*, Nos. 94-923, 94-924 (1995).

5. Rep. Milton Fitch, deposition testimony, 13 January 1994, *Shaw v Hunt,* No. 92-CV-202; *Shaw v Hunt,* 517 U.S. 899, 913 (1995).

6. Sen. Dennis Winner, deposition testimony, 11 January 1994, *Shaw v Hunt,* No. 92-CV-202.

7. Gerry Cohen, testimony, 29–31 March 1994, *Shaw v Hunt,* No. 92-CV-202; John R. Dunne, telephone conversation with author, 20 January 1998.

8. John R. Dunne letter to Tiare B. Smiley, 18 December 1991.

9. Thomas B. Edsall, "North Carolina Voting Plan Rejected," *Washington Post,* 20 December 1991.

10. John D. Merritt, testimony, 12 December 1993, *Shaw v Hunt,* No. 92-CV-202.

11. *Shaw v Hunt,* 861 F. Supp. 408, 457 (E.D. N.C. 1994); Smiley telephone conversation.

12. *Shaw v Hunt,* 861 F. Supp. 457.

13. North Carolina House of Representatives, *Floor Debates,* 23 January 1992; North Carolina Senate, *Daily Proceedings in the Senate Chamber,* 24 January 1992.

14. *Shaw v Hunt,* 861 F. Supp. 465–66.

15. Daniel T. Blue, "Justice Department Has the Last Word," submitted to Supreme Court in "Joint Appendix," *Shaw v Hunt,* Nos. 94-923, 94-924, 163.

16. *Shaw v Hunt,* 517 U.S. 920 (1996) (Stevens, dissenting).

17. *Shaw v Barr,* 808 F. Supp. 461 (E.D. N.C. 1992).

18. *Shaw v Reno,* 509 U.S. 630, 635–36 (1993) (citations omitted).

19. *Shaw v Reno,* 509 U.S. 647–48.

20. *Shaw v Hunt,* 861 F. Supp. 476.

21. U.S. Department of Justice, *Brief for the United States as Amicus Curiae Supporting Appellees,* submitted to the Supreme Court in *Shaw v Hunt.*

22. *Brief for the United States as Amicus Curiae Supporting Appellees,* submitted to the Supreme Court in *Shaw v Hunt.*

23. *Shaw v Hunt,* 517 U.S. 911–13.

24. *Busbee v Smith,* 549 F. Supp. 494 (D. D.C., 1982). The *Busbee* court upheld the Department's objection for racially discriminatory purpose. The objection was brought about, in part, by truly ugly racial comments made by the chair of the House Reapportionment Committee. Georgia had been forced to create a minority influence district by the Department in the 1970s, also on grounds of racial purpose. Andrew Young won the seat.

25. Robert A. Holmes, "Reapportionment Strategies in the Nineties: The Case of Georgia," in Bernard Grofman, ed., *Race and Redistricting in the 1990s* (New York: Agathon Press, 1998), 204–208.

26. *Johnson v Miller,* 864 F. Supp. 1354, 1361 (S.D. Ga. 1994). Although Rep. Brooks refers here to the "Attorney General," it appears that he is referring to the Office of the Attorney General, or the Assistant Attorney General for Civil Rights.

27. *Brief of the Appellees, Miller v Johnson,* Nos. 94-631, 94-797, 94-929 (1995); Davida Johnson, *Brief of Appellees,* submitted to the Supreme Court in *Abrams v Johnson,* Nos. 95-1460, 94-1425 (1996).

28. *Johnson v Miller,* 864 F. Supp. 1362.

29. Kathleen Wilde letter to John R. Dunne, 30 October 1991; *Johnson v Miller,* 864 F. Supp. 1363–64.

30. *Johnson v Miller,* 864 F. Supp. 1363; Wilde to Dunne, 30 October 1991; *Johnson v Miller,* 864 F. Supp. 1367.

31. *Johnson v Miller,* 864 F. Supp. 1363–67; Holmes, "The Case of Georgia," 206.

32. *Johnson v Miller,* 864 F. Supp. 1368; Wilde to Dunne, 30 October 1991.

33. *Johnson v Miller*, 864 F. Supp. 1369–93.

34. *Brief for the United States*, submitted to the Supreme Court in *United States of America v Johnson*, Nos. 94-631, 94-929, 94-797 (1995).

35. *Brief for the United States* and *Reply Brief for the United States*, submitted to the Supreme Court in *United States of America v Johnson.*

36. *Miller v Johnson*, 515 U.S. 900, 915–28 (1995).

37. *Johnson v Miller*, 922 F. Supp. 1552 (S.D. Ga. 1995); *Johnson v Miller*, 922 F. Supp. 1556 (S.D. Ga. 1995).

38. *Brief for the United States as Appellant*, submitted to the Supreme Court in *United States of America v Johnson*, Nos. 94-1460 and 94-1425 (1996).

39. *Brief of Appellees*, submitted to the Supreme Court in *United States of America v Johnson*, Nos. 94-1460 and 94-1425 (1996); *Abrams v Johnson*, 521 U.S. 74 (1997); *Reply Brief for the United States*, submitted to the Supreme Court in *United States of America v Johnson.*

40. *Abrams v Johnson*, 521 U.S. 74.

41. *Johnson v Miller*, 864 F. Supp. 1362; *Smith v Beasley*, 946 F. Supp. 1174, 1190–91 (D. S.C. 1996); *Johnson v Miller*, 864 F. Supp. 1362; James P. Turner, interview by author, tape recording, Accokeek, Md., 27 August 1997; Brenda Wright, telephone conversation with author, 13 January 1998; J. Gerald Hebert, telephone conversation with author, 7 January 1998.

42. Louisiana Senate and Governmental Affairs and Louisiana House and Governmental Affairs Committees, *Reapportionment Hearing* (Monroe, La., 16 March 1992), 42.

43. Ibid., 18, 24, 42, 59, 67, 96.

44. Jim Leggett, "Maps Take Odd Twists, Turns," *Alexandria Daily Town Talk*, 20 March 1992; Guy Coates, "Fields Slows Redistricting Push," *Baton Rouge Advocate*, 1 April 1992.

45. Bill McMahon, "Bankston Says Redistrict Split Not a Done Deal," *Baton Rouge Advocate*, 3 April 1992; "Redistricting: Leave Fort Polk Alone, Too," *Shreveport Times*, 16 April 1992.

46. Marsha Shuler, "House Reverses Remap Course," *Baton Rouge Advocate*, 8 May 1992; Marsha Shuler and Bill McMahon, "Congressional Remap Plans Advance in Legislature," *Baton Rouge Advocate*, 1 May 1992; Mike Hasten, "Surprised House Passes Remap Plan," *Lafayette Advertiser*, 6 May 1992; Glenn Koepp, testimony, reprinted in *United States' Post-Trial Brief*, submitted to the district court in *Hays v State of Louisiana*, CV95-1522S, CV95-1241 (1995).

47. *Hays v State of Louisiana*, 839 F. Supp. 1188 (W. D. La. 1993).

48. *Hays*, 839 F. Supp. 1196–97, note 21.

49. *Hays*, 839 F. Supp. 1203–04, note 48.

50. Deval L. Patrick letter to Brenda Wright and Robert B. McDuff, Washington, DC, 20 April 1994.

51. Angie LaPlace, telephone conversation with author, 30 December 1997; *Brief for Appellees Ray Hays et al.*, submitted to Supreme Court in *United States v Hays*, No. 94-558 (1995); *United States Post-Trial Brief*, submitted to the district court in *Hays v State of Louisiana*, CV92-1522S, CV95-1241 (1995).

52. *Hays v State of Louisiana*, 862 F. Supp. 119, 121–22 (W.D. La. 1994).

53. *Hays v State*, 936 F. Supp. 360, 369, 372 (W.D. La. 1996). Again, the court in *Hays I* had left an opening for the Department to take the position it had adopted. But it had to be a very optimistic outlook, or one reflecting the Department's "hunkering down."

54. Deval L. Patrick letter to E. Kay Fitzpatrick, Washington, DC, 12 August 1996.

55. *Reno v Bossier Parish School Board*, 520 U.S. 471 (1997).

7

Processes and Products of Voting Rights Act Enforcement

The Department of Justice is central to the redistricting process in covered jurisdictions. Following the 1990 census, from April 1991 to mid-1995, the CRD received almost 3,000 redistricting submissions. The preclearance process and the jurisdictions' acclimation to its requirements discourage the submission of plans that purposely discriminate on the basis of race or diminish existing minority electoral strength, but in the eyes of many voting rights advocates inside and outside of the Department, more could and should be accomplished through Section Five. In the nineties round of redistricting, the Division pushed the envelope to increase minority congressional representation.

The CRD has been under attack since the Supreme Court recognized a constitutional challenge to racial gerrymanders in *Shaw v Reno*. The Court has found that the Department adopted a maximization agenda in violation of the Equal Protection Clause of the Fourteenth Amendment. Congressional maximization plans have fallen across the nation as courts have complained of being placed in the "unenviable position of depriving black citizens of a privilege the Justice Department never had the right to grant: maximization of the black vote, whatever the cost."[1]

The Department's implementation of Section Five developed in a manner that seemed to be a natural progression to many participants in the process. Voting activists were hopeful that the 1982 results-test amendment, the Department's regulation incorporating Section Two into the Section Five process, and the Court's decision in *Gingles* provided a logical momentum to advocate for increased majority-minority districts. Initially unsure of the Department's commitment, they were won over by the Division's early objections. The activists held dear the ideal of proportional representation. Both political parties stood for increased minority representation; the Republicans aggressively so—Republican National Committee chairman Lee Atwater called for proportional representation. Within the Division, the failure to maximize came to be regarded as evidence of purposeful discrimination, a significant alteration of the Division's traditional approach, but one that raised little protest from political or professional staff. Only the state legislators who actually had to draw lines while accommodating multiple interests believed that maximization does not trump all other concerns, but state legislators were given little regard by the Department and held in disrespect by the issue network. The momentum for maximization was doubtless disruptive yet seemed natural.

But it wasn't. The Department sacrificed its historically balanced treatment of the states and interest groups, siding repeatedly with the public law advocates. The Department discarded statutory and precedential terms that stood in the way and attempted to redefine others. Its achievement was finally arrested and reversed by new players on the scene, local attorneys and voters who attacked the maximization plans through the courts on constitutional grounds.

In this final chapter I shall discuss those processes that most contributed to the Department's conduct, and the substantial if often unintentional products of the Department's choices. This discussion will return to the subtexts of voting rights enforcement, organizational culture, methods of legal interpretation, and the interest group environment that most impelled the Division along its path. In 1999, there was still ongoing litigation in North Carolina. As we approach yet another round of redistricting with the year 2000 census, I will discuss some of the consequences of the turmoil of the nineties for Department enforcement.

PROCESSES OF THE DEPARTMENT'S ENFORCEMENT

Three subtextual factors undergird critiques of the Department's enforcement: charges of politicized enforcement, the force of moral claim associated with voting rights, and changing notions of the meaning of equality. Each of these subtextual elements was at work in the nineties round of redistricting.

Politicization may be understood in either of two ways: as a policy approach governed by a philosophical or ideological understanding; or as a use of the policy process to achieve a less lofty, often partisan goal. Accusations of the latter sort of politicization were aimed at the Bush administration during the nineties round of redistricting. Some observers believed the administration intended to set aside a number of minority districts in each covered state as a condition of preclearance—providing proportional representation based on race. Yet the Bush administration pronounced itself ideologically opposed to quotas or racial preferences of any kind. The administration's critics, including many Democratic state legislators, accused it of betraying its ideological beliefs and using the Department of Justice as a tool to achieve redistricting plans that would favor Republican Party congressional prospects. The critics thus saw the Civil Rights Division as a pawn used by the Bush administration in a politicized enforcement to pursue a partisan advantage.

The two definitions of politicization were both at work at different levels of the Bush administration. Within the Division there was broad agreement concerning increasing the number of minority congresspersons; in the White House there was disdain for the philosophy but desire for the partisan effects.

Voting Section professionals who have a firm commitment to civil rights carry out enforcement policies. They are legal professionals; partisan machinations do not preoccupy them. In the early nineties they were led by chief of the Civil Rights Division John R. Dunne, a Bush appointee with a strong belief in the value of political participation. He became determined to enforce the Act aggressively. So the Division pushed the states toward maximization out of the sense of philosophical belief in increasing minority representation; by leaving Dunne and the Division alone to carry out a policy in opposition to its governing philosophy, the White House engaged in pursuit of partisan advantage.

The second subtextual element is the demand of moral right. The moral claim of the civil rights movement has sustained it against many challenges. Yet some of that force has seeped from the claim as civil rights transformed conceptually from the removal of discriminatory barriers against African-American citizens to claims of a right to proportional representation. One small measure of that diminution is the Department's argument that challenges to max-plans treat African Americans differently than other interests. Casting the debate as interest group politics lacks the moral power of an argument based upon the fundamental right to vote. Moreover, Section Five's intrusion into state decision making could only be justified by the moral necessity of assuring the franchise to African Americans, not by the goal of furthering an organized interest.

The CRD fulfills its responsibilities in an atmosphere of moral intensity. When Abigail Thernstrom challenged the established academic interpretation of the VRA, she had particularly harsh words for the CRD's enforcement practice, even accusing the Division of a "get-the-racist bastards" approach. Representative Earl Hilliard, Alabama's first African-American congressman this century, responded to *Shaw v Reno* by telling the Associated Press that "What the Supreme Court is doing is trying to placate those Nazis, those Klansmen, who want things to get back to where they were." Reverend Jesse Jackson accused the court of pursuing a "kind of ethnic cleansing."[2]

The third subtextual element concerns understandings of the proper framework for identifying and remedying discrimination. Affirmative action has had two meanings in separate phases of its development. In Phase One in the early and mid-sixties, the goal sought was the incorporation of African Americans into the general race for success. Affirmative action theory was grounded in the tenets of classical liberalism, that society should eradicate discrimination so that a person would have the opportunity to succeed based upon the individual's own merits. Phase Two transformed the meaning of affirmative action and the conception of equality. As the ideas of ineradicable historical and institutional racism began to take hold, proportional representation seemed to be the logical remedy.

Under the terms of Phase Two, racial preferences might be maintained if designed for a benign purpose, but the courts have been rejecting that view. The district court that heard the case of the Georgia congressional redistricting framed the debate:

> [B]y instruction of the United States Congress, racial concerns are DOJ's overriding criterion for approving a redistricting plan.

Shaw v Reno holds that if a plaintiff shows that racial concerns were the overriding criterion for drafting a redistricting plan, leading to the creation of dramatically irregular district boundaries, that plan is unconstitutional, unless it survives constitutionally strict scrutiny.

And therein lies the problem.[3]

There is interplay between the two meanings within Section Two of the Act, because the results test seeks to assure minority citizens an equal opportunity to participate in the political process and to elect representatives of their choice. The opportunity to participate encompasses the minority citizen's right to engage freely at every level of the political process in the same manner as white citizens, a Phase One type goal. This aspect of Section Two is almost never addressed in the Division's objection letters or court filings. The right to elect a representative of choice has been asserted by advocates to involve the right of a minority group to elect a candidate of its own racial or ethnic identification, which equates with proportional representation and Phase Two.

The Division repeatedly contended for the right to elect a candidate of choice in the nineties, implicitly accepting that a representative of choice is a member of the district's dominant racial or ethnic group. The Department pushed the states to create plans in which minority candidates of choice would represent the proportion of minority citizens within the state. The Supreme Court has rejected the position of the Department, cautioning it that the right to vote is an individual, not group, right and that the essence of the Act is opportunity and not guaranteed results.[4]

Voting Section professionals gravitate toward progressive policies. They are members of the voting rights issue network. The line staff regularly hears from lawyers and social scientists who promote emerging theories, and some Section attorneys regard these outside issue-network members as particularly prestigious. Some Section attorneys lack political sensitivity, a factor that, coupled with inexperience among line staff, contributed to the Section's problems in the nineties.

Dunne came to favor pushing greater opportunities for minorities to elect candidates, and the Voting Section professionals were comfortable with that direction. Dunne explains that maximization has unfortunately come to be used as a pejorative. His intent was to enhance minority voting rights. "I was looking to doing more but in my attempts to do more I guess I wandered into maximization which the courts determined to be improper. But I didn't start out with the idea of let's squeeze out as much as we possibly can in order to maximize the number of black districts."[5] He did wonder aloud at meetings about the correlation of minority districts with percentage of population, which could have conveyed a message of proportionality to staffers.

The critical task of the Division was established as the enhancement of minority voting strength by a process of pushing states to maximize districts. The sense of mission was broadly accepted within the Division. The Department had sufficient autonomy to pursue its critical task, despite being at the center of a political maelstrom involving the two political parties, public interest litigators, academic and social science participants, and a potentially hostile administration.

The ability to successfully sustain the mission could have been a precarious matter for the Division, but in the nineties, most of the important participants in the Division's universe saw it in their own best interest to be at least quiescent and at most enthusiastic about the push to create more minority districts. There is broad agreement among the members of the voting rights issue network of the propriety of achieving proportional representation by race. It also achieves one of their pet projects—the removal of the process of redistricting from the grubbily democratic hands of local officeholders. The litigators of the public interest advocacy groups likewise welcomed the willingness of the Division to reject state submissions in favor of plans created by their consultants. These public interest firm litigators regarded the results test as interpreted in *Gingles* and the incorporation of Section Two into the preclearance process as virtually requiring proportional representation. They had little to quarrel with in the Division's enforcement.

The Republican Party strategy was in accord with the wishes of the advocacy groups, although the interests of the two diverged significantly at times. The racial politics of redistricting cast the GOP, usually associated with opposition to racial preferences, into devoting resources toward a kind of quota plan for minority candidates. The Democrats could hardly mount opposition to new minority districts and risk alienating their most devoted constituency. They sought to accommodate the Department's demands and draw minority districts while preserving Democratic incumbents through creative gerrymanders.

The only real opposition came from the state legislators themselves, including some prominent African-American officeholders. Resistance was hearty in several locales, but the legislatures stood little chance; without preclearance, elections cannot be held. Each of the covered states where objections were lodged eventually succumbed. In several other states the mere threat of Department action, usually held out by activists implying a direct line to the Division, was enough to induce compliance.

The only remaining potential barrier to the CRD's design seemed a most likely opponent: the presidential administration of an avowed foe of racial preferences, George Bush. The White House and Attorney General Richard Thornburgh developed much of the administration's civil rights policy; the *New York Times* assessed Dunne as being out of the loop. Critics correlated the GOP's strategy to maximize minority districts with the Department's enthusiasm for a results approach and arrived at a conclusion of conspiracy—a Republican Plot.

The one policy area where Dunne was in command was voting rights. It was there that he was able to apply the lessons he had learned, and seek to remedy electoral unfairness in a manner he believed to be consistent with the law. The position was the capstone of his long career in public service and offered the opportunity to establish a legacy and record of accomplishment. Thornburgh made it clear to his Division chief that voting rights was to be entirely Dunne's responsibility, with no interference from up above. This independence was maintained throughout Dunne's tenure. It is quite likely, though, that the administration adjudged that there was much to be gained by the Division's approach, even if it was founded on an abhorrent political philosophy. This philosophical default permitted the Republicans to gain the partisan edge.

For over one-quarter of a century the Division performed in an environment of interest group politics in which the contending states and activists were relatively evenly matched. Interest group politics dissolved in the nineties. The Department's decision making veered decisively toward the positions favored by the advocacy groups. Their pet legal theories were adopted, their redistricting maps were accorded talismanic significance, and in some states they enjoyed an open alliance with Voting Section staff.

As the balance of power shifted to the advocacy groups, it seeped away from the states. In Dunne's 1991 speech to the National Conference of State Legislators, he reminded the assemblage of the near-certain futility of petitioning the court to reverse a Departmental objection. He indicated that the preferences of public interest litigation organizations would be treated with more deference than those of even state plans backed by minority legislators. The Department's tenacity was proven in Georgia, where the legislature needed three submissions before satisfying the federal government's requirements; and in Louisiana, where the Department was still objecting to the state's adoption of a court-imposed plan in 1996. In North Carolina it spurned a submission supported by minority legislators including the Speaker of the House and House Congressional Redistricting Committee co-chair in favor of an alternative developed by Republicans and modified by the NAACP. The North Carolina litigation continued into fall 1999.

Suspicion of state legislators is so strong within the voting rights issue network that even compromises worked out with the active leadership of powerful minority state legislators are disregarded. In North Carolina, the 1986 *Gingles* decision opened up state legislative seats to increased numbers of black legislators, contributing to a Democratic Party coalition that led in 1990 to the election of Daniel Blue as speaker of the house. He named Representative Fitch as one of three co-chairs of the Congressinal Redistricting Committee. Both Blue and Fitch were intimately familiar with the state's history of racial discrimination. They were also respected legislators who were cognizant of the need to form coalitions and inclined to protect those white Democrats who were willing to assist them, but the motivations of these legislators were suspect to the Department. The compromises forged by Blue and Fitch were the essence of the legislative process—a process that appears grimy and contemptible to the rational thinkers of the issue network but is nonetheless fundamental to democratic participation. It simply makes no sense for advocates and the Department to labor to bring minority officials into leadership positions, then nullify their ability to make their own choices about how to further their goals. The Department's oversight is essential to prevent backsliding and the implementation of new schemes to disenfranchise minority voters, but the preclearance power is not a kind of permanent receivership over state decision making. The progressive ideal seems to be that removing the democratic element can only purify the democratic process.

The Division continues to argue that the Supreme Court got it wrong in accusing the CRD of a maximization policy. They point out that there were a number of submissions where the CRD did not require maximization. Some courts have found no interference by the Department. In *Moon v Meadows* in 1997 the court reversed a majority-black congressional district in Virginia, but it found no indication that the Department had pursued a maximization agenda. The Department has also declined to pursue a maximization-at-all-costs approach for state legislatures in certain areas of

Virginia and Louisiana, and intervened in ways that disadvantaged Republicans in Virginia and in Los Angeles in the *Garza* litigation. In North Carolina, the intervention was less than in Texas, which was less aggressive than that in Georgia, Louisiana, and South Carolina. The CRD continues to deny any maximization policy, but the overall picture is one that supports Dunne's concession of an effort to increase minority districts in a manner that drifted into maximization.

There was certainly no memo that went to all Voting Section staff announcing a maximization policy, no herding of the personnel into a conference room to instruct them to pursue proportional representation. It is also true that within the Division there are attorneys who are more or less conservative or liberal, more or less diligent or inattentive, or even as *Compromised Compliance* would have it, more or less pragmatists or principled normativists. To agree that enforcement in the nineties did not have a monolithic character is not to depart from the conclusion of a maximization agenda.

Some of the CRD's traditional support system has been damaged as well. The prestige and credibility of the issue-network experts have suffered as its theories have fallen into disfavor with the Supreme Court. Issue-network notions of progressive reform have been influential in voting rights enforcement for nearly three and one-half decades and surely will continue to have influence, but as *Shaw* challenges have progressed through the courts, judicial deference to the experts has dissipated. The Supreme Court has shown a willingness to respect the testimony of state witnesses, especially legislators who are presumed to have particularized knowledge of local conditions.

The debate over how to interpret the Act has been reinvigorated in recent years by the calls of Justices Scalia and Thomas for a textual reading of the statute and abstention from engaging in representative theory. Justice Thomas has described the Court's vote-dilution decisions as relying upon "a sort of statutory construction through divination" in its reverence for legislative history. Justice Scalia protests that "Section Two of the Voting Rights Act is not some all-purpose weapon for well-intentioned judges to wield as they please in the battle against discrimination. It is a statute."[6] Justices Thomas and Scalia argue that interpretation of the Act must be confined to the language passed by the Congress and signed by the president. This approach conflicts with the method favored by many in the voting rights issue network, that legal decision making should promote social well-being. To look at the decision in such a case as *Allen v State Board of Elections,* it is apparent that the traditional method would have been inadequate to remedy the obstructions being placed in the path of African-American political participation. When we reflect upon the efforts of some states to continue disenfranchisement, it is harder to quarrel with the legal approach that seeks to assure social redress, but not every line shift betrays state-sponsored discrimination.

The Department's legal methodology was attendant to its results-oriented approach. The electoral reality the Division wished to promote was increased minority descriptive representation. In the wake of *Shaw,* Deval Patrick argued that the Court was ignoring the historical reality of disenfranchisement since Reconstruction and the importance of having the largest black and Hispanic congressional membership in the nation's history. In pursuing these goals, however, the Department's legal approach ignored other values such as federalism and compromises forged in passing the Act.

The Department conducted reverse engineering—it worked backward from the preferred result toward the useful interpretative method. Its defense of oddly shaped districts caused it to contort and even abandon the *Gingles* ruling. The Department read the Act to require equal results through Section Two's language that minorities should not be impaired in the ability to elect candidates of their choice. To the Department, wrote the *Hays* court, the statutory term "candidates of their choice" meant black candidates. The Department rarely presented its interpretation of what role Section Two's requirement of an equal opportunity to participate in the political process might play, or how to reconcile the Section Two proviso against a requirement of proportional representation, but the Supreme Court considers equal political opportunity to be the focus of Section Two.[7]

By far the most significant redefinition of a term was the acceptance of a state's failure to adopt an available alternative plan with more minority districts as evidence of discriminatory purpose under Section Five. This interpretation effectively incorporated the Section Two results test into Section Five, without the bother of setting forth how the state had failed to meet the *Gingles* preconditions or the totality-of-the-circumstances test. Dunne made clear in his speech to the National Conference of State Legislators that the Department did not consider a racially discriminatory purpose to require any degree of intent to discriminate on the basis of race. The Department had never before accepted the failure to maximize as evidence of purpose.

The altered definition of purpose was combined with the capacity of computer technology to search through census-block demographic data to link up minority populations across a state's landscape. Technology presented a revolutionary capacity to aggregate minority populations in previously unthinkable manners. Voting activists, public interest litigators, and the Republican Party were able to produce numerous alternatives that maximized minority districts. These alternatives were presented to the Department and often accepted as proof that the state could have done more. Computers made it possible. The problem for the states was that "the technology is so unbelievable that in some ways you could say that if you did not lasso concentrations of minorities . . . then you were deliberately ignoring significant concentrations. . . . and the Section Two law at that time, nobody worried about 'pretty' [districts]."[8] When the new definition of purpose was combined with reliance upon max plans as benchmarks, maximization was the only device that could secure preclearance.

The Department is certainly entitled to argue its interpretations of ambiguous phrases as a matter of fulfilling its advocacy functions. The problem with its role under the Voting Rights Act is that the Department is also entrusted with deciding submissions as would the district court. In the nineties, advocacy seeped, sometimes poured, into the preclearance function. Advocates argue that if the Voting Section practices client politics, it does so to favor the groups Congress intended to benefit by passage of the Act. This may be so concerning the litigation unit. But it makes no sense to suppose that Congress would grant the Department the authority of a surrogate court in the expectation that it would abandon judicial objectivity toward the parties. There is no question that the Act imposes upon the Department a high standard of diligence in guarding minority electoral participation. It does not impose a client relationship.

PRODUCTS OF THE DEPARTMENT'S ENFORCEMENT

There are three products of the Department's enforcement process in the nineties that are particularly significant; perhaps two of them are mostly unintentional effects. The first and intentional product is the effect on federalism. The two less intentional consequences are the effect on our system of representative democracy and the effect on the Department itself.

Federalism

In 1992 Grofman and Davidson wrote that the Voting Rights Act had put the "last nail in the coffin of the pre–Civil War concept of federalism."[9] To paraphrase Mark Twain, reports of the demise of federalism were premature. The Supreme Court has been breathing life back into the wounded notion for several years.

The balancing act required by Section Five is that minority voting power should be protected without untoward trespass into state decision making. Yet the issue of Department intrusion was joined early in the challenges to approved plans. Department intervention took different forms across the states. In North Carolina, the CRD did not suggest lines; in fact, the legislature adopted a plan with a second African-American district in a part of the state other than the location where the objection letter had pointed out a violation. In Georgia, however, the Voting Section line staff undertook deep involvement in the state legislative process. In Louisiana the Deval Patrick letter to litigators representing the Legislative Black Caucus was believed by state officials to be a clear signal that a two-seat plan would be required, and it had the effect of reversing the position held by the house.

It is obvious that Section Five preclearance has had a benign effect in most cases and will continue to be necessary for many years to come, but what level of federal intervention is supportable by the statute, and how much deference should be given state decision making? A concern expressed by Wilson Carey McWilliams in another context applies here: "In regimes that are not democratic, the culture of the ruling elite can be the foundation for political life; democracy presumes a much broader sharing of civic ethics and culture. Democratic debate is possible only about matters we are willing to submit to the judgment of majorities, and so presumes that we are minimally confident in the public's decency and idea of justice."[10] The South is not the place it was in 1965. The broader question lurking behind all preclearance decisions is, how much can or will the DOJ be minimally confident in the judgment of democratically elected legislatures, so that fair redistricting is one of those matters we are willing to submit to their judgment?

Former Department officials hold differing views concerning administrative enforcement and federalism. Dunne and former Special Litigation Counsel J. Gerald Hebert concede that the Department may have overstepped its bounds. But Patrick argues that the congressional will as expressed in Section Five countenances the intervention evident in the nineties. As the Louisiana congressional and South Carolina state legislature redistricting cases indicate, the Clinton CRD charts a course resistant to the judiciary's revived deference to federalism. If serious reflection and renewed respect for federalism is not undertaken within the Department, legal and ideological policy battles over the scope of the Department's reach into state decision making will continue.

Effect on Representation

The CRD's efforts to enhance minority representation equated color with interest. This point is related to the concept that a candidate of choice must be a minority candidate. The Georgia objection letter spoke of the state's failure to recognize communities of interest without identifying exactly what those interests were. In the Georgia appeal, the Department argued that the state should be permitted to prefer racial interests as it might any other interest group, but the Court held that making assumptions on the basis of race can be pernicious. After the courts exposed the Department's assumption, it resorted to arguments that indicated historical and socio-economic similarities among African-American citizens. The courts rejected the argument as a pretext, a "chicken-or-egg" fallacy. The maximization of congressional districts created a guarantee of near proportional representation based on presumed racial interest. The courts undid the result and the underlying supposition of racial interest.

In his dissent in *Allen v State Board of Elections* Justice Harlan questioned the competence of the judiciary to decide whether an at-large or a district system better serves the interests of black voters. "Under one system, Negroes have *some* influence in the election of *all* officers; under the other, minority groups have *more* influence in the selection of *fewer* officers."[11] There is little question but that in the choice of competing theories of representation, the Department selected a system in which minority candidates could win a maximum number of seats. In this, the Department abjured the system in which minorities might have influence in a greater number of districts, but a lesser chance of securing a victorious minority candidate.

Advocates of proportional representation argue that only where the legislature accurately reflects the composition of the whole populace does a truly representative body exist. The most forceful expression of this idea in America's early years may have come from John Adams, who argued that a representative body "should be an exact portrait, in miniature, of the people at large, as it should think, feel, reason and act like them."[12]

The Department's choice comports with the view of theorists who judge a legislature's legitimacy at least partially by how well the body corresponds in composition to the whole nation. Such a system is dependent upon the representative's characteristics; that is, the official is like his or her constituents. Proportional representation and descriptive representation go together. The metaphors that support a system of proportional representation are those of "portrait," "mirror," "map," "miniature," and "sample." Hannah Pitkin writes that "They constitute generally what we may call 'descriptive representation' in which a person or thing stands for others 'by being sufficiently like them.'" The representative does not necessarily act for others; he "stands for" them.[13] It is undoubtedly important that there be a descriptive presence in legislative bodies, especially for African Americans who have been historically denied that representation. Without African American representation in substantial numbers and adequate representation of black interests, questions of representative legitimacy come into play. (Some leaders seek not just descriptive representation in the legislature. President Clinton promised an administration "that looks like the American people.")

The other important form at issue in voting rights theory is substantive representation—"acting for." The focus is more complex and subtle than that of descriptive representation and considers whether the representative acts as an agent or a trustee, and how an official must regard the opinions of the constituency. Pitkin writes: "In the realm of action, the representative's characteristics are relevant only insofar as they affect what he does. Thus, for the activity of representing, the ideal of a perfect copy or likeness is chimerical." Descriptive representatives guarantee only black faces, argues political scientist Carol Swain. Substantive representation is a more useful goal.[14]

Presumably then, a candidate of choice might be a person of any race who effectively represents black interests. Patrick and Dunne have repeatedly stated this position, but a candidate of choice is an ambiguous term. In practice, the states and nearly all of the key players interpreted the Department's position to be that districts must be drawn that would almost assure that minority candidates would be elected.

Swain and David Lublin separately argue that white Democrats adequately represent black substantive interests. Each has also found that Republicans do a poor job of representing minority interests and that black interests suffer in a Republican-dominated House. Swain uses a number of standard indices of liberal voting such as AFL-CIO Committee on Political Education and Leadership Conference on Civil Rights scores as well as her own formulas to show that Democrats are almost always more supportive of civil rights and economic redistribution issues than are Republicans. Lublin finds that "racial redistricting results in the election of individual representatives who are much more responsive to black interests, but reduces aggregate support for policies favored by most African Americans on the floor of the House. Republicans gained 7–11 House seats [in 1992 and 1994] because concentrating black and Latino voters in majority-minority districts undermined the electoral bases of several white Democrats."[15] The value of descriptive representation—even where the individual substantive representation is favorable—may not aggregate favorably for minority interests.

Yet another scholar argues that the practice of equating black interests with liberal interests is misconceived. Eric John Narcisse asserts that there is no liberal consensus among African Americans on a good number of issues that come before the House in a given session. He shows that African Americans are conservative on a number of issues, including abortion, gay rights, school prayer, and the death penalty. Narcisse constructs his own "Black Representation Index" based on survey and public opinion polls of African Americans. While his measure varies according to what issues were before Congress at a given time, Narcisse finds that "African American representatives do not consistently provide higher levels of black substantive representation than white members. Similar assessments can be made about the Democratic Party and the most liberal members in general." Narcisse also suggests that before black substantive representation can be accurately understood, we must address other components of representation, including attaining benefits for individuals or groups in the district, attracting pork barrel projects, and cultivating trust.[16] It may also be that descriptive representation provides benefits that ideological rankings based on congressional votes do not measure. People may feel pride and a sense of belonging in having one of their own succeed. Descriptive representation may provide for greater comfort in approaching a member of Congress, or quicker and more understanding responses to constituent complaints, or availability of jobs and other patronage.

The states of Georgia and North Carolina argued that their plans advanced black substantive interests by providing for minority descriptive representation in addition to protecting Democrats who had voting records rated highly by civil rights organizations. For example, the plaintiffs in *Miller* showed that the 1994 congressional elections in Georgia, held with racially gerrymandered districts, had resulted in the election of a sufficient number of black congresspersons to bring the delegation into rough proportional representation by race. They pointed out, though, that the gerrymander had sundered the Democrats' biracial coalition and resulted in the Republicans' increasing their congressional delegation from one to seven, harming substantive representation.[17] The appellees reminded the Court that Justice Brennan, in his concurrence in *United Jewish Organizations v Carey*, had been concerned that superficially benign racial assignments might be used to disadvantage minority citizens. "An effort to achieve proportional representation . . . might be aimed at aiding a group's participation in the political processes by guaranteeing safe political offices or, on the other hand, might be a 'contrivance to segregate' the group . . . thereby frustrating its potentially successful efforts at coalition building across racial lines."[18]

There is little concern with these philosophical distinctions in the Department's legal writings, but their absence does not hide the underlying assumptions. Legal policy making by the Department is an inadequate basis for assessing what black interests are, how to measure them, and whether they are better served by maximizing the number of descriptive minority legislators or deploying minority voters among a greater number of districts where they might influence the partisan alignment. When the Department shifted from its professed case-specific approach to an effort to maximize minority descriptive representation, it thrust itself into a debate for which it was poorly suited.

Another representational issue is the degree of attachment and communication between the representative and constituents since so many of the gerrymandered districts traverse media markets, urban and rural areas, and local political boundaries. For example, Georgia's Eleventh Congressional District was "centered around four discrete, widely spaced urban centers that have absolutely nothing to do with each other, and stretch the district hundreds of miles across rural counties and narrow swamp corridors." In defending the North Carolina Twelfth Congressional District before the district court in *Shaw v Hunt*, the Department asserted that there was no difficulty in campaigning or in communicating with constituents, but a poll by the state in October and November of 1993 showed that less than 6 percent of residents in the Twelfth Congressional District could name their congressman.[19]

The contours of a district should be understandable to the constituents. Traditional redistricting criteria, including compactness and contiguity serve important democratic values. In *Vera v Richards*, where black congressional aspirants battled with white Democratic incumbents for reliably Democratic African American votes, the Democratic legislature devised a racial gerrymander that also assisted incumbents. The result was such an odd-looking map that Dunne's preclearance letter disavowed any implication of belief that the plan met statutory or constitutional standards other than those in Section Five. The district court found that values of compactness and cognizance were almost totally submerged:

> Traditional, objective districting criteria are a concomitant part of truly "representative" single member districting plans. Organized political activity takes place most effectively within neighborhoods and communities; on a larger scale, these organizing units may evolve into media markets and geographic regions. When natural geographic and political boundaries are arbitrarily cut, the influence of local organizations is seriously diminished. After the civic and veterans groups, labor unions, chambers of commerce, religious congregations, and school boards are subdivided among districts, they can no longer importune *their* Congressman and expect to wield the same degree of influence that they would if all their members were voters in his district. Similarly, local groups are disadvantaged from effectively organizing in an election campaign because their numbers, money, and neighborhoods are split. Another casualty of abandoning traditional districting principles is likely to be voter participation in the electoral process. A citizen will be discouraged from undertaking grass-roots activity if, for instance, she has attempted to distribute leaflets in her congressman's district only to find that she could not locate its boundaries.
>
> [A]s the influence of truly local organizations wanes, that of special interests waxes. Incumbents are no longer as likely to be held accountable by vigilant, organized local interests after those interests have been dispersed. The bedrock principle of self-government, the interdependency of representatives and their constituents, is thus undermined by ignoring traditional districting principles.[20]

Minority leaders and their allies in public interest law firms spurred the DOJ forward. They obviously have the best interests of minority citizens at heart. Nonetheless, minority leadership was not unanimously in their corner. Numerous African-American legislators believed that the creation of majority-black districts conflicts with the goal of maximizing substantive representation, or that progress would be best served by protecting their legislative allies. The Department chose to disregard minority elected officials, who after all are chosen democratically and answerable to their constituents.

The Department equated race with interest in its post-*Shaw v Reno* briefs. DOJ asserted that the interests of a racial minority are no different than those of other interests a legislature might take into consideration, such as those of farmers, labor, urban dwellers, or rural residents. It argued before the Supreme Court that Georgia should be free to give the same consideration to interests of racial minorities as to other interest groups. But the Georgia legislature was not free to choose among competing interests. It was forced to maximize by the Department, an advantage unavailable to other interests. The Department contended in *Hays v Louisiana* that if strict scrutiny were to apply to a state's effort to accommodate racial minorities, but not to "accommodating the interests of other politically cohesive groups," minority citizens would be disadvantaged, thus undermining the promise of the Equal Protection Clause.[21]

The Department has argued that *Shaw v Reno* leads to a result in which the group for whose interest the Fourteenth Amendment was adopted, African Americans, is the only group for which gerrymandered districts may not be created. This is not an insignificant concern. There is a quite understandable frustration that racial gerrymanders that favored whites throughout our history have rarely and only recently been questioned, but the courts have readily vacated new black districts. Oddly contorted districts that are designed for non-racial purposes, but may serve the interests of white officeholders, seem safe. Katharine Inglis Butler observes, however that all whites are not "represented by any white office holder. In reality, whites as whites are not represented at all."[22] It should be clear that a district drawn to aid a white candidate on the predominant basis of race would violate the Fourteenth Amendment.

The choice between competing theories of representation is one of political philosophy. The breadth of the choice must be an uncomfortable one for the attorneys of the Division, who prefer to see themselves as participating in a legal function, not one of political theory. It seems unlikely that the Congress intended to place such philosophical burdens on an administrative agency, and it is certain that the Department is poorly equipped to analyze and decide them.

Damage to the Department

Perhaps one of the most harmful products has been the diminution of the Department's own prestige. More is expected of the Department of Justice than of other litigants in terms of factual development, legal analysis, and probity. The courts, particularly the Supreme Court, rely upon the Department for these attributes.[23] Therefore when the Department commits errors or is credibly accused of wrongdoing, there is a great cost.

The Department has sustained a good deal of damage. The Supreme Court has accused it of pursuing a maximization policy. Lower courts have made detailed factual findings of Voting Section line staff, in partnership with public interest litigators, actively coercing state legislators to draw districts favored by minority interest groups. In finding that the Department lacked statutory justification for its regulation incorporating Section Two into the Section Five preclearance process, the Supreme Court expressed "little doubt" that the Department would completely subsume the results standard into Section Five, placing the burden on the states to prove the absence of dilution.[24] Departmental justifications have been dismissed as pretextual. Courts have even questioned the integrity of some line staff, as when the district courts in Georgia and South Carolina expressed disbelief at the lawyers' "professed amnesia" in answering questions about the preclearance process.[25]

There are differing assessments of how the Department might be affected. Concern is acute among members of the voting rights bar. ACLU voting rights litigator Laughlin McDonald has expressed alarm that opponents now feel free to "pummel" and "scapegoat" the Department. The late Frank Parker, longtime director of the Voting Rights Project, lamented that:

> The courts have traditionally relied on the Justice Department and in the past have accepted its interpretation of the Voting Rights Act.
>
> Given that the courts are no longer doing this, it puts a more difficult burden on the civil rights groups to try to take up the slack. It's a difficult task because the Justice Department is a

part of the government. The courts have never given the same weight to the interpretations advanced by the civil rights groups as they have to those advanced by the government.

The criticisms have had a deleterious effect on morale. Even those who believe that the criticism was not warranted note that it is hurtful.[26] Ironically, the collateral harm to the interest groups is in part attributable to the CRD's ready acceptance of the groups' interpretations and policy preferences.

The greatest concern was expressed in 1998 by longtime CRD attorney J. Gerald Hebert, now in private practice and continuing to litigate on behalf of minority interests for the Lawyers' Committee for Civil Rights Under Law:

> It has had a profound effect. The Department . . . has taken a step back and is not doing much voting rights enforcement, because every time it sticks its neck out, it keeps getting its head chopped off. The Department[,] I think is anxious to find an easy way to restore its credibility and regain some of its integrity that . . . has been under attack. . . . They are so overly cautious right now to the point where it is almost a paralysis at work. They don't really know what to do, and when to do it, and they are very skittish about flexing any muscles because they are afraid they will offend somebody or the case will get back up to the Supreme Court.
>
> The year 2000 is critical and presents an opportunity for the Voting Section, and maybe the last and only opportunity to regain its credibility.[27]

TOWARD A RESTORATION

The Department should search for ways to alleviate the structural difficulties that contributed to the failed policies of the nineties. A reduction in political and ideological pressure would render an obvious benefit. Heightened recognition of the incompatibility of the litigative and quasi-judicial functions would also help. As more jurisdictions acclimate themselves permanently to the nondiscriminatory norms of the VRA, the Division might look to restructure its decisional rules.

The job of chief of the Civil Rights Division has become one of the most politically charged posts in government. The chief has a portfolio much larger than the imposing field of voting rights. The appointee must manage a Division comprising no less than twelve sections. Voting rights, disability rights, educational discrimination, employment law, housing and fair credit cases, and fair employment for immigrants are all within the purview of the chief. The job requires a person of formidable political, legal, and management skills. The position often involves controversy, and the chief cannot afford to shy away from it.

The appointment has become plagued with an unusually high degree of ideological and partisan rancor over the past two decades. The controversial efforts to confirm William Lucas, Lani Guinier, and Bill Lann Lee are a testament to the difficulty. The post of the top civil rights enforcer in the nation has been left to an acting chief for over two years. The Senate has earned reproaches from both Democratic and Republican administrations for meddling in the appointment process. Partisans have developed a taste to "bork" each other's candidates. Controversial nominations for federal posts often fail to see the light of day because of informal communications between the executive branch and the Senate; this method of intercepting unacceptable candidates has not worked in the case of the chief of the Civil Rights Division. Greater consultation and less symbolism and confrontation between the president and Senate leaders should be pursued.

It is perhaps too much to hope that interest groups will absent themselves from the battle, but if political leaders were to show less fealty to them, the Division might be able to focus more on productive tasks and less on symbolic political battles. In recent years, Republicans have almost never been able to nominate a candidate with experience and respect in the civil rights community. Democrats have not been able to nominate anyone not delivered by the LDF.

In the days when civil rights policies carried moral force free of the association with racial preferences, presidents were less likely to nominate ideologically charged candidates. Former chiefs such as Burke Marshall, John Doar, and J. Stanley Pottinger were known for their moderation and ability to enforce the law. They were not in any way soft on civil rights. In the past, chiefs have been promoted from within the Division or from outside the ranks of the civil rights establishment. That practice might be useful again.

The appointee of the next president will face all the pressures of the job including the post-2000 census redistricting. A Republican might be wise to seek an appointee who has existing credibility with and respect from the civil rights community; it would be a healthy thing for the country. A Democrat might examine a candidate who enjoys civil rights community support but independence from it; such an appointee might be more alert to the dangers presented to the Division from overplaying a losing hand favored by the advocates.

It is critical that the Department separate the Section Five and litigation functions. Advocacy cannot mix with quasi-judicial decision making. Much has been right with the Department's implementation over the years. Division political appointees and professionals must regain the respect for the states and federalism that was almost forgotten. It should not hunker down, but should listen to criticisms. The voices the Voting Section hears most often and most loudly are those of the civil rights advocates, and they should listen to these veterans of electoral disputes, but they cannot listen solely to them or be guided by them in the manner that occurred too often in the nineties. The preclearance process is vitally concerned with the protection of minority interests but does not render the Division the champion of those interests. It makes the Division a quasi-judicial decider of submissions, subject to the decisional parameters of a court. The objective independence implied by a quasi-judicial function must be reinvigorated.

In other administrative reviews, such as those governed by the Administrative Procedures Act (APA), scrupulous separation is observed between agency counsel and those responsible for quasi-judicial decisions. Agency hearings under the APA are presided over by independent members of the agency or administrative law judges. The advocacy functions of the agency are kept separate. A party is entitled to present evidence through counsel and cross-examine opposing witnesses. Anonymous communications are limited as they would be by a court. The administrative law judge's decision must be in writing and include findings of fact and conclusions of law based upon substantial evidence in the record. Decisions are reviewable by a court of law.[28] Heightened formality could also foster greater stability in the definition of important terms—such as the definition of discriminatory purpose—which would make the process more transparent and more balanced.

The problem with such an arrangement, however, is time. It would be difficult to complete such an examination in sixty days. Some accommodation between time pressures, workload, and process should be pursued in the interest of a fairer proceeding.

The process might also benefit from rethinking decisional rules. When the Warren Court upheld the VRA in *South Carolina v Katzenbach,* it recognized that "Congress exercised its authority under the Fifteenth Amendment in an inventive manner." Keith J. Bybee argues that the Court approved that inventive manner in recognition of the detailed consideration Congress had given the problem of assuring the constitutional right to vote. He asserts that Chief Justice Earl Warren saw the extensive congressional deliberation as a model for what should occur in state legislatures making redistricting decisions. Bybee offers that courts might honor that model by focusing their decisions on the inclusiveness and seriousness with which state legislatures consider election-law legislation. This avenue might serve CRD decision making as well. The model would require the Division to be concerned with sufficient diversity within state legislatures and the realization of deliberative procedures in the determination of fundamental political rules.[29]

The cases recounted here show that the battles over maximization themselves exacerbated the worst of racial politics. In North Carolina, the ACLU accused African-American politicians who backed the legislature's first plan of racial treason. When the Louisiana legislature met to adopt a plan in 1996 that would eliminate the district of African-American Congressman Cleo Fields, Fields testified against the plan. "[H]e showed the committee a tee-shirt with a likeness of him being chased by hooded figures, one carrying a board with a nail and one with a rope and accompanied by a dog. The shirt had lettering which said, 'Run, Cleo, run.' " During floor debate on a congressional redistricting proposal in the Georgia state senate following the Supreme Court's *Miller* decision, a white state senator urged the body to support his plan "if you're tired of paying for the sins of your fathers and grandfathers." In Georgia, an African-American state senator who opposed the max-plan was charged with being an "Uncle Tom." A Republican state legislator in Georgia fretted that the races would break up into separate parties, a white Republican Party and a black Democratic Party.[30]

Inclusive decision making and cooperation does not come easily but does occur, as it did in North Carolina, at least until the CRD dismantled its result. Take the involvement of Representative Fitch as one of three co-chairs of the North Carolina house committee with redistricting responsibility. He worked across racial lines to produce a plan with the first African-American congressional district in the twentieth century, an effort that also protected cooperative white Democrats. He harbored regrets about the plan because he would have liked another African-American district, but he fought for the leadership's plan in the house and with the CRD. He accommodated what might have been his preferred result for a manageable compromise and kept his eye on maintaining comity in the legislature and on the multiple concerns of legislative leadership.

There was a seat at the table for African-American legislators. It is an irony that racial redistricting contributes to Republican gains in Congress and state legislatures because African Americans are an integral component of the Democratic Party establishment. If Democrats hold legislatures—and the North Carolina Legislative Black Caucus sensed this when the CRD did not—then African-American legislators will be in leadership and African-American substantive concerns will be addressed. If Republicans hold legislatures, those spoils of the system will be far more remote.

Adoption of the deliberative model with its dependence upon evidence of cross-racial cooperation should also encourage legislators to build inclusive coalitions, a benefit that can devolve to the citizenry at large. People understand when racial considerations dominate policy judgments. The original model of VRA enforcement, which was followed from the passage of the Act up until the eighties, relied upon community involvement, particularly the energy of African-American political leadership to mobilize registration and voting—and, as the Court put it in *DeGrandy*, the "obligation to pull, haul and trade to find common political ground."[31] The model of achieving maximization through litigation or the threat of litigation has produced a withered politics. In fact, litigation has contributed to political polarization. Bybee's model may help restore political deliberation among the people's representatives in place of litigation among elites.

The Supreme Court has repeatedly stated that "reapportionment is primarily the duty and responsibility of the State through its legislature or other body."[32] Bybee's approach offers a hopeful manner for the Division to consider whether the states have met their responsibilities. The Division already requires evidence of minority participation in crafting voting rights plans, and it makes a worthy effort to reach out to communities to assure that racial minorities are not shut out of the process. The deliberative model offers no certainty that a given proportion of minority seats would be produced by legislative deliberation, but there would be assurance that minority arguments are granted full consideration. Of course, the Voting Section should be on guard that state claims of minority participation are real and not based upon sham. The states have an enduring obligation to earn the trust of the Division and minority citizens. They would continue to have the burden of proof to show the DOJ that their redistricting plans are free of discriminatory purpose and effect. The 1990s problem that needs to be cured for this approach to work is that in states such as North Carolina there was significant evidence that the legislature was considering African-American input, but the DOJ was imposing objections based upon pretextual reasoning developed at the behest of interest groups. The nineties cycle, however, was something of a deviation. If the CRD should return to its historical sense of balance and avoid being trapped by interest group ideology, the idea of legislative deliberation has promise.

Can the CRD restore its tattered prestige? It is essential that it do so.

James Turner calls the Voting Rights Act a wonderful statute, one that he was proud to have enforced. In impressive terms, the Division chiefs whose tenures have been under review here express similar regard and optimism about the cause of voting rights. John Dunne expresses confidence that "the ballot box is the way that minorities in this country are going to realize opportunity." Deval Patrick regards the Civil Rights Division as the "champion of American ideals."[33]

If these hopes are to be fulfilled, the Department must heal its credibility, and to do so, it must restore its balance.

NOTES

1. *Johnson v Miller*, 864 F. Supp. 1354, 1369 (S.D. Ga. 1994).

2. Abigail Thernstrom, *Whose Votes Count? Affirmative Action and Minority Voting Rights* (Cambridge, Mass.: Harvard University Press, 1987), 168; Rep. Hilliard to Associated Press, in author's files; David G. Savage, "Despite Redistricting Dispute, Black Lawmakers Win Reelection," *Los Angeles Times*, 9 November 1996.

3. *Johnson v Miller*, 864 F. Supp. 1360 (citation omitted).

4. *Miller v Johnson*, 515 U.S. 900 (1995); *Johnson v DeGrandy*, 512 U.S. 997 (1994).

5. John R. Dunne, telephone conversation with author, 20 January 1998.

6. *Holder v Hall*, 512 U.S. 874, 931 (1994); *Chisom v Roemer*, 501 U.S. 380, 404 (1991).

7. *Hays v State of Louisiana*, 839 F. Supp. 1188, 1197 note 21 (E.D. La. 1993); *Johnson v DeGrandy*, 512 U.S. 1014 note 11.

8. Tiare B. Smiley, telephone conversation with author, 31 December 1997.

9. Bernard Grofman and Chandler Davidson, "The Enforcement of the Voting Rights Act by the U.S. Department of Justice: Compromised Compliance? Republican Plot? Or Great American Success Story?" note 17 (paper presented at the annual meeting of the American Political Science Association, 1992).

10. Wilson Carey McWilliams, "Enchantment's Ending: The Election of 1988," in Wilson Carey McWilliams, *The Politics of Disappointment* (Chatham, N.J.: Chatham House, 1995).

11. *Allen v State Board of Elections*, 393 U.S. 544, 587 (1969).

12. Hanna F. Pitkin, *The Concept of Representation* (Berkeley, Calif.: University of California Press, 1967), 60.

13. Pitkin, *Concept of Representation*, 60, 80.

14. Pitkin, *Concept of Representation*, 142; Carol M. Swain, *Black Faces, Black Interests: The Representation of African Americans in Congress* (Cambridge, Mass.: Harvard University Press, 1993), 211.

15. Swain, *Black Faces, Black Interests*, 14–19. Swain also constructed indexes of her own composition aimed at showing liberal voting scores; David Lublin, "Racial Redistricting and Public Policy in the U.S. House of Representatives" (paper presented at the annual meeting of the American Political Science Association, Washington, DC, September 1997); see also David Lublin, *The Paradox of Representation: Racial Gerrymandering and Minority Rights in Congress* (Princeton, N.J.: Princeton University Press, 1997), 73; Kevin A. Hill, "Does the Creation of Majority Black Districts Aid Republicans? An Analysis of the 1992 Congressional Elections in Eight Southern States," *Journal of Politics* 57 (May 1995), 384–401.

16. Eric John Narcisse, "Reanalyzing Black Substantive Representation: Whither the Interest Group Scores?" (paper presented at the 1997 annual meeting of the American Political Science Association, Washington, DC, September 1997).

17. *Brief of Appellees*, submitted to Supreme Court in *Miller v Johnson*, Nos. 94-929, 94-631, 94-797 (1995); Gerry F. Cohen letter to United States Department of Justice, 14 October 1991 (supporting North Carolina's first submission; copy in author's files).

18. U.S. Department of Justice, *Brief of the Appellees*, submitted to the Supreme Court in *Miller v Johnson*, Nos. 94-929, 94-631, 94-797, 46, and note 43, citing *United Jewish Organizations v Carey*, 430 U.S. 144, 172 (1977) (Brennan, concurring).

19. *Johnson v Miller*, 864 F. Supp. 1389; U.S. Department of Justice, *Post Trial Brief for the United States*, submitted to the district court in *Shaw v Hunt*, No. CV-92-202 (1995); Ruth O. Shaw et al., *Brief of Appellants Shaw, et al., on the Merits*, submitted to the Supreme Court in *Shaw v Hunt*, Nos. 94-923, 94-924 (1995).

20. *Vera v Richards*, 861 F. Supp. 1304, 1334–35, note 43 (S.D. Tex. 1994). Bernard Grofman has written that districts should be "cognizable" to residents. Bernard Grofman, "Would Vince Lombardi Have Been Right If He Had Said: 'When It Comes to Redistricting, Race Isn't Everything, It's The Only Thing?'" Cardozo Law Review 14 (1993), 1237, 1262.

21. U.S. Department of Justice, *Brief for the United States*, submitted to the Supreme Court in *Miller v Johnson*; Department of Justice, *Reply Brief for the United States*, submitted to the Supreme Court in *United States v Hays*, Nos. 94-558, 94-627 (1995).

22. Katharine Inglis Butler, *Affirmative Racial Gerrymandering: Rhetoric and Reality*, Cumberland Law Review 26 (1995), 313, 361.

23. Brian K. Landsberg, *Enforcing Civil Rights: Race Discrimination and the Department of Justice* (Lawrence, Kans.: University Press of Kansas, 1997).

24. *Reno v Bossier Parish School Board*, 520 U.S. 471(1997).

25. *Johnson v Miller*, 864 F. Supp. 1362 and *Smith v Beasley*, 946 F. Supp. 1174, 1190–91 (D. S.C. 1996).

26. Southern Regional Council, "Justice, Section Five Targeted—Limits on Race Cost Minority State Seats," *Voting Rights Review* (Atlanta, Ga.: Southern Regional Council, summer 1996); Southern Regional Council, "High Court Rules—Dismantling of Minority Districts to Continue," *Voting Rights Review* (Atlanta, Ga.: Southern Regional Council, summer 1996); Brenda Wright, telephone conversation with author, 13 January 1998; James P. Turner, interview by author, tape recording, Accokeek, Md., 27 August 1997.

27. J. Gerald Hebert, telephone conversation with author, 7 January 1998.

28. *Administrative Procedures Act*, U.S. Code, vol. 5, secs. 554, 556, 557 (1994); Martin Shapiro, *Who Guards the Guardians: Judicial Control of Administration* (Athens, Ga.: University of Georgia Press, 1988), 39–41.

29. Keith J. Bybee, *Mistaken Identity: The Supreme Court and the Politics of Minority Representation* (Princeton, N.J.: Princeton University Press, 1998), 154–55, 164–65.

30. Jim Leggett, "Racial Split: La. House Panel Moves to Abolish Fields' District," *Alexandria Daily Town Talk*, 29 March 1996; Robert A. Holmes, "Reapportionment Strategies in the Nineties: The Case of Georgia," in Bernard Grofman, ed., *Race and Redistricting in the 1990s* (New York: Agathon Press, 1998), 219; Cathy Geyso, "Senator Talks About Reapportionment Woes," *Augusta Chronicle/Herald*, 8 September 1991.

31. *Johnson v DeGrandy*, 512 U.S. 1020.

32. *Growe v Emison*, 507 U.S. 25, 35 (1993).

33. Turner interview; Dunne telephone conversation; Deval L. Patrick, telephone conversation with author, 20 January 1998.

Afterword

On 24 January 2000 the Department of Justice suffered another critical blow to its enforcement of Section Five of the Voting Rights Act. In a five to four opinion authored by Justice Scalia in *Reno v Bossier Parish II*, the Supreme Court virtually eviscerated the provision under which the Department is to preclear plans that do "not have the purpose and will not have the effect of denying or abridging the right to vote on account of race or color."[1]

The Court had already limited the utility of the effect condition in 1976 in *Beer v United States*.[2] In *Beer* the Court had determined that the effects test was restricted to matters in which a jurisdiction effected a retrogression in the ability of racial minorities to exercise the vote. The effects test became a nearly toothless enforcement tool; few covered jurisdictions have submitted redistricting proposals that actually diminish minority voting rights. So for nearly a quarter of a century, the weight of Section Five objections has fallen on plans that the DOJ has adjudged to have the purpose of abridging the right to vote on "account of race or color." This book has argued that the Department adopted a virtually unrestrained definition of purpose in the nineties. In *Bossier Parish II*, the Court held that the purpose condition applies only to election law changes that have the intent of retrogression. Existing discriminatory practices cannot be touched by Section Five objections, but must be pursued by Section Two litigation.

The Department argued strenuously against such a narrow interpretation of purpose. It contended that unless a purpose objection could get at existing unconstitutional discrimination, egregious forms of bias could be perpetuated. The Department reminded the Court that *Beer* had expressed that even an ameliorative change could be denied preclearance if it "so discriminates on the basis of race or color as to violate the Constitution."[3] The Department recounted for the Court the historical utility of Section Five in dismantling the regime of white supremacy in the covered jurisdictions. Moreover, Congress had entrusted the Department with enforcement of Section Five and "in 34 years of administering Section 5, the Justice Department has never limited its 'purpose' analysis in the administrative preclearance process to an examination of a covered jurisdiction's 'retrogressive purpose.' "[4]

The Court rejected the Department's arguments. The majority expressed the view of statutory construction that where *Beer* retrogression analysis qualifies the term "have the effect of . . . abridging the right to vote," it must necessarily qualify the term "have the purpose . . . of . . . abridging the right to vote." The Court majority read the Department's arguments as a continuing resistance to the decision in *Beer.* Indeed, Justice Souter in dissent contended that *Beer* was wrongly decided but that he would respect the precedent. Nonetheless, Justice Souter found ample reasons why *Beer* should not be followed in *Bossier Parish II,* including reasons proffered by the Department. Among those reasons was Justice Souter's belief that "particular deference" should be accorded the Department's longstanding practice of objecting to changes that show an unconstitutionally discriminatory purpose, "in light of the Department's 'central role' in administering Section 5."[5] Justice Souter as well recounted the utility of Section Five in doing away with discrimination in voting, and he noted the "relentless bad faith" of the white power structure's efforts in Bossier Parish to limit black political power (though Justice Thomas interjected that three black officials had recently been elected from white majority districts in Bossier Parish). Neither the Department nor Justice Souter, however, was able to dissuade the Court majority from its preoccupation with textualism.

The lack of deference accorded the Department by the Court majority is notable. In *Miller v Johnson,* the Court declined to grant deference where the Department's interpretation of the VRA would compel race-based redistricting, implicating the Court's constitutional responsibilities under the Fourteenth Amendment. In *Bossier Parish II,* the Court went further and refused to grant deference to the DOJ's long held statutory interpretation. R. Shep Melnick points out that the key question in statutory interpretation is whether administrative enforcement agencies or courts should exercise greater authority over statutory interpretation. The Supreme Court established a practice of deference to administrative agencies in *Chevron v NRDC.* The Court's adherence to Justice Scalia's textualism, however, cuts against following *Chevron,* especially where federal agencies try to expand power over state governments. Melnick also asserts that judges are more likely to grant deference to administrative bodies they regard as "trustworthy and attentive to congressional concerns" rather than those they regard as "parochial, myopic, malicious or excessively loyal to the White House. . . . "[6] It is risky to try to read the minds of the Justices. But the majority's language in cases such as *Miller* and the two *Bossier Parish* decisions certainly reflect sharp disagreement with DOJ enforcement strategies and tactics and perhaps distrust of the Civil Rights Division. In *Bossier Parish II,* the Court warned that the Department's persistent efforts to read Section Two dilution into Section Five preclearance so implicate federalism that doubts about Section Five's constitutionality might arise. The advantages of balance and credibility that buttressed the Department in voting rights matters before the courts have disintegrated to a dangerous degree.

The Department's Section Five enforcement powers have eroded apace. At the beginning of the nineties' redistricting cycle, the Civil Rights Division adopted a muscular definition of purpose: that if a covered jurisdiction refused to adopt an available maximization plan, declination would serve as evidence of discriminatory purpose, with state justifications dismissed as pretextual ruses. Explicit and implicit adoption of Section Two into Section Five preclearance decisions were standard. But beginning with *Shaw v Reno* in 1993, through *Miller v Johnson, Shaw v Hunt, Bush v Vera, Abrams v Johnson* and *Bossier Parish I* and *II*, the Department has been defeated over and over again. As the defeats have mounted, the Section Five authority has shrunk to the point where the Department is all but powerless to affect existing plans, no matter how discriminatory. For years the threat of a Section Five objection prevented many covered jurisdictions from submitting discriminatory election law changes. The Department lost an immense amount of power in the past decade and faces the post-2000 redistricting cycle in a startlingly weak position.

NOTES

1. *Reno v Bossier Parish School Board,* 120 S. Ct. 866 (2000) (*Bossier Parish II*); *Voting Rights Act, Section Five,* U.S. Code, vol. 42, sec. 1973 (1994).
2. *Beer v United States,* 425 U.S. 130 (1976).
3. *Brief on Reargument for the Federal Appellant,* submitted to the Supreme Court in *Reno v Bossier Parish School Board II,* Nos. 98-405 and 98-406 (1999), citing *Beer v United States,* 425 U.S. 141.
4. U.S. Department of Justice, *Brief on Reargument for the Federal Appellant* and *Reply Brief on Reargument for the Federal Appellant,* in *Reno v Bossier Parish School Board II.*
5. *Reno v Bossier Parish School Board II* (Souter, J., dissenting).
6. R. Shep Melnick, *Between the Lines: Interpreting Welfare Rights* (Washington, DC: Brookings Institution, 1994); *Chevron v NRDC,* 467 U.S. 837 (1984).

Selected Bibliography

CASE LAW

Abrams v Johnson, 521 U.S. 74 (1997).
Allen v State Board of Elections, 393 U.S. 544 (1969).
Baker v Carr, 369 U.S. 186 (1962).
Beer v United States, 425 U.S. 130 (1976).
Bossier Parish School Board v Reno, 907 F. Supp. 434 (D. D.C. 1995).
Burns v Richardson, 384 U.S. 73 (1966).
Busbee v Smith, 549 F. Supp. 494 (D. D.C. 1982).
Bush v Vera, 517 U.S. 917 (1996)
Chevron v NRDC, 467 U.S. 837 (1984).
Chisom v Roemer, 501 U.S. 380 (1991).
City of Mobile v Bolden, 446 U.S. 55 (1980).
Evers v State Board of Election Commissioners, 327 F. Supp. 640 (S.D. Miss. 1971).
Garza v County of Los Angeles, 918 F.2d 763 (9th Cir. 1990).
Gaston County, North Carolina v United States, 395 U.S. 285 (1969).
Growe v Emison, 507 U.S. 25 (1993).
Hays v State of Louisiana, 839 F. Supp. 1138 (W.D. La. 1993); 862 F. Supp. 119 (1994); 936 F. Supp. 360 (1996).
Holder v Hall, 512 U.S. 874 (1994).
Johnson v DeGrandy, 512 U.S. 997 (1994).
Johnson v Miller, 864 F. Supp. 1354 (S.D. Ga. 1994); 922 F. Supp. 1552; 922 F. Supp. 1556 (1995).
Johnson v Mortham, 926 F. Supp. 1460 (N.D. Fla. 1996).
Jordan v Winter, 541 F. Supp. 1135 (N.D. Miss. 1982).
Ketchum v Byrne, 740 F.2d 1398 (7th Cir. 1984).

Major v Treen, 574 F. Supp. 325 (E.D. La. 1983).
Metro Broadcasting, Inc. v Federal Communications Commission, 497 U.S. 547 (1990).
Miller v Johnson, 515 U.S. 900 (1995).
Moon v Meadows, 952 F. Supp. 1141 (E.D. Va. 1997).
Presley v Etowah County Commission, 502 U.S. 491 (1992).
Reno v Bossier Parish School Board, 520 U.S. 471 (1997).
Reno v Bossier Parish School Board II, U.S. 120 S. Ct. 866 (2000).
Shaw v Barr, 808 F. Supp. 461 (E.D. N.C. 1992).
Shaw v Hunt, 517 U.S. 899 (1996).
Shaw v Hunt, 861 F. Supp. 408 (E.D. N.C. 1994).
Shaw v Reno, 509 U.S. 630 (1993).
Smith v Beasley, 946 F. Supp. 1174 (D. S.C. 1996).
South Carolina v Katzenbach, 383 U.S. 301 (1966).
Thornburg v Gingles, 478 U.S. 30 (1986).
Turner v Arkansas, 784 F. Supp. 553 (E.D. Ark. 1991).
United Jewish Organizations v Carey, 430 U.S. 144 (1977).
Vecinos De Barrio Uno v City of Holyoke, 72 F.3d 973 (1st Cir. 1995).
Vera v Richards, 861 F. Supp. 1304 (S.D. Tex. 1994).
Voinovich v Quilter, 507 U.S. 146 (1993).
Watkins v Mabus, 771 F. Supp. 789 (S.D. Miss. 1991).

REFERENCES

Atwater, Lee. "Altered States: Redistricting Law and Politics in the 1990s." *Journal of Law and Politics* 6 (1990): 661.

Baker, Nancy V. *Conflicting Loyalties: Law and Politics in the Attorney General's Office, 1789–1990.* Lawrence, Kans.: University Press of Kansas, 1992.

Ball, Howard, Dale Krane, and Thomas P. Lauth. *Compromised Compliance: Implementation of the 1965 Voting Rights Act.* Westport, Conn.: Greenwood Press, 1982.

Barone, Michael, and Grant Ujifusa. *Almanac of American Politics, 1994.* Washington, DC: National Journal, 1993.

Biskupic, Joan. "Bush's Civil Rights Nominee Wins Senate Confirmation." *Congressional Quarterly*, vol. 48, No. 10, 10 March 1990.

———. "Panel Delays Vote on Lucas at Sen. Heflin's Urging." *Congressional Quarterly*, vol. 47, No. 30, 29 July 1989.

"Black Caucus Grows, Moves Toward Center." *1992 Congressional Quarterly Almanac* (1992).

Blackstone, William. *Commentaries on the Laws of England.* Sec. 2, 1765.

Bloom, Richard A. "Justice's Dunne and the Voting Rights Act." *National Journal*, 4 May 1991.

Bragdon, Peter. "Eyes on Dunne at Justice." *Congressional Quarterly*, Vol. 48, No. 22, 2 June 1990.

Bullock, Charles S. III, and Katharine Inglis Butler. "Voting Rights." In *The Reagan Administration and Human Rights*, edited by Tinsley E. Yarbrough. New York: Praeger, 1985.

Butler, Katharine Inglis. "Affirmative Racial Gerrymandering: Rhetoric and Reality." *Cumberland Law Review* 26 (1995): 313.

Bybee, Keith J. *Mistaken Identity: The Supreme Court and the Politics of Minority Representation.* Princeton, N.J.: Princeton University Press, 1998.

Caldeira, Gregory A. "Litigation, Lobbying and the Voting Rights Bar." In *Controversies in Minority Voting: The Voting Rights Act in Perspective*, edited by Bernard Grofman and Chandler Davidson. Washington, DC: Brookings Institution, 1992.

Clayton, Cornell. "Introduction: Politics and the Legal Bureaucracy." In *Government Lawyers: The Federal Legal Bureaucracy and Presidential Politics*, edited by Cornell Clayton. Lawrence, Kans.: University Press of Kansas, 1995.

———. *The Politics of Justice: The Attorney General and the Making of Legal Policy*. Armonk, N.Y.: M. E. Sharpe, Inc. 1992.

Cohen, Richard E., and Carol Matlack. "All Purpose Loophole." *National Journal*, 9 December 1989, 2980.

Cohen, Richard E., and Carol Matlack. "For the Republic or for the Republicans?" *National Journal*, 9 December 1989, 2986.

Davidson, Chandler, ed. *Minority Vote Dilution*. Washington, DC: Howard University Press, 1984.

———. "The Voting Rights Act: A Brief History." In *Controversies in Minority Voting: The Voting Rights Act in Perspective*, edited by Bernard Grofman and Chandler Davidson. Washington, DC: Brookings Institution, 1992.

Davidson, Chandler, and Bernard Grofman. *Quiet Revolution in the South: The Impact of the Voting Rights Act, 1965–1990*. Princeton, N.J.: Princeton University Press, 1994.

Days, Drew S. III. "Section 5 Enforcement and the Role of the Justice Department." In *Controversies in Minority Voting: The Voting Rights Act in Perspective*, edited by Bernard Grofman and Chandler Davidson. Washington, DC: Brookings Institution, 1992.

Days, Drew S. III, and Lani Guinier. "Enforcement of Section 5 of the Voting Rights Act." In *Minority Vote Dilution*, edited by Chandler Davidson. Washington, DC: Howard University Press, 1984.

Dolan, Michael W. "Political Influence on the Department of Justice: Are the Pressures Only External?" *Journal of Law and Politics* 9 (1993): 309.

Donovan, Beth. "Nation Watches as Texas Struggles to Create Minority Districts." *Congressional Quarterly*, Vol. 49, No. 33, 17 August 1991.

Elliott, Ward E. Y. *The Rise of Guardian Democracy: The Supreme Court's Role in Voting Rights Disputes, 1845–1969*. Cambridge, Mass.: Harvard University Press, 1974.

Foster, Lorn. "Section 5 of the Voting Rights Act: Implementation of an Administrative Remedy." *Publius* 16, fall (1986): 37.

Gallup News Service. "Social Audit: Black/White Relations in the U.S." Princeton, N.J.: Gallup Organization, 1997.

Garrow, David J. *Protest at Selma: Martin Luther King, Jr., and the Voting Rights Act of 1965*. New Haven, Conn.: Yale University Press, 1978.

General Accounting Office. "Voting Rights Act Needs Strengthening." Washington, DC: General Accounting Office, 1978.

Genovese, Michael A. *The Nixon Presidency: Power and Politics in Turbulent Times*. New York: Greenwood Press, 1990.

Graham, Hugh Davis. *The Civil Rights Era: Origins and Development of National Policy, 1960–1972*. New York: Oxford University Press, 1990.

———."Voting Rights and the American Regulatory State." In *Controversies in Minority Voting: The Voting Rights Act in Perspective*, edited by Bernard Grofman and Chandler Davidson. Washington, DC: Brookings Institution, 1992.

Grofman, Bernard. "An Expert Witness Perspective on Continuing and Emerging Voting Rights Controversies: From One Person, One Vote to Partisan Gerrymandering." *Stetson Law Review* 21 (1992): 783.

———. "Race and Redistricting." *Washington Post* 21 October 1991.

———. "Would Vince Lombardi Have Been Right if He Had Said: 'When It Comes to Redistricting, Race Isn't Everything, It's the Only Thing'?" *Cardozo Law Review* 14, No. 5 April (1993): 1237.

———, ed. *Race and Redistricting in the 1990s*. New York: Agathon Press, 1998.

Grofman, Bernard, and Chandler Davidson. "The Enforcement of the Voting Rights Act by the U.S. Department of Justice: Compromised Compliance? Republican Plot? Or Great American Success Story?" Paper presented at the annual meeting of the American Political Science Association, 1992.

———, eds. *Controversies in Minority Voting: The Voting Rights Act in Perspective*. Washington, DC: Brookings Institution, 1992.

Grofman, Bernard, and Lisa Handley. "1990s Issues in Voting Rights." *Mississippi Law Journal* 65, No. 2, winter (1995): 205.

Guinier, Lani. "No Two Seats: The Elusive Quest for Political Equality." *Virginia Law Review* 77, No. 8, (November 1991): 1413.

Gurwitt, Rob. "The Messiest Job in Politics." *Governing*. November 1993.

Hamilton, Alexander, James Madison, and John Jay. *The Federalist Papers*. New York: Mentor, 1961.

Handley, Lisa, and Bernard Grofman. "The Impact of the Voting Rights Act on Minority Representation: Black Officeholding in Southern State Legislatures and Congressional Delegations." In *Quiet Revolution in the South: The Impact of the Voting Rights Act, 1965–1990*, edited by Chandler Davidson and Bernard Grofman. Princeton, N.J.: Princeton University Press, 1994.

Heclo, Hugh. "Issue Networks and the Executive Establishment." In *The New American Political System*, edited by Anthony King. Washington, DC: American Enterprise Institute, 1978.

Hill, Kevin A. "Does the Creation of Majority Black Districts Aid Republicans? An Analysis of the 1992 Congressional Elections in Eight Southern States." *Journal of Politics* 57 No. 2 (May 1995): 384.

Holmes, Robert A. "Reapportionment Strategies in the Nineties: The Case of Georgia." In *Race and Redistricting in the 1990s*, edited by Bernard Grofman. New York: Agathon Press, 1998.

Issacharoff, Samuel. "The Constitutional Contours of Race and Politics." In *The Supreme Court Review 1995*, edited by Dennis J. Hutchinson, David A. Strauss, and Geoffrey R. Stone. Chicago: University of Chicago Press. 1996: 45.

Jones, Augustus J. Jr. "Kinder, Gentler? George Bush and Civil Rights." In *Leadership and the Bush Presidency*, edited by Ryan J. Barilleaux and Mary E. Stuckey. Westport, Conn.: Praeger, 1992.

Karlan, Pamela S., and Peyton McCrary. "Without Fear and Without Research: Abigail Thernstrom on the Voting Rights Act." *Journal of Law and Politics* 4 (spring 1988): 751.

Kousser, J. Morgan. *Colorblind Injustice: Minority Voting Rights and the Undoing of the Second Reconstruction*. Chapel Hill, N.C.: University of North Carolina Press, 1999.

Landsberg, Brian K. *Enforcing Civil Rights: Race Discrimination and the Department of Justice*. Lawrence, Kans.: University Press of Kansas, 1997.

———." The Role of Civil Service Attorneys and Political Appointees in Making Policy in the Civil Rights Division of the United States Department of Justice." *Journal of Law and Politics* 9 (1993): 275.

Lawson, Steven F. *Black Ballots: Voting Rights in the South, 1944–1969.* New York: Columbia University Press, 1976.

———. *In Pursuit of Power: Southern Blacks and Electoral Politics, 1965–1982.* New York: Columbia University Press, 1985.

Lawyers' Committee for Civil Rights Under Law. "Justice Department Voting Rights Enforcement: Political Interference and Retreats." Washington, DC: Lawyers' Committee for Civil Rights Under Law, 1982.

———. "Without Justice: A Report on the Conduct of the Justice Department in Civil Rights in 1981–82." Washington, DC: Lawyers' Committee for Civil Rights Under Law, 1982.

Lublin, David. *The Paradox of Representation: Racial Gerrymandering and Minority Rights in Congress.* Princeton, N.J.: Princeton University Press, 1997.

———. "Racial Redistricting and Public Policy in the U.S. House of Representatives." Paper presented at the annual meeting of the American Political Science Association, Washington, DC, August 1997.

Matlack, Carol. "Questioning Minority-Aid Software." *National Journal*, 23 June 1990, 1540.

McCloskey, Paul N. Jr. *Truth and Untruth: Political Deceit in America.* New York: Simon and Schuster, 1972.

McCrary, Peyton, and J. Gerald Hebert. "Keeping the Courts Honest: The Role of Historians as Expert Witnesses in Southern Voting Rights Cases." *Southern University Law Review* 16 (1989): 101.

Melnick, R. Shep. *Between The Lines: Interpreting Welfare Rights.* Washington, DC: Brookings Institution, 1994.

Narcisse, Eric John. "Reanalyzing Black Substantive Representation: Whither the Interest Group Scores?" Paper presented at the annual meeting of the American Political Science Association, Washington, DC, August 1997.

"103rd's Hispanic Contingent Largest Ever." *1992 Congressional Quarterly Almanac* (1992).

O'Rourke, Timothy G. "*Shaw v Reno*: The Shape of Things to Come." *Rutgers Law Review* 26 (1995): 723.

Parker, Frank R. *Black Votes Count: Political Empowerment in Mississippi After 1965.* Chapel Hill, N.C.: University of North Carolina Press, 1990.

———. "Voting Rights Enforcement in the Reagan Administration." In *One Nation Indivisible: The Civil Right Challenge for the 1990s*, edited by Reginald C. Govan and William L. Taylor. Washington, DC: Citizen's Commission on Civil Rights, 1989.

Pertschuk, Michael. *Giant Killers.* New York: W. W. Norton, 1986.

Phillips, Kevin P. *The Emerging Republican Majority.* Garden City, N.Y.: Anchor Books, 1970.

Pitkin, Hanna Fenichel. *The Concept of Representation.* Berkeley, Calif.: University of California Press, 1967.

Posner, Mark A. "Post-1990 Redistrictings and the Preclearance Requirement of Section 5 of the Voting Rights Act." In *Race and Redistricting in the 1990s*, edited by Bernard Grofman. New York: Agathon Press, 1998.

Rabkin, Jeremy. *Judicial Compulsions: How Public Law Distorts Public Policy.* New York: Basic Books, 1989.

Raines, Howell. *My Soul Is Rested: Movement Days in the Deep South Remembered.* New York: Putnam, 1977.

Reynolds, William Bradford. "The Reagan Administration and Civil Rights: Winning the War Against Discrimination." *University of Illinois Law Review* 4 (1986): 1001.

Schlozman, Kay Lehman, and John T. Tierney. *Organized Interests and American Democracy.* New York: Harper & Row, 1986.

Selig, Joel. "The Reagan Justice Department and Civil Rights: What Went Wrong." *University of Illinois Law Review* No. 4 (1985): 785.

Shapiro, Martin M. *Who Guards the Guardians: Judicial Control of Administration.* Athens, Ga.: University of Georgia Press, 1988.

Sniderman, Paul M., and Edward G. Carmines. *Reaching Beyond Race.* Cambridge, Mass.: Harvard University Press, 1997.

Southern Regional Council. "High Court Rules—Dismantling of Minority Districts to Continue." *Voting Rights Review* (Atlanta, Ga.: Southern Regional Council), summer 1996.

———. "Justice, Section Five Targeted—Limits on Race Cost Minority State Seats." *Voting Rights Review* (Atlanta, Ga.: Southern Regional Council), summer 1996.

———. "Substantial Gains Are Seen in State Legislative Redistricting." *Voting Rights Review* (Atlanta, Ga.: Southern Regional Council), fall 1991.

Spears, Ellen. "The Republicans Go to Court." Atlanta, Ga.: Southern Regional Council, April 1992.

Stephanopoulos, George. *All Too Human: A Political Education.* Boston: Little, Brown & Co., 1999.

Swain, Carol M. *Black Faces, Black Interests: The Representation of African Americans in Congress.* Cambridge, Mass.: Harvard University Press, 1993.

Thernstrom, Abigail. *Whose Votes Count? Affirmative Action and Minority Voting Rights.* Cambridge, Mass.: Harvard University Press, 1987.

Turner, James P. "Case-Specific Implementation of the Voting Rights Act." In *Controversies in Minority Voting: The Voting Rights Act in Perspective,* edited by Bernard Grofman and Chandler Davidson. Washington, DC: Brookings Institution, 1992.

United States Commission on Civil Rights. "Political Participation: A Study of Participation by Negroes in the Electoral and Political Processes in 10 Southern States Since the Passage of the Voting Rights Act of 1965." Washington, DC: United States Commission on Civil Rights, 1968.

———. "The Voting Rights Act: Ten Years After." Washington, DC: United States Commission on Civil Rights, 1975.

U.S. Department of Justice. Civil Rights Division. *County Council of Sumter County, South Carolina v United States,* No. 82-912 (D. D.C.). *Post-Trial Brief.*

———. *Hays v State of Louisiana,* CV-92-1522S and CV-95-1241 (W.D. La.). *Post-Trial Brief.*

———. *Shaw v Hunt,* No. 92-CV-202 (E.D. N.C.). *Brief for the United States in Opposition to Plaintiff-Intervenor's Motion for a Preliminary Injunction.*

———. *Shaw v Hunt,* No. 92-CV-202 (E. D. N.C.). *Post Trial Brief for the United States.*

U.S. Department of Justice. Office of Solicitor General. *Abrams v Johnson,* Nos. 95-1460 and 95-1425. *Brief for the United States as Appellant.*

———. *Allen v State Board of Elections,* Nos. 3, 25, 26, and 36. *Memorandum for United States as Amicus Curiae.*

———. *Beer v United States,* No. 73-1869. *Brief for the United States.*

———. *Beer v United States,* No. 73-1869. *Motion To Affirm.*

———. *Bush v Vera*, Nos. 94-805, 94-806, and 94-988. *Brief for the United States.*
———. *Bush v Vera*, Nos. 94-805, 94-806, and 94-988. *Reply Brief for the United States.*
———. *City of Mobile v Bolden, No. 77-1844. Brief for the United States as Amicus Curiae.*
———. *Gaston County, North Carolina v United States*, No. 701. *Motion To Affirm.*
———. *Growe v Emison*, No. 91-1420. *Brief for the United States as Amicus Curiae Supporting Appellants.*
———. *Holder v Hall*, No. 91-2012. *Brief for the United States as Amicus Curiae.*
———. *Holder v Hall*, No. 91-2012. *Brief for the United States as Amicus Curiae Supporting Respondents.*
———. *Johnson (Wetherell) v DeGrandy, No. 92-519. Motion To Affirm in Part and Vacate in Part.*
———. *Metro Broadcasting, Inc. v Federal Communications Commission*, No. 89-453. *Brief for the United States as Amicus Curiae Supporting Petitioner.*
———. *Miller v Johnson*, Nos. 94-929, 94-631, and 94-797. *Brief for the United States.*
———. *Miller v Johnson, Reply Brief for the United States.*
———. *Presley v Etowah County Commission*, Nos. 90-711 and 90-712. *Brief for the United States as Amicus Curiae Supporting Appellants.*
———. *Reno v Bossier Parish School Board*, Nos. 95-1455 and 95-1508. *Brief for the Federal Appellant.*
———. *Reno v Bossier Parish School Board*, Nos. 98-405 and 98-406. *Brief on Reargument for the Federal Appellant.*
———. *Reno v Bossier Parish School Board*, Nos. 98-405 and 98-406. *Reply Brief on Reargument.*
———. *Shaw v Gerson*, No. 92-357. *Brief for the Federal Appellees.*
———. *Shaw v Hunt*, No. 94-923 and 94-924. *Brief for the United States As Amicus Curiae Supporting Appellees.*
———. *South Carolina v Katzenbach*, No. 22. *Brief for the Defendants.*
———. *State of Louisiana v Hays*, No. 91-1539. *Brief for the United States as Amicus Curiae.*
———. *Thornburg v Gingles*, No. 83-1968. *Brief for the United States as Amicus Curiae Supporting Appellants.*
———. *Thornburg v Gingles*, No. 83-1968. *Brief for the United States as Amicus Curiae.*
———. *United States of America v Hays*, No. 94-558. *Brief for the United States.*
———. *United States of America v Hays*, No. 94-558. *Brief in Opposition to Motion to Affirm.*
———. *United States of America v Hays, Reply Brief for the United States.*
———. *United States of America v State of Florida*, Nos. 92-767 and 92-593. *Brief for the United States in Opposition to Motion to Dismiss or Affirm.*
———. *United States of America v State of Florida, Reply Brief for the United States.*
———. *Voinovich v Quilter*, No. 91-1618. *Brief for the United States As Amicus Curiae Supporting Appellants.*
Wasby, Stephen L. *Race Relations Litigation in an Age of Complexity*. Charlottesville, Va.: University Press of Virginia, 1995.
Weaver, Suzanne. *Decision to Prosecute: Organization and Public Policy in the Antitrust Division*. Cambridge, Mass.: MIT Press, 1977.
Wilson, James Q. *Bureaucracy: What Government Agencies Do and Why They Do It.* New York: Basic Books, 1989.
Wilson, James Q., ed. *The Politics of Regulation*. New York: Basic Books, 1980.
Wolters, Raymond. *Right Turn: William Bradford Reynolds, the Reagan Administration, and Black Civil Rights.*. New Brunswick, N.J.: Transaction, 1996.

Index

About the Author

MAURICE T. CUNNINGHAM is Chairman of the Political Science Department at the University of Massachusetts at Boston. He is a former assistant attorney general in Massachusetts and participated as co-counsel in Voting Rights Act litigation.